The origins of the Scottis

MANCHESTER
1824
Manchester University Press

Politics, culture and society in early modern Britain

General Editors

PROFESSOR ANN HUGHES
DR ANTHONY MILTON
PROFESSOR PETER LAKE

This important series publishes monographs that take a fresh and challenging look at the interactions between politics, culture and society in Britain between 1500 and the mid-eighteenth century. It counteracts the fragmentation of current historiography through encouraging a variety of approaches which attempt to redefine the political, social and cultural worlds, and to explore their interconnection in a flexible and creative fashion. All the volumes in the series question and transcend traditional interdisciplinary boundaries, such as those between political history and literary studies, social history and divinity, urban history and anthropology. They thus contribute to a broader understanding of crucial developments in early modern Britain.

The origins of
the Scottish
Reformation

ALEC RYRIE

Manchester
University Press
Manchester and New York

distributed exclusively in the USA by Palgrave

Published by Manchester University Press
Oxford Road, Manchester M13 9NR, UK
and Room 400, 175 Fifth Avenue, New York, NY 10010, USA
www.manchesteruniversitypress.co.uk

Distributed in the United States exclusively by
Palgrave Macmillan, 175 Fifth Avenue,
New York, NY 10010, USA

Distributed in Canada exclusively by
UBC Press, University of British Columbia, 2029 West Mall,
Vancouver, BC, Canada V6T 1Z2

British Library Cataloguing-in-Publication Data is available

Library of Congress Cataloging-in-Publication Data is available

ISBN 978 0 7190 7106 5 paperback

First published by Manchester University Press in hardback 2009

This paperback edition first published 2010

Printed by Lightning Source

FOR MY PARENTS

Contents

Preface

◆

I embarked on this project with some trepidation. Scottish history has traditionally been the preserve of Scots, mostly working in Scottish universities – often in separate departments of Scottish history. I am a Scot by birth and by other profound connections; but I have lived in Scotland for only one year of my life, I cut my teeth as a researcher on English history and I now work at an English university. Worse, perhaps, I am instinctively sympathetic to the 'British' perspectives which are becoming as contentious now as they were in the sixteenth century. My hope is that these vantage points have allowed me to achieve some insights into Scottish history while also maintaining critical distance. Readers will judge if I have been successful on either count.

My excuse is that the history of Scotland is too important to be left exclusively to Scottish historians. The Scottish Reformation was an event of international significance, and one of the purposes of this book is to see it on that wider stage. The nationalist flavour of much Scottish history has not only distorted the subject, but (in places) failed to do justice to it. Histories of the Scottish Reformation have been coloured not only by nationalist special pleading, but also by the religious controversies which have died harder in Scotland than elsewhere. In recent decades both of these biases have receded: a reflection of the worldwide retreat of academic historians from such dubious agendas, but also of political change in a country which no longer feels the same need to compensate for a disempowered present with a glorious past. The story which is emerging is one in which none of the religious or political players can usefully be described as heroes or villains, and in which events followed a twisting and unpredictable course. This book's aim is to contribute to this retelling, in the confidence that this untidy story is not only truer but more interesting than the traditional, partisan grand narratives. Indeed, some of what I have argued about what happens to idealism in war, about the success and failure of moderation, and about how small groups of violent provocateurs can effect political change, seems to me to be uncomfortably topical.

It is five years since I first began digging into the Scottish Reformation, and I have accumulated numerous debts along the way. Several historians of early modern Scotland have helped me to find my newcomer's way around the subject, and have saved me from mistakes even worse than the ones which this book still contains: J. H. Burns, Marcus Merriman, Laura Stewart, Jenny Wormald and particularly Martin Dotterweich. Peter Marshall and William Wizeman helped to straighten out my theology and cool down my rhetoric. Michael Mullett, the reader for Manchester University Press, made wise suggestions as well as helping to civilise some of my more barbarous writing. For four successive years, the European Reformation Research Group's annual meeting heard drafts of sections of this book, and that group's breadth and generosity has provided insights I would otherwise have missed. The Centre for Reformation and Early Modern Studies at the University of Birmingham has proved both supportive and stimulating; I am grateful to colleagues who, so far from groaning when they hear the words 'Ah, but in Scotland . . .', have helped me to place my work in clearer perspective. Students in my Scottish Reformation and Mary, Queen of Scots special subjects teased out many of the ideas here with me; I hope they have found these classes as stimulating as I have, and I am grateful to them all. Thank you.

Other debts are more personal. Eilidh Whiteford and Sarah Nicholson taught me – a long time ago, now – something about how to see the world through Scottish eyes. Warren and Vicky Leat, Mo and Jimmy Calder, and Richard Rickford were gracious hosts to their self-invited guest during my research trips, and listened patiently to my post-archival enthusiasms. As always, Victoria's support and strength are fundamental. My final thanks, however, must go to my parents: British Scots of (to my eyes!) the best kind. It is to their care for me that this book owes whatever of breadth or depth it has; it belongs to them.

Notes for the reader

A few words on religious terminology may be helpful for those unfamiliar with recent histories of the Reformation. Both 'Protestant' and 'Catholic' are used here as broad terms, each encompassing a considerable variety of beliefs. I have also used the vaguer label 'evangelical', mostly when discussing the early Reformation period (up to the mid-1540s or thereabouts). This refers to those whose beliefs we, with hindsight, can recognise as proto-Protestant, but which the 'evangelicals' themselves did not necessarily recognise as such. Even vaguer are the terms 'reformer' and 'reformist', which are applied to both Protestants and Catholics (the enthusiasm of some Catholics for radical reforms of their Church is a significant theme of this book). A little more precision is intended by the terms 'Lutheran' and 'Reformed', each of which refers to distinct Protestant groupings: 'Reformed' Protestantism is the multi-faceted tradition often, but misleadingly, referred to as 'Calvinism'.

All quotations have been rendered into modern English. My own inclination is to a more austere style, but while the English of the sixteenth century is accessible enough to the modern reader, the Scots language is another matter. Its distinctive spellings, usages and vocabulary can be daunting, even for modern Scots. I hope those who share my fondness for those usages will forgive me.

Throughout, the year is reckoned to begin on 1 January. All sums of money are, unless otherwise noted, in Scottish pounds (of which there were roughly four to the (English) pound sterling for much of this period, but values fluctuated).

Much of chapter 5 is based on my article, 'Reform without frontiers in the last years of Catholic Scotland', *English Historical Review* 119 (2004), 27–56. I am grateful for permission to draw on that material here.

List of abbreviations

ALC	Robert Kerr Hannay (ed.), *Acts of the Lords of the Council in Public Affairs 1501–1554* (Edinburgh, 1932)
AM	John Foxe, *Actes and monuments of matters most speciall in the church* (RSTC 11225: London, 1583)
APS	*The Acts of the Parliaments of Scotland, vol. II: 1424–1567* (1814)
BL	British Library
CCCC	Corpus Christi College, Cambridge
CSP Foreign 1547–53	William B. Turnbull (ed.), *Calendar of State Papers, Foreign Series . . . 1547–1553* (London, 1861)
CSP Foreign 1558–59	Joseph Stephenson (ed.), *Calendar of State Papers, Foreign Series, of the reign of Elizabeth, 1558–59* (London, 1863)
CSP Foreign 1559–60	Joseph Stephenson (ed.), *Calendar of State Papers, Foreign Series, of the reign of Elizabeth, 1559–60* (London, 1865)
CSP Foreign 1560–61	Joseph Stephenson (ed.), *Calendar of State Papers, Foreign Series, of the reign of Elizabeth, 1560–61* (London, 1865)
CSP Scotland	Joseph Bain *et al.* (ed.), *Calendar of State Papers relating to Scotland and Mary, Queen of Scots, vol. I: 1547–1563* (Edinburgh, 1898)
HP	Joseph Bain (ed.), *The Hamilton Papers: Letters and Papers Illustrating the Political Relations of England and Scotland in the XVIth Century*, 2 vols (Edinburgh, 1890–92)
IR	*Innes Review*
Knox	John Knox, *The Works of John Knox*, ed. David Laing, 6 vols (Edinburgh, 1846–64)
LP	James Gairdner and R. H. Brodie (eds), *Letters & Papers, Foreign & Domestic, of the Reign of Henry VIII*, 21 vols (London, 1862–1932)
LPL	Lambeth Palace Library
NA	National Archives, Kew (formerly Public Record Office)
NAS	National Archives of Scotland
NLS	National Library of Scotland
ODNB	*Oxford Dictionary of National Biography*
RPC	John Hill Burton (ed.), *The Register of the Privy Council of Scotland, vol. I: 1545–69* (Edinburgh, 1877)
RSCHS	*Records of the Scottish Church History Society*

List of abbreviations

RSS	David Hay Fleming *et al.* (eds), *Registrum Secreti Sigilli Regum Scotorum: The Register of the Privy Seal of Scotland*, 5 vols (Edinburgh, 1908–57)
Sadler SP	Arthur Clifford (ed.), *The State Papers and Letters of Sir Ralph Sadler*, 2 vols (Edinburgh, 1809)
SHR	*Scottish Historical Review*
TA	T. Dickson *et al.* (eds), *Accounts of the Lord High Treasurer of Scotland*, 13 vols (Edinburgh, 1877–1978)
Wodrow Misc.	David Laing (ed.), *The Miscellany of the Wodrow Society* (Edinburgh, 1844)

Timeline

1528   Execution of Patrick Hamilton for heresy at St Andrews

        James V's personal rule begins

1534   Henry VIII of England breaks with Rome

1542   Death of James V: accession of Mary Queen of Scots, aged six days

1543   Earl of Arran becomes Governor of Scotland and briefly pursues Protestant policies

        Treaty of Greenwich pledging Mary Queen of Scots in marriage to Edward Tudor. The treaty is quickly repudiated by Scotland

1544–50 War with England (the 'Rough Wooings')

1546   Execution of George Wishart for heresy at St Andrews

        Murder of David Beaton, cardinal-archbishop of St Andrews

1547   Death of Henry VIII: Edward VI King of England

1548   Treaty of Haddington. Mary Queen of Scots is pledged in marriage to Francis, the Dauphin of France, and is taken to France

1549   First reforming general council of the Catholic Church under Archbishop Hamilton of St Andrews

1553   Death of Edward VI: Mary Tudor Queen of England

1554   Mary of Guise becomes Regent of Scotland

1557   Brief and inconclusive war with England

1558   Mary Queen of Scots marries the Dauphin Francis

        Death of Mary Tudor: Elizabeth I Queen of England

1559   Reformation-rebellion against Mary of Guise breaks out

1560   Protestant victory and 'Reformation' parliament

Scotland at the time of the Reformation

Introduction

———◆———

This book is about one of the most extraordinary national transformations in European history. During 1559 and 1560, the kingdom of Scotland experienced what was arguably the first modern revolution. The turmoil was sparked by religious conflict, but its impact was far wider. Scotland's political culture, social structure and international position were all profoundly affected by these events.

Like most revolutions, the Scottish Reformation was chaotic and unpredictable, in its course and in its consequences. It began unexpectedly: an attempt by the government to arrest dissident preachers provoked protest which blew up into riot and armed confrontation with frightening speed, surprising foreign observers, the regime and the rebels themselves. The year-long civil war that followed was a bewildering switchback of changing fortunes and foreign intervention. And the rebels' apparently total victory in the summer of 1560 masked their own divisions and the continued strength of some of the forces that had opposed them. For more than a century, religious revolutionaries in Scotland and elsewhere would be inspired by what had been started in 1559–60, and would try to bring it to some kind of completion.

Historians of Scotland have long recognised the Reformation as a pivotal event in Scottish history – perhaps *the* pivotal event. It is nowadays fashionable amongst historians to stress underlying continuities over visible changes, but the sharp break with the past in 1559–60 cannot easily be effaced. For historians with religious axes to grind, the Reformation has represented the moment that Scotland stepped from popish servitude into the light of Christ – or its passage from the true Catholic Church into the outer darkness of heresy. More secular historians of Scotland have also treated 1560 as a watershed.[1] An outstanding recent study by Margo Todd has reminded us of the dramatic social change brought about by Reformed Protestantism (the movement often, misleadingly, dubbed 'Calvinism').[2] The political upheavals of

1559–60 and the corrosive ideologies which Calvinism fomented permanently changed the terms of trade of Scottish politics. Perhaps most importantly, 1560 marked a sharp, unprecedented and (so far) permanent shift in Scotland's international relations, and so in the history of north-western Europe as a whole.

Geography ensured that during the Middle Ages (as indeed since), Scotland's view of the rest of the world was dominated by a single problem: that of relations with its uncomfortably powerful southern neighbour. Obviously enough, there were two clear-cut solutions to this problem available, neither of them particularly attractive. Defiance of England carried the risk of bloody conquest, or (which was little better) repeated, bloody and failed attempts at conquest. At the other extreme, alliance with England might become a bloodless conquest, or at least a 'special relationship' bringing little profit or honour to the junior partner. Both of these solutions had their advocates in medieval Scotland, but when forced to choose, the Scots consistently chose defiance. England's record of aggression was too well known for it to be trusted as an ally. Scotland instead spun itself a wider international web: trading across the North Sea to the Netherlands, Germany, Scandinavia and even Poland; sending scholars to the Netherlands and France; sealing royal marriages with Denmark and France. And it was with France above all that Scotland formed an alternative, and remarkably long-lived, 'special relationship'. The French alliance could not always deter the English, and indeed sometimes provoked them, but it did secure Scottish independence. When war came with England, as it did often enough during the fourteenth and fifteenth centuries, Scotland's formidable defensive geography, its pugnacious and independent aristocrats and its sometimes fickle ally ensured that the invaders were unable to convert battlefield victories into conquest.

During 1559–60 it became clear that this bloody status quo could not last. The Scots' political classes became convinced, perhaps rightly, that France had altered the terms of the 'special relationship' from alliance to colonisation. Many Scots also allowed themselves to be persuaded that England no longer harboured imperial ambitions. This change of heart ensured that Scotland, improbably, became the focus for a major international crisis. Every prince in Western Europe understood that if Scotland replaced its French alliance with an English one, the international balance of power would shift significantly. Indeed, in the spring of 1560 it briefly seemed possible that a Spanish army might intervene in Scotland, on top of the English and French forces already there. However, the decision to renounce the French alliance was a matter not only of politics but also of religion. For many Scots (not all), the choice between France and England had become the choice between Catholicism and Protestantism. By the spring of 1560, the Scottish political establishment had opted decisively for the English–Protestant alignment.

Scotland's basic foreign-policy question remained after 1560 – alliance with or defiance of England? – but its answer changed, swiftly and permanently. The nature of the Anglo-Scottish alliance has proved and continues to prove contentious. Minorities within Scotland have periodically questioned whether the alliance is worth its costs. For all that, however, the maintenance of that alliance in some form as the cornerstone of Scotland's place in the world has been the settled will of the Scots ever since 1560, and, for the time being, remains so. This remarkable alliance eventually created – as some of its founders hoped it would – a new identity and a new country.[3] Whether or not Britain and Britishness are ideas whose time is now passing, during their four centuries of existence they have shaped the peoples of both countries, and of the world beyond them.

The Scottish Reformation was not simply Britain's midwife, however. It also has a broader importance in the history of European religion and politics. Reformed Protestantism in Scotland was not, as it boasted, uniquely pure;[4] but its success was uniquely thorough. Beyond the religious laboratories of the Swiss city-states, Reformed Protestantism never won plainer or more lasting victories. In Scotland, unlike in France or Hungary, Calvinism succeeded in converting widespread support into political dominance. Unlike in England, Calvinism was not neutered and shackled by a state which shared its doctrines but did not trust its ambitions. Unlike in the Netherlands, the established Protestant Church in Scotland laid claim to the allegiance of all inhabitants, and did a remarkably good job of turning that claim into a reality. Scottish Catholicism was not merely politically defeated. It virtually disappeared from lowland Scotland and from the majority of the Highlands, until it returned with Irish immigrants in the eighteenth century. In its place, an astonishingly complete cultural revolution took place, as the model of religious life which Calvin had pioneered in a city of ten thousand people was rolled out across a sparse and sprawling country of a million or more souls. In 1559–60, this project was neither complete (of course) nor clearly defined, but the ambitions of those who began it are unmistakable.

The thoroughness of the Scottish Reformation was a consequence not only of its leaders' religious convictions but also of their political radicalism. Scottish Protestants first established their churches in defiance of established authority, as did Reformed Protestants in France and the Netherlands. In Scotland, however, that defiance extended into the political sphere. The reformers' theologians, notably but not exclusively John Knox, provided robust theoretical and rhetorical justifications for rebellion in the name of the Gospel. Their aristocratic leaders were ready to wrap themselves in such justifications, alongside older beliefs which asserted their own political rights and the consensual nature of the Scottish state. One consequence of this was that the Scottish Reformation took the form of a political rebellion, which powerfully reinforced the long Scottish tradition of mulish political independence. For nearly a century and a half after 1560, Scottish Protestants resisted attempts by the state to control religious life, while insisting that their rulers were liable to correction (and, ultimately, deposition) by the Church. This unsentimental, uncompromising and sometimes surly tradition of political independence was of lasting importance. Scottish Protestants' loathing of royal control over the Church sparked the civil wars which convulsed the British Isles in the seventeenth century. Scottish political traditions fed into North American ideals; Scottish theorists such as George Buchanan were acknowledged by the political thinkers of the Enlightenment.[5]

For all the Scottish Reformation's importance, however, its causes remain remarkably obscure. This is partly a simple matter of sources. The early history of an underground movement such as Scottish Protestantism is, inevitably, largely hidden from us. This book draws on two kinds of sources, neither of them satisfactory. The first, contemporaneous documents, are frustratingly thin. The informal nature of the Scottish state meant that it left a meagre paper-trail. We also have very few private letters, sermons or treatises. What we do have, in abundance, is English official documentation on Scottish affairs. This is enormously valuable, given England's intimate involvement in the Scottish Reformation, but its perspective is obviously skewed, and the English themselves lamented the unreliability of their information.[6] No other foreign government was nearly so interested in Scottish religious affairs, although we still await a truly thorough study of the relevant French archives.

Secondly, there are memoirs, histories and chronicles written after the fact, by witnesses of varying degrees of reliability. The most important of them is John Knox's gossipy, cantankerous and enthralling *History of the Reformation*.[7] The heart of Knox's history, recording the events of 1558–60, is a near-contemporaneous account; the sections on the earlier Reformation were actually written later, mostly in 1566. Knox was a poor historian: self-important, uninterested in detail and alarmingly ready to base sweeping generalisations on a single event. Yet his *History* is invaluable, not only for his eyewitness testimony but also for his inclusion of a great many documents which would otherwise have been lost. Other Protestant chronicles include the wildly unreliable histories of Robert Lindsay of Pitscottie and of George Buchanan; the English martyrologist John Foxe, whose Scottish material probably reflects the eyewitness testimony of the senior Scottish cleric John Winram;[8] and – a generation later – the Presbyterian polemicist David Calderwood. The most important Catholic history of the Reformation was the trenchant and bitter work of John Leslie, bishop of Ross, although John, Lord Herries' chatty and occasionally reliable chronicle is also coloured by the Catholicism to which he converted.

Almost all of these sources are well known to historians. Any archival discoveries, or rediscoveries, in this book do not change the picture dramatically. Indeed, thanks to the colossal efforts of nineteenth- and twentieth-century editors, most of these sources are in print. This book does not, therefore, claim to reveal unknown facts about the origins of the Scottish Reformation. Its originality, if it has any, lies not in the sources it uses but in the questions it asks of them and the links it can draw between them. For easy answers to questions about the origins of the Scottish Reformation will no longer do.

The search for 'causes' of great events has a bad name amongst some historians, and with good reason. It is altogether too easy to read history backwards to produce 'just-so stories', which start with what happened and then look for the reasons why it must inevitably have been so. The half-century before 1560 thus becomes the overture to the Reformation, rather than a period worth studying in its own right.[9] This 'inevitabilist' history tells us more about historians' metaphysics, and perhaps also their politics, than it does about the events it purports to describe. It is a bastard child of the determinist and social–Darwinist assumption that historical 'success' is always deserved, and grandchild of the corrupted theologies which read historical 'success' as a sign of God's favour. Nowadays historians prefer other (perhaps equally dubious) analogies, often to the dimly understood mathematics of chaos theory. The argument is that the causes of complex events consist of so many interwoven but independent variables as almost to defy analysis. 'Monocausal' explanations are derided as oversimplifications – sensibly enough, although some historians seem alarmingly fond of complexity for its own sake. The concept of 'contingency' is invoked to argue that events need not have turned out how they did, had even minor chance events fallen out differently. It is an appealing idea which has made the old genre of imagined history respectable under the name of 'counterfactuals'.[10] Although the metaphysics of 'contingency' are scarcely better than those of 'inevitability', this idea does at least recognise that great events can sometimes have trivial causes. And if causes are trivial, so, surely, is the search for them? Historians are increasingly turning to examine processes, consequences and historical relationships. Searching for causes seems increasingly futile.

This is doubly so when dealing with events such as the Scottish Reformation, for here the question of 'causes' has been usually been openly partisan. The dominant interpretation of the Scottish Reformation has been the heroic Protestant narrative, whose fundamental answer to the question of why the Reformation happened is that God willed it (which may be true, but is unverifiable). In its more recent forms this narrative has been thoroughly 'inevitabilist'. The classic Protestant history of David Hay Fleming, and the more recent work of James Kirk, belong in a tradition which stresses the profound corruption of the Catholic Church in Scotland; the fertile soil on which the seed sowed by the first reformers fell; the steady growth of Protestant belief in the dark years of persecution; and the sudden dawn of open Protestantism in 1559–60 banishing the night of popery.[11] Intriguingly, however, the earlier versions of this narrative look more 'contingent' to modern eyes. John Knox stressed that the reformers' cause often seemed hopeless and that even their successes were fragile. He believed that the outcome was in the balance until very late in the day, and that it was by no means secure after 1560. Indeed, Knox believed that the Scottish Reformation was, literally, inexplicable – that it had no worldly causes at all. Its success could thus be ascribed only to the mere will of God. This was an 'inevitability' which was theological, not historical.

Meanwhile, if Protestant histories of the Scottish Reformation have been triumphalist, Catholic histories have either been denunciations of the reformers as venal and godless conspirators; or laments for a lost world, in which the disaster is ascribed penitentially to the old Church's failure to live up to its principles. Modern Catholic histories – best represented in a splendid collection of *Essays on the Scottish Reformation* – have been subtler and more elegiac, but they have not challenged the basic claim that the Reformation was a matter of Protestant activism and Catholic failure.[12]

In the past two generations, historians of Scotland have moved away from these views, although partly by paying the question of origins comparatively little notice. Gordon Donaldson's pathbreaking survey of the Reformation questioned many of the old certainties, as he tried – not entirely successfully – to save Reformation history from being 'the plaything of ecclesiastical polemic'. He described an amorphous Reformation which only slowly and fitfully evolved (or degenerated) into Presbyterianism. Donaldson also argued, influentially, that the Reformation crisis arose 'less from religion than from the resentment which was building up against the government's pro-French policy'.[13] This view of the Reformation as a slow process in which the turning-points were more political than religious has informed a number of local studies of religious change, as well as Ian Cowan's powerful attempt to write a general history of the Reformation which takes full account of local diversity.[14] The best of these local studies, Michael Lynch's magisterial survey of Edinburgh, not only stresses how slowly and painfully the new Church put down roots in Edinburgh after 1560. He argues that the 1559–60 crisis was scarcely rooted in the town at all, but was imposed on it by force from outside.[15] If the religious crisis has been thus dissolved into a gradual process, it has been replaced by a political one. This, in turn, has been questioned by one important recent study casting doubt on the strength of anti-French feeling.[16] The Scottish Reformation almost seems to be in danger of vanishing altogether.

This book aims to present a new synthesis of ideas on the origins of the Scottish Reformation, building on this recent scholarship but also suggesting some new directions. It asks not only why the Scottish Reformation took place, but why *this* Reformation took place, rather than one of the many other 'Reformations' – and, indeed, counter-Reformations – that seemed possible in sixteenth-century Scotland. It tries to reconnect religion and politics, and to trace their interaction. In particular, it emphasises how acts or threats of violence drove political processes and shaped religious culture. Violence isolated moderates and aggravated division. Sometimes it discredited those who applied it. Equally often, it managed to destroy its targets, and those who refused to use violence were outmanoeuvred. As such this is a tale of few villains and fewer heroes. (If I have shown bias, I hope it is for or against individual characters in the story, rather than the parties to which some of them belonged.) The book also tries to place the Scottish Reformation on the wider stage of the European Reformation. Despite the nationalism of the traditional accounts, and of much Scottish history in general, the Reformation's natural stage was all Europe. The Scottish Reformation can be illuminated by international comparisons, and it was itself an international phenomenon. Religious developments in England and France, in particular, were a decisive influence on Scottish events.

The classic explanation for the Reformation is that the pre-Reformation Church was 'corrupt', and that its corruption created a moral vacuum which Protestantism filled. However, as a good deal of recent scholarship has argued, the late medieval Church cannot be dismissed so easily, and the first chapter of this book assesses the state of this question. Although some aspects of the pre-Reformation Church's administration can be described as 'corrupt', it is not at all clear that this 'corruption' was actually damaging. Rather, the Church had bought itself powerful protectors – albeit at some cost to its moral authority. Against this background, chapter 2 assesses the impact of the first arrival of Protestant ideas in the 1520s. As almost everywhere in Europe, this was initially a movement of clerics, scholars and merchants, and as such a rather limited threat to the Scottish religious establishment.

The new heretical movement became dangerous because it intersected with politics. In the 1530s, some members of the nobility, as well as lairds (that is, the landed magnates without noble titles) began to be drawn towards it. Perhaps they wished to do no more than mock the pretensions of the clergy, as they always had, but the Protestant presence and the Church's heavy-handed response to it provided a fresh impetus to such mockery, and a new language in which to mock. Worse, as chapter 2 also describes, the regime of James V (1513–42) was ambiguous towards the reformers. James was vehement in his opposition to heresy, for reasons of conviction and of convenience, but like other Renaissance monarchs he also gave some houseroom to moderate reformers, intrigued by the nature of their piety and entertained by their withering satires of clerical pomposity. The result was that by the time of his death, Protestantism had gained a foothold in the Scottish state.

James V's unexpected death in wartime pitched Scotland into a major political crisis, the subject of chapter 3. He was succeeded by an infant girl: Mary, Queen of Scots. During 1543, it seemed as if a Reformation of sorts might take place in Scotland. Mary's regent, the Earl of Arran, tried to forge an alliance with Henry VIII's England, and to reform the Scottish Church along English lines. He failed. Facing a broad Scottish consensus against any such deal, Arran reversed his policy in order to salvage his own authority. However, the few months of relative toleration which Scottish Protestantism enjoyed won the movement new recruits, and also raised its hopes. This helped to engender a bitterer and more confrontational mood when those hopes were defeated.

Many of those reformers still looked to England, which continued to aim at a Scottish alliance even when it became clear that such an 'alliance' could only be imposed by force. The so-called 'Rough Wooing' – England's attempt to extort a marriage alliance from Scotland by military means between 1544 and 1550, which is the subject of chapter 4 – proved to be the most intensive period of Anglo-Scottish warfare for over a century. It was a war with a religious dimension; England held out the prospect of a Protestant union between the two neighbours (especially after Henry VIII's death in 1547). However, Scottish Protestant hopes were defeated by England's reluctance to pay more than lip-service to such ideas. There were some notable Protestant achievements during the wars – most spectacularly, the murder of David Beaton, the Cardinal-Archbishop of St Andrews, in 1546 – but they came to nothing. In the end, large-scale French intervention ensured that the English were soundly defeated. Scottish Protestants were discredited by association with them. Their hopes seemed more distant than ever.

The 1550s were less obviously eventful. With the young Queen Mary now in France, Scotland became in effect a French satellite state – an arrangement whose immediate fruits were security and stability. In this context, the old Church, long criticised for its shortcomings and battered by war damage, set about an ambitious programme of reform, which is examined in chapter 5. The Catholic reformers' project was a bold one: they took on board some of the doctrinal, as well as disciplinary criticisms of their Church and attempted what amounted to a relaunch of Scottish Catholicism. It turned out to be self-defeating, largely because the new government of the Queen Mother, Mary of Guise, who became Regent in 1554, was unwilling to give the old Church the support it needed. Instead, she tolerated Protestantism, for her own, dangerously short-sighted reasons. The result was that the old

Church had its certainties shaken, while the Protestant minority, already radicalised by the bitter experiences of the 1540s, grew more aggressive in its beliefs and its mood. The underground Protestant movement, whose spread is discussed in chapter 6, was still small, but it was acquiring both anger and self-confidence.

How this situation toppled into crisis is the subject of chapter 7. It was not a simple matter of anti-French feeling, which in 1550s Scotland was no more than a background problem. The Scottish political classes had some specific grumbles about their ally's conduct, but not enough to question the alliance itself. They were merely becoming suspicious of France's methods and its trustworthiness. When the crisis came, it came for religious reasons. From the convoluted and partial accounts which survive, it is possible to piece together a decent account of religious politics during 1557–59. The picture which emerges is one of a religious peace process. Encouraged by Catholic reform and by political toleration, some of the Protestant lords pressed for a religious compromise which would formally allow some degree of co-existence. The negotiations helped to legitimate Protestant hopes; they failed, however, partly because neither Church nor regime was fully ready to compromise in a changing international climate, and partly because the more radical Protestants deliberately sabotaged the process through a series of provocative and high-profile acts of violence. The last of these, an iconoclastic riot in Perth in May 1559, finally polarised the situation and produced a military confrontation.

Chapter 8 examines the rebellion which followed. The Protestant rebels, styling themselves 'the Congregation', quickly managed to secure either active or tacit support from most of Scotland's political class. The religious issue was at the rebellion's heart, and was the priority for most of its key leaders, to a greater extent than some recent historians have allowed. However, Mary of Guise's clumsy military response to it, and the perceived tyranny of her French troops, also helped to mobilise Scottish opinion in favour of the rebels. Only now did the latent suspicion of France come to the fore. By contrast, the new, Protestant, English regime of Elizabeth I managed to intervene in the rebellion while convincing most Scots that it did not have any imperial ambitions. After a war which lasted into the summer of 1560, and whose end was grimly fought, the Congregation and their English allies managed to extract a surrender from Guise's French forces, not least because the growing religious turmoil in France itself prevented the dispatch of further reinforcements. However, alongside the military confrontation, the Congregation were also beginning the process of building a Reformed Protestant Church in Scotland's parishes. The book concludes by looking at the dubious process by which that Church was established in law in August 1560.

By that stage, the Protestant cause had acquired an extraordinary degree of moral authority and political momentum within Scotland. It is true that, as plenty of scholars have demonstrated, the new Church was not built in a day. It is also true that some Catholic structures and institutions maintained a shadowy afterlife for many years; that a few clergy remained publicly loyal to the old ways, not all of them from exile; and that in some regions, Catholic worship continued for a time. Yet given the limited resources of the Scottish state and of the new Church, it is surely the dramatic change in 1560 which is more striking. The rebellion of 1559–60 was accompanied by a cascade of conversions – politically convenient, but often sincere too. And the destruction of Scottish Catholicism as a living system of piety was remarkably sudden and complete. The Protestant Reformation was a long time coming to Scotland, but when it came, it came decisively. This does not mean that it was, as used to be assumed, the result of a slow and inevitable process of gathering strength, a wave which suddenly crested in 1559–60. Nor does it mean that this was an essentially political process in which religion was little more than a convenient badge of allegiance. The religious explosion was as genuine as it was sudden, as the products and residues of three decades of volatile religious politics combined in an unpredictable way. It was, indeed, a contingent process. It was not, however, a fluke or an accident. Above all, it is a story of political change driven by violence and the fear of violence: violence which made compromise impossible, which both produced and undermined rival claims to moral authority, and which forced Scotland's ruling classes to make political choices most of them would have preferred to avoid. It was not inevitable that this process would produce a Protestant Reformation; perhaps it was inevitable that it would destabilise Scotland's political and religious culture. How this process took shape, and how it unexpectedly produced a religious revolution, is the subject of this book.

NOTES

1 T. C. Smout, *A History of the Scottish People 1560–1830* (London, 1969).

2 Margo Todd, *The Culture of Protestantism in Early Modern Scotland* (New Haven and London, 2002).

3 Linda Colley, *Britons: Forging the Nation 1707–1837* (New Haven and London, 1992); Roger Mason, 'Scotching the Brut: politics, history and national myth in sixteenth-century Britain' in Roger Mason (ed.), *Scotland and England 1285–1815* (Edinburgh, 1987), 60–84; Jane Dawson, 'Anglo-Scottish Protestant culture and integration in sixteenth-century Britain' in Steven G. Ellis and Sarah Barber, *Conquest and Union: Fashioning a British State, 1485–1725* (New York, 1995), 87–114.

4 Knox, II, 263–4.

5 George Buchanan, *A Dialogue on the Law of Kingship Among the Scots*, eds Roger Mason and Martin Smith (Aldershot, 2004), xv–xvi.

6 *HP*, I, 298.2. The most important documents are found in *LP*; *HP*; *CSP Scotland*; *CSP Foreign*.

7   Knox, I and II; cf. John Knox, *History of the Reformation in Scotland*, ed. and tr. William Croft Dickinson, 2 vols (Edinburgh, 1949). See also Maurice Lee, 'John Knox and his History', *SHR*, 45 (1966), 79–88; Roger Mason, 'Usable pasts: history and identity in Reformation Scotland', *SHR*, 76 (1997), 54–68.

8   Thomas Freeman, ' "The reik of Maister Patrik Hammyltoun": John Foxe, John Winram and the martyrs of the Scottish Reformation', *Sixteenth Century Journal*, 27 (1996), 43–60.

9   Janet P. Foggie, *Renaissance Religion in Urban Scotland: The Dominican Order, 1450–1560* (Leiden and Boston, 2003), 2.

10 For 'counterfactual' history in full flood, see Niall Ferguson (ed.), *Virtual History: Alternatives and Counterfactuals* (London, 1997).

11 David Hay Fleming, *The Reformation in Scotland: Causes, Characteristics, Consequences* (London, 1910); James Kirk, *Patterns of Reform: Continuity and Change in the Reformation Kirk* (Edinburgh, 1989).

12 David McRoberts (ed.), *Essays on the Scottish Reformation* (Glasgow, 1962). On sixteenth-century Catholic views, see below, 12–13.

13 Gordon Donaldson, *The Scottish Reformation* (Cambridge, 1960), esp. 27; cf. Donaldson, *All the Queen's Men: Power and Politics in Mary Stewart's Scotland* (London, 1983), esp. 28; Donaldson, *Scotland: James V to James VII* (Edinburgh and London, 1965), 86–7.

14 Ian B. Cowan, *The Scottish Reformation: Church and Society in Sixteenth-Century Scotland* (London, 1982). For a recent local study along these lines, see Linda Dunbar, *Reforming the Scottish Church: John Winram (c. 1492–1582) and the Example of Fife* (Aldershot, 2002).

15 Michael Lynch, *Edinburgh and the Reformation* (Edinburgh, 1981).

16 Pamela E. Ritchie, *Mary of Guise in Scotland, 1548–1560: A Political Career* (East Linton, 2002).

Chapter 1

———◆———

A 'corrupt' Church?

'CORRUPTION' AND ITS IMPORTANCE

After 1560, when Roman Catholics looked back on the disaster that had engulfed their Church in Scotland, they knew who to blame. There was the greed of the nobles, the lassitude of the common people and – of course – the depravity of the Protestants. Above all, however, they blamed themselves. Lord Herries, who had repented of his own former Protestantism, described the years before the crisis in a tone of lamentation:

> It is certain that in these days the Church in this kingdom was in a lethargy. . . . Prelates and bishops, who should have governed the Church here, were turned lazy in spiritual exercises; priests and the inferior clergy were become loose and idle, and lascivious, many of whom with a greedy appetite embraced those liberties newly preached. In a word, all was out of frame; for the people in general (as it were) [were] wearied with the old Church government, and willing to accept of any novelties that agreed with their humours.[1]

Closer to the time, other Catholics were more biting in their assessments. The Dutch Jesuit Nicholas de Gouda visited Scotland in 1562, to see if anything might be salvaged from the wreckage. He was appalled by what he found. The lives of the Catholic clergy, he wrote, had been 'extremely licentious and scandalous', a state of affairs which was tolerated by 'the absolutely supine negligence of the bishops'. He singled out one central abuse for criticism. The highest (and wealthiest) offices in the Church had effectively been monopolised by the Crown and the nobility. Men who were entirely unqualified, and even children, had regularly been appointed as bishops and abbots.[2] The previous year, the Catholic controversialist Quintin Kennedy had posed the question: 'What is the cause of this great variance of opinion which is risen lately amongst Christian men for matters of the faith?' His answer, too, dwelt on the habit of granting offices in the Church 'to unqualified men as temporal reward'. And he asked: 'When such monstrous ministers, blinded in ignorance, drowned in lusts, are appointed to have authority in the Church of God, what wonder is it that the world be confounded with heresies, faction, and opinion as it is?'[3] Such criticism had all the more force coming from Kennedy, who owed his lucrative office as commendator of Crossraguell Abbey not to his spiritual qualities but to his being the son of an earl.

So perhaps the origins of the Scottish Reformation are not a puzzle at all. The guilty party has already confessed. The Catholic Church brought disaster on itself through its corruption. It was led by men who saw it as a mere milch cow, and staffed by priests who learned lessons in corruption and indiscipline from their fathers in God. It had forfeited the respect of the people. Some modern Catholic historians have agreed that this was a Church sunk too deep in sin to be able to reform itself.[4] Or as a Protestant described it: 'Like a hoary giant of the forest, it was rotten within and doomed to collapse ignominiously before the approaching storm.'[5]

This has been a common theme of histories of the Scottish Reformation – reasonably enough. If Catholics blamed the Reformation on their own failings, Protestant historians were even readier to harp on the corruption of the pre-Reformation Church – and they provided more gory detail. Nor can there be any serious doubt that the pre-Reformation Church had some serious and intractable problems. However, most recent historians have become increasingly wary of any simple link between the Church's perceived 'corruption' and its collapse in 1559–60. This chapter will re-examine the state of the late medieval Scottish Church, to ask whether its problems contributed to its downfall – and if so, how.

There are good reasons to be suspicious of the attempt to scapegoat the old Church. Both its Protestant and Catholic critics had ulterior motives. Protestants throughout Europe accused the Catholic Church of being riddled with corruption almost by default (every medieval reform movement had done the same). This made for good propaganda, but there was a theological rationale too. The reformers argued that the corruption of the clergy's lives revealed the corruption of the doctrine by which they lived. The Catholic Church was an evil tree bringing forth evil fruit. Catholics, however, drew the opposite conclusion from the same 'facts'. They blamed the Reformation on the Catholic Church's failure to live up to its own principles. This meant that they could criticise their 'corrupt' predecessors – and so distance themselves from their misdeeds – while claiming that Catholic doctrine itself was not to blame. Both sides shared an interest in denigrating the medieval Church. No-one had an interest in defending it.

This is a debate which goes beyond Scotland. In an attempt to explain the Reformation, the late medieval Church across most of Europe has been described as corrupt and ripe for renewal. Those wider debates suggest that the Scottish Church's undoubted difficulties should be approached with caution. There may not, in practice, have been an easy connection between ecclesiastical corruption and the growth of Protestantism. Corruption and (more importantly) the perception of corruption were widespread in Germany and the Swiss Confederation, but in neither case did Protestantism sweep the board. By contrast, the late medieval Church in England was well funded, well disciplined, led by exceptionally able men and genuinely popular. Yet this was not enough to save England from Protestantism. It is a comparison worth pausing over, because, paradoxically, it may have been the very 'quality' of the English Church which made it vulnerable. Everywhere in Europe, princes and nobles hoped to take advantage of the Church's wealth. If, as in England, the Church happened to be well disciplined and in good financial order, it could often resist attempts at quiet encroachment. However, an immensely wealthy institution led by low-born scholars and administrators lacked the social clout to repel an all-out attack. It was necessary for Henry VIII and Edward VI to ransack the English Church, seizing most of its property, because that Church was insufficiently 'corrupt' to be plundered by more subtle means. It was possible for them to do so because the lands of the English Church had no powerful defenders. Instead, the country's secular magnates themselves stood to profit from the looting.

Scotland's situation was very different.[6] By one set of definitions, the Scottish Church was measurably more 'corrupt' than its English counterpart. That is, Scotland's nobles and lairds exercised a great deal of control over the Church in general and its wealth in particular. The high nobility were extremely well represented amongst the senior bishops and abbots. Some bishops, especially of the more remote dioceses, scarcely troubled to visit their sees. William Cunningham, son of the Earl of Glencairn, was elected Bishop of Argyll in 1539. He retained the see for fourteen years without even being consecrated, effectively running the bishopric as part of his family's estate.[7] Likewise, those noblemen appointed to head monastic houses were often commendators rather than abbots: that is, they were not required to take religious vows, or indeed to be ordained as priests. The first Scottish commendator was appointed in 1430, and by 1560 some two-thirds of Scotland's religious houses were headed by commendators, most of them noblemen by birth. Such offices could become effectively hereditary.[8] The most spectacular 'abuse' of this system was the appointment of four of James V's infant (and illegitimate) sons to head Scotland's richest religious houses during the 1530s, with the revenues passing directly to their father. Once in office, the normal rules did not apply to such men. Even amongst well-regulated orders, a noble surname attracted incomes and multiple benefices regardless of regulations.[9] Most damagingly of all, these men did not simply exploit ecclesiastical revenues themselves, but transferred lands from the Church to their own relatives, permanently undermining the Church's finances.[10]

These problems did not merely impoverish the Church's wealthiest institutions, but were passed on down the hierarchy into Scotland's thousand or so parishes. The foundation of Church finance across Christendom was the tithe (in Scots, the 'teind'): a form of income tax in which, in theory, a tenth of all agricultural produce or other 'increase' was owing to the rector of the parish, the fabric of the church building and the support of the poor. The practice had become rather different. Many teinds had been negotiated into fixed customary payments, a process which slowly eroded parishes' incomes. More significant, however, was impropriation. This was the process by which an institution – a monastic house, collegiate foundation or cathedral – might permanently acquire the rectory of a parish, and so claim the teind income which went with it. The institution would then in theory be required to provide a priest to serve the parish (a vicarious representative, or vicar). However, even when a vicar was appointed, only a fraction of the teind income would be returned to him. Impropriation, in other words, was a means of sucking wealth away from the parishes to support larger institutions. This was not always damaging. Sometimes institutional rectors used the funds productively and took their responsibilities to their impropriate parishes seriously. However, in practice, these institutions were often the same ones whose wealth was being diverted into noble pockets. The overall effect of impropriation on the Scottish Church was thoroughly malign, as senior churchmen recognised.[11] However, the scale of the problem defied any easy reform. Over 85 per cent of Scottish parishes were impropriate, a proportion only rivalled in the rest of Europe by the equally troubled Church of Switzerland. The 148 parishes which did retain their own teind income were, as a result, more lucrative appointments; as such, they were often held by pluralist or profiteering absentees.[12] Despite the efforts of ecclesiastical reformers, the parish clergy were systematically impoverished. They were, as a consequence, driven to financial expedients which further undermined their moral authority.[13] The customary freewill offerings given to the clergy at Easter had, it seems, been allowed to solidify into a compulsory requirement. This was widely agreed to be bringing the Church into disrepute, creating the impression that the sacraments were for sale and causing the poor 'to murmur greatly against the State Ecclesiastic'. We are told of one priest reprimanded by his bishop for refusing to exact some of the more inflammatory traditional dues from his people.[14] It is plausible enough. A well-meaning priest could not be allowed to start a price war among the clergy, if that meant that vital sources of income would be eroded. The burden which those dues laid on the common people was a secondary concern.

In other words, the Scottish Church's finances were shot through with practices which violated the spirit and, in some cases, the letter of the law. More important, perhaps, was the widespread perception that this was so. It was a truism that whenever a major benefice fell vacant, 'the great men of the realm will have it for temporal reward'.[15] The poet William Dunbar asked, in a satire on the seizure of valuable benefices by the powerful:

> Whether it is merit more
> To give him drink that thirsts sore
> Or fill a full man till he burst
> And let his fellow die for thirst.[16]

Such sympathy for the lower clergy was unusual, however. A generation later, the conservative poet Richard Maitland dismissed the clergy indiscriminately as little more than armed ruffians. 'To preach and teach they will not learn / The church goods they waste away.'[17] Another satirist writing in the 1550s depicted the entire clerical estate as obsessed with plunder and embezzlement, from the lowly parish priest who would stir from his sloth only in order to extort the last scrap of food from a widow, through the monks who preferred gluttony to study, to the bishops who saw preaching the Gospel as beneath their dignity.[18]

However, neither the undoubted problems of the Scottish Church nor the lively conventions of anticlerical rhetoric meant that this was a Church vulnerable to potential Protestant attack. Many of the fiercest attacks came from those whose commitment to the old Church and to traditional piety was in no doubt. The 1550s satirist who condemned the clergy as a whole insisted that their priority should have been to pray for souls in purgatory instead – an activity which, in Protestant eyes, was a blasphemy far more damnable than mere venality. Richard Maitland, too, grounded his criticism of his own times in the lament that 'churchmen before were good of life' and that there had been a time when 'devotion was not away'.[19] They were trying to provoke the Church to reform itself, and as such their rhetoric should not be taken at face value. The faults they criticised were widespread but not universal. If the senior clergy were usually noblemen, noble birth did not automatically equate to venality or negligence. The high nobility continued to provide committed and able churchmen up to and beyond 1560. Moreover, the presence of so many powerful men amongst its leaders could be of positive benefit to the Church. The Crown, nobles and lairds came to have a strong vested interest in the status quo. They were the chief beneficiaries of the Church's 'corruption'. After the dissolution of the English monasteries, Henry VIII tried to tempt Scotland to follow his example, but no such seizure of Church lands was ever remotely possible in north of Border. The system as it stood simply benefited Scotland's landed elite too much for it to be directly challenged.

If the Scottish Reformation was a reaction against a 'corrupt' Church, we might expect that when it came the 'corruption' would be swept away. During and after the crisis of 1559–60, however, noble control of Church wealth was actually entrenched. In November 1559, the Protestant lords did denounce the pattern of appointment to major benefices, but their complaint was that the richest pickings were being taken by Frenchmen rather than coming to themselves.[20] The following year, the Protestant nobles vetoed plans to use ecclesiastical incomes to support the Reformed ministry. They were enthusiastic for the reform of doctrine, but they had no intention of allowing such reform to undermine the 'corruption' from which they and their peers had benefited for so long.

The point is not that the late medieval Scottish Church's irregularities were unimportant, still less that they were wholly advantageous. They did not, however, produce a Church which was unstable or 'weak'. With hindsight it may appear that the Church had sold its soul to the nobility. If it did so, it secured a good price; but it is not in fact clear that the bargain was quite so deadly. A Church is a large and a complex organisation, and cannot be neatly plotted on a scale between 'weakness' and 'strength'. Our concern is not, primarily, to gauge the Scottish Church's moral standing, but to ask whether the condition and quality of its various constituent parts contributed to the process of Reformation in the sixteenth century – and if so, how.

PIETY IN PRE-REFORMATION SCOTLAND

The Scottish Church changed dramatically in the century before 1560, and these changes cannot be measured simply against a yardstick of 'corruption'. During the reigns of James III (1460–88) and James IV (1488–1513) the Scottish Church became a fully independent province, in parallel with those kings' nation-building projects. The vestigial jurisdiction of the archbishops of York and Trondheim over parts of the Scottish Church was ended and the bishoprics of St Andrews and (later) Glasgow were raised to metropolitan status. During the fifteenth century the Church's intellectual life was underpinned by the foundation of three universities. The founder of the last of these, Bishop Elphinstone of Aberdeen, also produced a new national liturgy for the whole Scottish Church, the *Aberdeen Breviary*, published in 1509–10. New monastic foundations had dried up in Scotland as they had in much of the rest of Europe, but – as elsewhere – this was because benefactors were tending to favour other forms of the religious life. Collegiate churches were one such form. These were, in effect, informal, stripped-down monasteries, or perhaps miniature cathedrals. They were staffed by secular priests, who had not taken monastic vows, who received stipends and who were free to resign if they wished to do so, but who were required to observe the statutes of the colleges while they were members of them, and to live quasi-monastic lives of intercession. There were more than twenty new collegiate foundations between 1450 and 1550.[21] All these foundations were made possible through the impropriation of parish churches, a process which could be more than mere plundering. Some of the classic religious orders were also prospering. Christendom's most self-consciously austere order, the Carthusian monks, had one Scottish house, at Perth, founded by James I in 1426. The Carthusians were not immune to the Scottish Church's acquisitive and litigious habits (the priorship of the house was contested at law for twelve years in the 1540s and 1550s) but the monks themselves were recognised as being exceptionally pious and disciplined even by the daunting standards of their own order.[22]

The healthiest religious orders, however, were clearly the Franciscan and Dominican friars. They were largely free of financial scandal, and their relative poverty also saved them from being staffed by nobles.[23] Everywhere in Latin Christendom, the friars were the Church's preachers. Most parish clergy, in Scotland as elsewhere, did not preach, aside perhaps from a brief homily at Mass. The set-piece sermon, an address lasting over an hour (often well over), was an occasional highlight which called for an expert. In the towns where they were based, the friars' preaching was almost commonplace. Beyond them, for anyone other than a friar to preach was a novelty. Protestants criticised the rest of the clergy for their failure to preach, but there was merit in creating a corps of itinerant specialist preachers.[24] This expertise fitted them to be in the front line of the Reformation struggles – on both sides. Pope Leo X famously described the turmoil provoked by Martin Luther as 'a quarrel among friars', and in Scotland as elsewhere, friars were both the earliest converts to and the earliest opponents of the new doctrines. When the Earl of Arran was looking for evangelical preachers in 1543, it seemed obvious to look amongst 'poor friars that are well learned in the Holy Scriptures'. The most vigorous opponent of the men he appointed was another friar.[25] Theologically aware and rhetorically skilled, the friars were valuable allies and dangerous enemies.

Indeed, while Protestants spoke of monks with contempt, they paid the friars the compliment of hatred. Reformers vied with friars for the religious affection of the towns. The reformist clique in Perth in 1543–44 saw the town's friars as their chief opponents. In radical Dundee, violence was being threatened against friars a decade earlier. The friaries were the most consistent recipients of Protestant iconoclastic violence, and not, as Gordon Donaldson suggested, simply because they were conveniently located in towns.[26] Seven of the Franciscans' sixteen Scottish friaries were Conventual houses, where a less stringent interpretation of the Franciscan rule was observed; the Order's real spiritual and scholarly rigours were confined to its Observant wing, which controlled the other nine houses. In 1559–60, only one of the Conventual houses (in the Protestant heartland of Dundee) may have been attacked, while only two of the Observant houses (in isolated Elgin and Jedburgh) escaped.[27] Across Scotland, iconoclastic violence during 1559–60 was directed at the healthiest and best ordered institutions. The more lax houses posed no threat, and could usually be persuaded to co-operate with the reformers – even when their heads were not members of noble families that had turned to Protestantism.[28] The best-documented case in which a traditional monastery was sacked – that of Scone Abbey, near Perth – also seems to be one of the few occasions on which the violence was sparked by local resentment rather than being co-ordinated by the Protestant leadership.[29] In most cases, Protestant violence is a testament to the strength of its targets.

The friars' power was grounded on the respect which they commanded from the laity. This was the critical battleground. There may have been widespread contempt for the abuses of the old Church and resentment of its financial exactions, but this did not easily translate into distaste for its doctrines – any more than, in modern times, contempt for particular politicians automatically leads to distaste for democracy or affection for the alternatives. Whatever the problems of the old Church, traditional pieties were widespread across the social scale and until the very end. James IV was famously devoted to the Franciscan Observants, a piety which his son did something to emulate.[30] In the mid-1540s we find the Earl of Eglinton establishing a splendid set of memorial Masses for himself from a range of different friars; and Lord Fleming founding a collegiate Church in which any educational purpose was eclipsed by the emphasis on Masses for the dead and prayer to the Virgin Mary. Parliaments routinely and fulsomely reaffirmed the Church's rights and privileges.[31] In all of the principal towns, even those normally seen as Protestant strongholds, investment in traditional pieties continued into the 1550s. In Ayr, approximately two-fifths (sometimes as much as two-thirds) of the burgh council's expenditure went on gifts to the local Dominican house, stipends for chaplains in the parish church and other pious purposes. In 1547, the burgh council of Perth granted burgess status to one priest, in recognition of his 'faithful labour in daily rising to say the first Mass regularly at the same hour for the great help of the whole community'.[32]

There is also plenty of evidence of colourful popular piety in pre-Reformation Scotland: a piety which sometimes strained Catholic orthodoxy but whose vibrancy is unmistakable. Semi-official celebrations such as liturgical dramas were at least as popular as anticlerical satires – probably with the same audiences. In 1545 the Protestant preacher George Wishart lamented that scarcely a hundred would come to hear him preach, in a town where two thousand would regularly turn out to see a mystery play. The plays were stamped out with some difficulty after 1560. Other popular devotions, such as pilgrimages, also persisted stubbornly in some parts of the country.[33] The relic of the Holy Cross held by the Trinitarian monastery at Peebles was a magnet for pilgrims, and even attracted a measure of devotion from James V.[34] In 1542 his wife, Mary of Guise, herself went on pilgrimage to the chapel of Our Lady of Loretto, at Musselburgh, the site of an image of the Virgin which had been received from heaven by a hermit. This image was named for the more famous shrine in Italy popularised by Pope Julius II, and it received 'great devotion of the people' for its healing powers. (And Guise was, indeed, safely delivered of the daughter she was carrying.)[35] The hermit himself, Thomas Douchtie, had acquired a considerable reputation for holiness on his extensive travels, not least because of his imprisonment by the Turks. He seems to have been the talk of the country after his return to Scotland with the image in the early 1530s. If reformers lampooned him, it is only a sign of how seriously he was taken.[36] Itinerant, 'freelance' holy men of this kind seem to have had a particular appeal. A few years before Douchtie, another wandering ascetic, John Scot, had returned to Scotland. His reputation for miraculous feats of fasting quickly became a 'rumour through all the Realm . . . rife in all men's mouths'.[37] Such purported miracle-workers were periodically exposed as frauds, but these occasional scandals were a regular feature of medieval Catholicism, and testify less to popular scepticism than to a widespread willingness to believe.[38]

There also seems to have been a robust respect for the saints. The *Aberdeen Breviary* had introduced dozens of new Scottish saints into the liturgy, part of the Stewart kings' deliberate attempt to link piety and patriotism. Often, however, saints' cults were more local. When the Earl of Caithness was killed during a failed attempt to seize the Orkney Islands in 1529, the islanders ascribed the victory to St Magnus, 'whom they ever honour patron of their whole Isle and liberty, with all piety and Religion'. It was said that they saw the saint fighting alongside them. They were not alone in turning their piety against their neighbours. William Dunbar, in the course of an exuberantly traditional description of Heaven and Hell, claimed that Hell was filled with Highlanders, so much so that the devil was vexed by their Gaelic 'clatter'. Like the practice of swearing blasphemous oaths by the blood, body, passion or wounds of Christ, or the fear of being buried on the northern side of a church, this was not exactly piety. Nor did the more po-faced Catholic reformers approve of such beliefs and practices.[39] They are, however, testament to the vitality and depth of traditional beliefs.

By contrast, there is very little evidence of heresy – of real religious dissidence – in Scotland before the arrival of Protestantism. The English heresy of Lollardy was noticed north of the Border in the early fifteenth century, but the handful of cases does not suggest any deep penetration of the country.[40] Lollard activity surfaces only twice in Scotland after the 1430s. In 1494, a group of Ayrshire lairds were accused of Lollard heresies. One of the suspect families, the Campbells of Cessnock, was later said by the Scottish Lutheran

Alexander Alesius to have had heretical sympathies. It is hard to know what to make of this case. It may have been the tip of a heretical iceberg in the south-west, or it may itself have been grossly exaggerated by the later (Protestant) Campbells' pride in their foresighted ancestors.[41] More concrete, but probably less important, is the one surviving Scots version of the Lollard New Testament, now in the British Library. A very late family tradition ascribes its authorship to the Ayrshire notary Murdoch Nisbet, and claims that he had also instructed small conventicles of heretics.[42] There was some heretical presence in late medieval Scotland, then, but it was clearly confined to one corner of the country, and there is no reason to believe that it had any real significance even there.

If there were few real heretics in late medieval Scotland, however, there was certainly a *fear* of heresy. Lollardy caused some alarm to the Church and even to James I in the early fifteenth century, and even in the 1480s the royal councillor John Ireland warned James III that 'in thy realm has been, and yet, as I understand, are, errors and heresies lurking'.[43] Even early Protestants could be found speaking slightingly of 'Lollards' – which suggests that dislike of the heresy had spread much further than real Lollardy.[44] Such suspicions may account for the Church's hair-trigger readiness to fire heresy accusations at those who strayed into apparent unorthodoxy. An Aberdeen Dominican who preached on the contentious subject of the immaculate conception of the Virgin Mary in 1520 found himself reported to the Sorbonne, which duly rapped him across the knuckles.[45] A more obscure case arose in Aberdeen the following year. The schoolmaster, John Marschell, had made comments about papal jurisdiction which the burgh council found unacceptable, and which he was forced to recant, although they may have been protecting their own privileges as much as Rome's.[46] The inquisitorial instinct was flourishing in the universities as well. In 1541, during one of the regular rounds of public disputations at the University of St Andrews, David Guild, a Regent of St Leonard's College within the university, strayed into the theological minefield of Christological definitions. Perhaps his speculations on the meaning of the Father's begetting of Christ were ill advised, but it was disproportionate to blow up this piece of isolated academic conjecture into a full-scale heresy charge. It took the personal intervention of the venerable John Mair (or Major), Dean of the Faculty of Theology and the university's most celebrated scholar, to end the case. Mair claimed he was determined to vindicate an innocent man and put a stop to malevolent rumour.[47] Guild was probably never in any real danger, but the case illustrates the readiness with which the charge of heresy could be brandished in situations that had nothing to do with real religious dissidence.

These confrontational habits reached down to the parishes. The hierarchy could not, or would not, distinguish between different kinds of threats to their authority. Financial disputes and knee-jerk anticlericalism were lumped together with genuine heresy. One effect of this was to spread contempt for the Church's disciplinary processes, both because of their overuse and because they were frequently unenforceable. The Church's most important sanction was excommunication, or 'cursing'. In theory this was a fearsome excision from the body of Christ. Excommunicates were denied access to the sacraments, and if they died unrepentant were destined for Hell. In the meantime, they should have suffered social ostracism, and in particular exclusion from commercial or civic life. In practice, however, the overuse of excommunication seems to have fostered a blasé attitude amongst many late medieval Scots. The heretic who claimed in the 1530s that cursing was used 'only to terrify simple persons and extort the goods of laymen' had struck a nerve. William Arth (a friar whom Knox insisted was 'papist in his heart') condemned the abuse of excommunication in the early 1530s, insisting that it was being used inappropriately, as a weapon of first rather than last resort, and was consequently being brought into contempt.[48] Catholic reformers also worried that it was being seen as destructive and vindictive, rather than as an act of loving correction.[49] When the entire town council of Edinburgh was excommunicated in 1558 during a financial spat with the Archbishop of St Andrews, they chose not to back down but rather to embark on the lengthy process of an appeal to Rome. Clearly, for these councillors – few of whom can be associated with any kind of Protestantism – excommunication was an annoyance, but little more than that.[50]

This was despite efforts to bolster the spiritual penalties of excommunication with more concrete sanctions. In 1552, parish clergy were ordered to read out the names of local excommunicates week by week, to heighten the social pressure on the unrepentant, but this plainly had the capacity to backfire.[51] There were repeated parliamentary acts against 'them that wilfully, obstinately or arrogantly incurs the pains of cursing'. In cases where someone was excommunicated for refusing to honour a debt, creditors were promised royal letters to enforce the settlement of the account. Those who remained obdurately excommunicate for more than a year were to forfeit all their goods to the Crown. These acts, it is worth emphasising, were in no way aimed at heresy. Parliaments worried that some excommunicates continued to receive communion, or even compelled priests to say Mass for them by force.[52] Such practices testify to a lively faith in the old Church's sacraments, and to an equally lively contempt for the old Church's strictures.

If there is a common thread running through the varied difficulties of the late medieval Church in Scotland, it is this: not that there was contempt for the Church as an institution, still less for Catholic doctrine, but that there was widespread disrespect for the clergy. The Church's acknowledged financial problems were a part of this, but it was not a simple matter of money. The moral standards of the clergy are open to challenge in every age, but the problem was the more acute in sixteenth-century Scotland because the lives of the bishops themselves were scandalous as often as they were exemplary. The last two Catholic Archbishops of St Andrews, David Beaton and John Hamilton, were committed churchmen and each, in their different ways, devoted real effort to the defence of the Church,[53] but both men laid themselves open to accusations of pride and hypocrisy. In July 1545, Beaton allowed a dispute with the Archbishop of Glasgow over precedence in the latter's cathedral to turn into a public scuffle in which both men's processional crosses were damaged: one did not need to be malicious to be shocked by this.[54] Or again, the catechism published in Hamilton's name in 1552 roundly denounced clerical immorality, and the general provincial councils of 1549–59 over which he presided legislated against the sexual incontinence of the clergy.[55] Yet the long-standing relationship between Hamilton himself and Lady Grisel Sempill was an open secret. Nor was Hamilton the only such offender amongst the bishops. William Gordon, Bishop of Aberdeen, was even petitioned by the chapter of his own cathedral to rid himself 'of the gentlewoman by whom he is greatly slandered; without the which be done, divers that are partakers say they cannot accept counsel and correction of him which will not correct himself'. His half-brother Alexander Gordon was a candidate for several bishoprics before eventually securing that of Galloway, as well as the glamorous and empty title of Archbishop of Athens. Throughout these career manoeuvres he was living with one Barbara Logie, and indeed they later claimed that they had married in secret in the 1540s.[56] The sexual misdemeanours of the clergy have always attracted comment, but it is perhaps no surprise that this was such a consistent theme of anticlerical polemic in Scotland.

In 1549, the Catholic author of the *Complaynt of Scotland* told the clergy that 'the abuse and the sinister ministration of thy office is the special cause of the schism and of divers sects that troubles all Christianity'.[57] Yet this link is in fact far from clear. There is no easy correlation between 'corruption' and heresy, as even Protestant historians have recognised.[58] For example, the diocese of Aberdeen had an even higher rate of impropriation than the rest of the country (95 per cent), but remained a redoubt of religious conservatism throughout the Reformation period.[59] The dangers which the Scottish Church's systemic problems and popular reputation posed – and the limits of those dangers – are well summarised in John Knox's tale of David Stratoun of Lauriston. Stratoun owned a fishing boat, and in the early 1530s he fell into a dispute with the vicar of Ecclesgreig over the teinds owing on his fish. Teind disputes of this kind were part of the normal friction of Catholic life, but the financial distortion of the Scottish Church served to exacerbate them. Teinds seemed less like a spiritual duty than a tax. Stratoun, fired by 'hatred against the pride and avariciousness of the priests', justified his non-payment with contemptuous mockery. If clergy wanted their share of the fish, he said, 'it were but reason, that they should come and receive it where he got the stock' – and he explained that he had thrown every tenth fish overboard. The vicar was understandably unhappy with this, and Stratoun was excommunicated for non-payment. Excommunication, as so often, was a flash-point. Stratoun denounced the excommunication as illegitimate, and this attracted an accusation of heresy.

So far this was a normal tale of knockabout anticlericalism, and while Knox clearly enjoyed it (and embellished it), he was quite clear that Stratoun was no evangelical reformer. Indeed, Knox wrote that he was 'a man very stubborn, and one that despised all reading (chiefly of those things that were godly)', who was distinguished only by his hatred of the clergy. It was only after Stratoun's delation for heresy that he fell in with certain godly lairds, who led him to reading the Scriptures in the vernacular, and thus to a dramatic conversion. It was for these new convictions that he was burned outside Edinburgh in August 1534.[60] Knox's highly stylised account may not be particularly credible, but the model he suggests is clear. Stratoun's aggressive anticlericalism did not make him a heretic. It was only when the Church's response to his anticlericalism pushed him into heretical company that he was converted.

Stratoun's case shows us one route by which the Church's institutional problems could give rise to doctrinal dissidence. The heavy-handed use of the heresy laws against those whose offences were merely matters of discipline could prove a self-fulfilling prophecy. This, in its turn, was perhaps a consequence of the debasement of the Church's main disciplinary weapon – excommunication. The path that Stratoun took was, however, an unusual one. The most earnest converts to Protestantism were more commonly won from the heart of the old faith, not its fringes. The Church's difficulties may have produced laymen who scoffed at and despised it, but scoffing and despising were not the habits of mind which made Protestant converts.

If the Church's systemic problems did feed into the rise of heresy, it is more likely that they did so in a negative way. Its financial and disciplinary shortcomings left it ill fitted to mount a counterattack against a genuine heretical challenge. Its moral authority was compromised, and many of its financial resources had been seized. It was not powerless by any means. The strength of the friaries and the active leadership of some senior clergy were genuinely valuable. However, the Church was clearly better equipped to provide small numbers of first-class itinerant preachers and theologians than to maintain a broad defensive front in the parishes. The Church's own reforming councils had no illusions on this score. They were unsure whether parish clergy could even read aloud with any fluency, and forbade them to make any attempt to defend controversial doctrines.[61] This made defence against a heretical advance difficult – although, as we shall see, not impossible.

On one level, the 'corruption' of the late medieval Church in Scotland was simply a fact. It was shot through with financial sharp practice; many of its leaders were careerists at best and simoniacs at worst; its parish clergy were under strength, impoverished and sometimes inadequate to their responsibilities. These flaws were recognised across Scottish society, and indeed across the Church. But they were also duplicated, to a greater or lesser extent, across most of Christendom. Not all of them were novelties, and not all of them were worsening. Parts of the Church were in excellent health and, more importantly, popular piety appears to have been robustly loyal to traditional religion. If the clergy – or some of the clergy – were despised, it is principally because they failed to live up to the standards that traditional religion expected. It is not at all clear that a Church suffering from these problems would be a natural seedbed for heresy. The existing heresy of Lollardy had made only the faintest mark in Scotland. The Crown and nobility had a strong vested interest in protecting a status quo from which they profited so handsomely. If annoyance at the financial exactions of the clergy, or disgust at their abuses or incompetence, sparked contempt for the Church as an institution – in particular, if the widely despised penalty of excommunication brought ecclesiastical authority into disrepute – this in itself was unlikely to foster heresy. Indeed, the perceived failings of the clerical estate spurred some, especially the clergy themselves, to work and campaign for reform. Much of the criticism came, as it always does, from pious laymen and perfectionist clerics railing against their laxer colleagues. The anticlerical hyperbole mostly came from those who wished to renew the Church, not to overthrow it. If its defences were weak, this was partly because it did not obviously need defending. Until heresy began to be imported from abroad in the 1520s, the Scottish Church was entirely stable. Plenty of its critics were calling for reform, but there was no demand for Reformation.

NOTES

1 John, Lord Herries, *Historical Memoirs of the Reign of Mary Queen of Scots and a Portion of the Reign of King James the Sixth* (Edinburgh, 1836), 14.

2 J. H. Pollen (ed.), *Papal Negotiations with Mary Queen of Scots During her Reign in Scotland* (Scottish History Society 37: Edinburgh, 1901), 138.

3 *Quintin Kennedy (1520–1564): Two Eucharistic Tracts*, ed. Cornelis Henricus Kuipers (Nijmegen, 1964), 171.

4 Brother Kenneth, 'The popular literature of the Scottish Reformation' in McRoberts (ed.), *Essays*, 178–9; Thomas Winning, 'Church councils in sixteenth-century Scotland' in McRoberts (ed.), *Essays*, 332–58.

5 Hay Fleming, *Reformation in Scotland*, 171.

6 There are several detailed overviews of the state of the late medieval Church, ranging from the unrelenting condemnation to be found in Hay Fleming, *Reformation in Scotland*, to the more nuanced assessments in Donaldson, *Scottish Reformation*, 1–28; Cowan, *Scottish Reformation*, chs 1–3; Jenny Wormald, *Court, Kirk and Community: Scotland 1470–1625* (Edinburgh, 1981), 75–94. See also the useful discussion in Michael Mullett, *Catholics in Britain and Ireland, 1558–1829* (Basingstoke, 1998), 33–54.

7 Robert Kerr Hannay, 'Some Papal Bulls among the Hamilton Papers', *SHR*, 22 (1925), 37; Margaret H. B. Sanderson, *Ayrshire and the Reformation: People and Culture 1490–1600* (East Linton, 1997), 73.

8 Mark Dilworth, *Scottish Monasteries in the Late Middle Ages* (Edinburgh, 1995), 14–16, 21–3; Donaldson, *Scottish Reformation*, 39–40.

9 Foggie, *Renaissance Religion*, 40.

10 Pollen, *Papal Negotiations*, 7, 529.

11 *Ibid.*, 529.

12 Wormald, *Court, Kirk and Community*, 88; Cowan, *Scottish Reformation*, 65.

13 David Patrick (ed.), *Statutes of the Scottish Church 1225–1559* (Scottish History Society 54: Edinburgh 1907), 112, 169; Donaldson, *Scottish Reformation*, 13–14.

14 Patrick, *Statutes*, 159, 185–6; *AM*, 1266.

15 *Wodrow Misc.*, 151; cf. similar comments in John Hamilton?, *The Catechisme, That is to Say, ane Instructioun set furth be Johne Aschbischop of Sanct Androus* (RSTC 12731: St Andrews, 1552), fo. 58v; Patrick, *Statutes*, 176–7.

16 W. A. Craigie (ed.), *The Maitland Folio Manuscript*, vol. I (Scottish Text Society 2nd series, 7: Edinburgh, 1919), 6.

17 *Ibid.*, 37.

18 Cosmo Innes (ed.), *The Black Book of Taymouth, With Other Papers from the Breadalbane Charter Room* (Edinburgh, 1855), 165–8.

19 *Ibid.*, 166; Craigie, *Maitland Folio Manuscript*, 38.

20 *CSP Foreign 1559–60*, 42.

21 Cowan, *Scottish Reformation*, 60–1.

22 Mary Black Verschuur, 'Perth and the Reformation: Society and Reform 1540–1560' (PhD thesis, University of Glasgow, 1985), 292–5; Dilworth, *Scottish Monasteries*, 31.

23 William Moir Bryce, *The Scottish Grey Friars* (Edinburgh and London, 1909), I, 139; Foggie, *Renaissance Religion*, 233; Donaldson, *Scottish Reformation*, 9–10; Wormald, *Court, Kirk and Community*, 86–7.

24 Knox, I, 246; *AM*, 1266.

25 Richard Rex, 'The Friars in the English Reformation' in Peter Marshall and Alec Ryrie (eds), *The Beginnings of English Protestantism* (Cambridge, 2002), 38–59; *HP*, I, 303. On evangelical friars, see below, ch. 2.

26 Foggie, *Renaissance Religion*, 232–5; David Calderwood, *The History of the Kirk of Scotland*, ed. Thomas Thomson, 8 vols (Edinburgh, 1842), I, 175; *ALC*, 372; Donaldson, *Scottish Reformation*, 7–10.

27 Bryce, *Scottish Grey Friars*, I, 149.

28 Michael Yellowlees, 'Dunkeld and the Reformation' (PhD thesis, University of Edinburgh, 1990), 229–31.

29 Knox, I, 359–62.

30 See below, 41.

31 *Historical Manuscripts Commission: Report*, X, App. 1 (1885), 26; John Stuart (ed.), *Miscellany of the Spalding Club*, V (Aberdeen, 1852), 26–8, 299, 308–15; *APS*, 267–8, 282, 286, 294, 301.

32 George S. Pryde (ed.), *Ayr Burgh Accounts 1534–1624* (Scottish History Society 3rd series, 28: Edinburgh, 1937), lviii–lix; Lynch, *Edinburgh*, 30; *Extracts from the Council Register of the Burgh of Aberdeen 1398–1570* (Aberdeen, 1844), 325; Verschuur, 'Perth and the Reformation', 281–2.

33 Bruce McLennan, 'The Reformation in the burgh of Aberdeen', *Northern Scotland* 2:2 (1976–77), 140; Knox, I, 138; Cowan, *Scottish Reformation*, 6–7; James Kirk, 'Iconoclasm and Reform', *RSCHS*, 24 (1992), 369–70.

34 James V, *The Letters of James V*, eds Robert Kerr Hannay and Denys Hay (Edinburgh, 1954), 204–5.

35 John Leslie, *The Historie of Scotland*, tr. James Dalrymple, eds E. G. Cody and William Murison (Scottish Text Society 19, 34: Edinburgh, 1895), II, 253; Wormald, *Court, Kirk and Community*, 91.

36 *A Diurnal of Remarkable Occurents that have Passed within the Country of Scotland since the Death of King James the Fourth till the Year MD.LXXV* (Edinburgh, 1833), 17; Knox, I, 72–5.

37 Leslie, *Historie*, II, 220; see below, 45. Douchtie and Scot may have worked together: George Buchanan, *The History of Scotland*, tr. James Aikman, 4 vols (Glasgow, 1827), II, 304–5.

38 James M. Aitken, *The Trial of George Buchanan before the Lisbon Inquisition* (Edinburgh, 1939), 17.

39 Wormald, *Court, Kirk and Community*, 82; Mullett, *Catholics*, 34; Leslie, *Historie*, II, 218–19; Craigie, *Maitland Folio Manuscript*, 16; *APS*, 485; Hamilton, *Catechisme*, fo. 23r.

40 James H. Baxter (ed.), *Copiale Prioratus Sanctiandree: The Letter-book of James Haldenstone, Prior of St Andrews (1418–1443)* (St Andrews, 1930), 230–6; Knox, I, 5–6. On Lollardy in Scotland generally, see John A. F. Thomson, *The Later Lollards 1414–1520* (Oxford, 1965), 202–10; Margaret H. B. Sanderson, 'The Lollard trail: some clues to the spread of pre-Protestant dissent in Scotland, and its legacy', *RSCHS*, 33 (2003), 1–33.

41 Knox, I, 7–12; Martin Dotterweich, 'The Emergence of Evangelical Theology in Scotland to 1550' (PhD thesis, University of Edinburgh, 2002), 26–54; D. E. Easson, 'The Lollards of Kyle', *Juridical Review*, 48 (1936), 123–8.

42 BL Egerton MS 2880; Dotterweich, 'Emergence of evangelical theology', 58–61.

43 Baxter, *Copiale Prioratus Sanctiandree*, 3–4, 382; J. H. Burns, *The True Law of Kingship: Concepts of Monarchy in Early-Modern Scotland* (Oxford, 1996), 124.

44 Martin Dotterweich, 'Emergence of evangelical theology', 112.

45 A. Clerval, *Registre des procès-verbaux de le Faculté de Théologie de Paris* (Paris, 1917), I, 283–4, 303.

46 *Extracts from the Council Register of Aberdeen*, 97–8, 107; cf. McLennan, 'Reformation in the burgh of Aberdeen', 124.

47 John Herkless and Robert Kerr Hannay (eds), *The College of St Leonard* (Edinburgh and London, 1905), 220–2. For a more dramatic interpretation of this case, see John Durkan, 'Heresy in Scotland: the second phase, 1546–58', *RSCHS*, 24 (1992), 325.

48 Gordon Donaldson (ed.), *St Andrews Formulare 1514–1546* (Edinburgh, 1944), II, 370; Knox, I, 36–9.

49 Hamilton, *Catechisme*, fo. 164r.

50 Peter J. Murray, 'The excommunication of Edinburgh town council in 1558', *IR*, 27 (1976), 27–8.

51 Patrick, *Statutes*, 140–1.

52 *APS*, 342, 482, 485–6.

53 On Beaton, see below, ch. 2; on Hamilton, see below, ch. 5.

54 *LP*, XX(i), 1127; *Diurnal of Occurents*, 39; Knox, I, 146–7.

55 Hamilton, *Catechisme*, fo. 93v; Patrick, *Statutes*, 91, 163–4.

56 *Registrum Episcopatus Aberdonensis* (Edinburgh, 1845), I, lxiv; NAS B59/1/1 fo. 184r.

57 Robert Wedderburn, *The Complaynt of Scotland*, ed. A. M. Stewart (Scottish Text Society 4th series, 11: Edinburgh, 1979), 126.

58 Hay Fleming, *Reformation in Scotland*, 172.

59 Wormald, *Court, Kirk and Community*, 88.

60 Knox, I, 58–60; cf. *AM*, 982.

61 Patrick, *Statutes*, 146–7, 157.

Chapter 2

Playing with fire:
the Reformation under James V

THE BEGINNINGS OF SCOTTISH PROTESTANTISM

The Reformation in Scotland began as it did across most of the rest of Europe: with books and universities, with merchants and friars. It began as a self-consciously foreign and a self-consciously intellectual movement. Its adherents and its opponents alike looked abroad, principally to Germany, for its origins. Many of those early adherents were drawn from the learned elite; for others, the new movement's greatest attraction was the possibility of becoming 'learned', through study and discussion of the newly available vernacular Bible. The Bibles themselves were foreign imports, for whose producers the Scottish market was at best an afterthought. However, over the course of James V's reign, the reformist movement's rhetoric, its doctrines and especially its social shape did begin to reflect the Scottish situation. More importantly, James V's own double-edged policy towards the emerging problem of heresy set patterns which would persist after his death in 1542.

The eruption of revolutionary heresy in Germany in the early 1520s forced itself onto the attention of every province of Christendom. Even in those territories where the Lutheran threat remained no more than a possibility, there were excellent reasons to take pre-emptive action against it. If nothing else, being seen to defy heresy would attract favourable international attention. Therefore, the mere fact that a Scottish parliament legislated against Lutheranism in 1525 does not tell us very much. The act reads more like prevention than cure, lamenting the spread of Luther's heresies in 'divers countries' while boasting that Scotland had 'never as yet admitted any opinions contrary the Christian faith'. Those bringing heretical books into any Scottish port were to have their ships seized. The act was to be proclaimed in the ports, but – perhaps more importantly – it was also sent to Rome, where a few months later Pope Clement VII was commending the Scots' zeal for orthodoxy.[1]

Even in 1525, however, the regime saw the Lutheran threat as more than theoretical. The royal letter notifying the burgh of Aberdeen of this legislation warned that 'sundry strangers and others within [the] diocese of Aberdeen, has books of that heretic Luther, and favours his errors and false opinions'.[2] Aberdeen was not alone. In February 1527, an English agent in the Netherlands heard that Scottish merchants were buying quantities of heretical books and shipping them to Edinburgh and St Andrews.[3] Seven months later, the parliamentary act against heresy was bolstered by a clause extending its penalties to Scottish subjects as well as to foreigners.[4] 'Evangelical' ideas (for there was not yet anything as clearly defined as 'Protestantism') had a foot in the door at the universities. Catholic rebuttals of Luther were certainly circulating at St Andrews, and it is likely that Lutheran works had also found their way there.[5] More worryingly for the authorities, Latin treatises were beginning to be supplemented by heresy in the vernacular. In 1534 the King denounced the appearance of 'divers tracts and books translated out of Latin in our Scots tongue by heretics', which were arriving in half a dozen east coast towns.[6] The King's outrage was probably sparked by the only Scots-language evangelical book which survives from this early period: *The Richt Vay to the Kingdome of Heuine is Techit Heir*, a Lutheran handbook translated from a Danish original by the Scot John Gau, and published in October 1533.[7] In 1534, another Scottish evangelical, John Johnsone, published *An Confortable Exhortation of our Mooste Holy Christen Faith*, a simple exposition of the essentials of Lutheranism. Oddly, this book's language is thoroughly anglicised, although it was explicitly aimed at the Scottish market.[8] A more pressing danger in 1534 concerned the friar Alexander Alesius, who had fled to Germany before a charge of heresy, and who was reported to be translating heretical works for a Scottish readership. The Catholic theologian Johannes Cochlaeus wrote to James V to warn him that Alesius was a persuasive writer, and to urge that all German merchandise coming into Scotland be searched.[9]

However, as the Scottish establishment realised, the danger posed by books specifically aimed at the Scottish market was dwarfed by the threat of evangelical works spilling over from England.[10] A talented group of English evangelical exiles was producing a steady stream of vernacular printed works for the edification of their own countrymen, and much of this material also reached Scotland. William Tyndale understood his audience to include 'the faithful brethren of Scotland'; ever the linguist, he was aware that the Scots might find English texts hard going, and stated his intention to produce books in their vernacular.[11] If this promise was not kept, it is partly because Scottish readers learned to cope with English, a pattern which would become fixed over the generations that followed. English evangelical books turn up repeatedly in 1530s Scotland. In 1539 one Edinburgh merchant was found to have something of a collection of them.[12] Another 1530s heretic seems to have owned Simon Fish's rabble-rousing anticlerical diatribe, *A Supplicacyon for the Beggers*. Fish's text was to remain popular, and may have influenced the 1558–59 'Beggars' Summons'.[13] In 1531, a priest from Leith was arrested in London for having bought books by Luther, Tyndale and others. He was probably intending to take these north with him.[14] Some texts came from even further afield. In 1536, the English ambassador to Scotland, William Barlow, brought some printed anti-Catholic propaganda to edify his hosts: woodcuts, probably German in origin, disparaging the pope and monasticism.[15] However, the most important imported texts were, of course, the new translations of the New Testament. From its earliest days, the Scottish Reformation was built on English Bibles.

All the earliest evidence of evangelical activity in Scotland, then, is linked directly to foreign influences. The very first recorded trace of Lutheranism dates from 1524, possibly even earlier, when a French man-at-arms in the Duke of Albany's entourage was spreading Lutheran heresies in Scotland – an offence for which he was executed by order of the *parlement* of Paris.[16] James V himself was keen to emphasise that heresy was an alien import, stressing in 1530 that its source was foreign merchants. Even in 1541, when describing (and exaggerating) the danger heresy presented to his kingdom, he did so in terms of Scotland's proximity to heretical Germany and schismatic England. John Knox agreed that the upsurge in interest in evangelicalism in the early 1530s was due to 'merchants and mariners, who, frequenting other countries, heard the true doctrine affirmed'.[17] Nor was it only merchants. The Dominican and Franciscan orders were both worried about cases in which their friars had been allowed 'to pass forth of the realm in apostasy', some of them then returning to preach heresy.[18] The three most notorious heresy cases of the early Scottish Reformation all centred on individuals who had spent time in Lutheran Germany. James Melville was an Observant Franciscan friar who left his order as early as 1526, and after a spell in England found his way to Luther's home city of Wittenberg. He returned home in 1534, travelling in secular dress and preaching heresy to the people with all the rhetorical skill for which his order was famed. His case was, at that time, sufficiently exceptional for the King to take a personal interest in it.[19] Perhaps less dangerous, but certainly more scandalous, was the case of George Gilbert, a priest who had not only spent time in the Lutheran city of Regensburg but had gone so far as to marry there. Arrested by the Bishop of Brechin in 1534, he was sprung from custody by an armed gang of supporters, provoking outrage from the Court of Session.[20]

However, the most important early heresy case was that of Patrick Hamilton. In many ways he fits the stereotype. As the Catholic chronicler John

Leslie put it, he 'venom very poisonous and deadly in Germany had sucked out of Luther'.[21] Hamilton probably first encountered heresy in print when a student at St Andrews, and was confirmed in it when he fled to the Lutheran city of Marburg before a heresy charge in 1527. While there, he published a set of Latin commonplaces crisply summarising the Lutheran doctrine of justification by faith alone. These commonplaces (*Patrick's Places*) won him considerable fame in England, through a translation which was made after his death, but there is no evidence of their being known in Scotland until the late 1540s.[22] He was honoured in his home country for other reasons. He returned to Scotland after only a few months in Germany, and the summons against him was soon renewed. In January 1528 he came up to St Andrews and surrendered.

His case was, as Jane Dawson has pointed out, badly mishandled. All our sources agree that the rushed trial and condemnation were intended to frighten Hamilton into a recantation. He was taken directly from court to the stake, where a fire was already lit, ready for him. He was pressed to give way, his captors striving to talk him back from the brink. Some thought that they did not have the stomach to go through with a burning. Hamilton, however, knew what he was about. One sympathetic eyewitness believed that he was eager to embrace the honour of martyrdom: God had chosen him 'to suffer for his name', vindicating his faithfulness and his doctrine. He refused to change his mind 'for the awe of your fire'. The Archbishop's men could hardly back down. Hamilton was burned there and then, an outcome which, it seems, no-one except the martyr himself had really expected. The process was made even grimmer and more protracted than usual by the difficulties of kindling a bonfire on a stormy February day in Fife.[23]

Archbishop James Beaton had gambled that Hamilton would recant, and he had lost. We cannot easily tell how damaging this error really was, as we are reliant chiefly on later hagiographies. Yet the execution unmistakably caused a stir. Even if we doubt Knox's cheerily gruesome claim that 'the reek of Master Patrick Hamilton . . . infected as many as it blew upon' with heresy, we do know that the burning was a milestone for some reformers. Alexander Alesius, an eyewitness, first fell under suspicion of heresy for his refusal to condemn Hamilton posthumously. John Johnsone, who was also present at the burning, wrote movingly of the contrast between the martyr's composure and his persecutors' frenzied and fearful conduct. More significantly, however, Knox claimed that when the news began to spread, 'there was none found who began not to inquire, Wherefore was Master Patrick Hamilton burnt?'.[24] And the news did indeed spread. None of the major histories or chronicles of the period omits the event. Hamilton's steadfastness at his death helped to make it memorable, as did the stories of terrible fates being visited providentially on his persecutors.[25] More importantly, Hamilton was more than just a scholar. He was a scion of one of Scotland's most powerful families, a kinsman of royalty (albeit neither close nor legitimate) who could realistically have looked forward to a lucrative career in the Scottish Church. Even though he was not yet ordained, he already held the title of Abbot of Ferne in the 1520s. For such a prominent youngster to be condemned so publicly and so ferociously was a scandal; and it was a dangerous sign of worse to come. Hamilton's brother, Sir James Hamilton of Kincavil – another eyewitness of the burning – was soon to embrace evangelical views himself, and to be exiled for much of the 1530s as a result.[26]

These were only the first of what would become a flood of lairds and nobles who embraced the reformist cause, and who became the driving force behind the Scottish Reformation. In about 1533 Lord Ochiltree's brother Walter Stewart was accused of heresy; he had mutilated an image in Ayr Parish Church. In 1534 David Stratoun of Lauriston was burned; his brother organised the rescue of George Gilbert from the Bishop of Brechin's custody in the same year. Stratoun was said to have been converted by another laird, John Erskine of Dun. The unorthodox views of a Breadalbane laird, Robert Menzies of Weem, were causing a stir amongst his neighbours by the late 1530s. The laird of Arngibbon's brother was burned for heresy in 1539; the laird himself had earlier stood surety for him and his fellow accused. In 1539, Scottish gentlemen were said to be fleeing to England almost daily 'for reading of Scriptures in English'.[27] And men of higher status still were being infected. Lord Methven's son was convicted of heresy, perhaps after protesting against the burnings of 1539, and was pardoned early in 1540.[28] Alexander Cunningham, the grandson of the Earl of Glencairn who was himself to succeed to the title in 1548, was later to be one of the most steadfast Protestant nobles. He had certainly been converted by early 1543, and perhaps as much as a decade earlier. In 1533 or soon after, he wrote a lively anticlerical poem lampooning the popular holy man Thomas Douchtie, in which he also defended Lutherans and the reading of the New Testament. Either he or one of his cousins was accused of heresy in the late 1530s.[29] Archibald Campbell, the fourth Earl of Argyll, may have been another early convert. The evidence here is shakier, and Argyll was not the most constant of politicians; but as his family later remembered it, Argyll had been converted long before his death in 1558, during a trip to France. As Jane Dawson has argued, this points towards James V's state visit to France in 1536–37.[30] It is clear, however, that there was at least one evangelical nobleman in James's entourage during that trip. John Borthwick, the younger brother of the stout conservative Lord Borthwick, was a soldier in the French king's Scots guard. By the time he attended his own king in 1536–37 he was unmistakably reformist in his religion, sending evangelical protégés to the English court and despising the gifts James V had received from the Pope. Back in Scotland in 1540, he fled before a detailed charge of heresy.[31]

How did evangelical reform break out of its clerical and mercantile ghetto to secure so much early support from lairds and nobles? There is no clear answer to this vital question. The pattern was not uncommon. From the farce of the 'Knights' War' in Germany in 1522–23 through to the tragedy of the French Wars of Religion, Reformation ideas won support from aristocrats. In most of Europe, however, noble converts were accompanied by urban support, whereas in Scotland's burghs there is very little evidence of early reformism. Of the country's four principal towns, Edinburgh and Aberdeen were redoubtably conservative, and Perth showed only faint hints of evangelical activity before James V's death.[32] Only in Dundee was there more than scattered or individual support for the new ideas. In the early 1530s the provost and bailies there harboured two evangelical fugitives, although even this may have reflected their strained relations with the Bishop of Brechin rather than any enthusiasm for heresy.[33] Scotland's reformist nobles were not an element of a broader coalition; they were the movement's backbone from the very beginning – despite their strong vested interest in the status quo. The evangelicals' proficiency in winning noble converts remains mysterious. If we are to reach even a partial understanding of it, we must examine quite what these noblemen were converted to.

The regime described the heretics as an organised and coherent group: the 'sect and followers' of Luther, or the 'sect of heresies'. Such views, however, tell us more about official paranoia than the reality of Scottish heresy.[34] Lutheran doctrine was indeed influential, especially amongst the clergy. Patrick Hamilton's views on justification by faith alone aligned him very closely with Luther. The charges against his brother, James Hamilton of Kincavil, suggest similar views: he was said to have denied the existence of free will and the practice of prayer for the dead, both of which were rejected by evangelicals as incompatible with justification by faith alone.[35] Two heretics burned in 1534 are likewise said to have denied free will.[36] The Dominican friar Alexander Seton apparently also preached on justification, emphasising the all-sufficiency of Christ and making no mention of the traditional works of penance which evangelicals rejected as worthless.[37] George Buchanan fled into exile in 1539, before charges which included claiming that Luther's doctrine of the sacraments was orthodox. He also admitted having been attracted by the doctrine of justification by faith alone, having read St Augustine on the subject. One of Buchanan's associates, Canon Thomas Forret, was likewise converted by reading Augustine.[38] The early exiles also embraced unambiguously Lutheran views: the books written by Johnsone and Alesius, and translated by John

Gau, make their doctrinal allegiance unmistakable. The spreading of explicitly Lutheran doctrines, then, was a prominent theme in early Scottish reformism. It was, however, neither the only nor perhaps the most compelling part of the early reformers' message.

As in many parts of Europe, part of the excitement of evangelicalism lay not in the reformers' specific doctrines but in the open Bible. The mere opportunity to read Scripture in the vernacular was attractive and always had been. This did not necessarily entail embracing heretical beliefs; but the heretical provenance of the translations and the Church's anti-Lollard habits ensured that Bible-reading became entangled with heresy willy-nilly. The parliament of 1541 denounced 'private conventions . . . made to dispute on the Scripture'. The English understood that the chief offence of the Scottish religious refugees who reached them in 1539 was mere Bible-reading. Alexander Cunningham's anticlerical poem spoke of 'Lutherans', but had nothing to say about their theology. Rather, their 'whole intent' was 'to read this English New Testament'.[39] The regime, perhaps unwisely, gave no quarter to such activities. The second martyr of the Scottish Reformation, Henry Forrest, was allegedly burned simply for owning an English New Testament.[40] The ban on vernacular Scripture was Alesius' chief concern when he protested against James V's religious policies. Cochlaeus, it seems, was a little embarrassed by the sweeping nature of the Scottish Church's ban, but Archbishop Dunbar of Glasgow had no such doubts, blithely bracketing vernacular Scripture with heresy.[41] This policy may well have helped some Scots to quell the temptation to read the English New Testament. The price was that those curious and pious souls who yielded to that temptation were driven into the company of more doctrinaire evangelicals.

Alongside such learned pursuits, however, early Scottish evangelicalism also had a more rumbustious side. The early reformers were bluntly and sometimes viciously anticlerical. It is not a coincidence that iconoclasts in the 1530s repeatedly targeted the Franciscan friaries. They were attacking not only the images, but also their owners.[42] Likewise, much evangelical preaching was dominated not by theology, but by criticisms of the morals and learning of the clergy – or at least, this was what their audiences found most memorable. For all Alexander Seton's Lutheranism, it was a sermon maligning the Scottish bishops which led to his arrest. John Keillor, a friar executed in 1539, was made notorious not by his doctrines, but by a play he wrote comparing the clergy to Christ's persecutors. The Carthusian monk Andrew Charteris left his order and spent a year at Wittenberg, but when he wrote home to his brother, he did not speak about the Gospel but 'inveighed vehemently against bishops, priests, abbots, monks, friars', complaining specifically that anyone who challenged their abuses was swiftly charged with heresy.[43] There was justice in this last charge. The accusation of heresy was, Buchanan wrote, 'a weapon [the clergy] were wont to brandish against all to whom they were ill-disposed'. A high-minded rebuke of clerical failures, or a personal vendetta against a priest accused of fraud and adultery, could lead to a heresy charge even where there was no whisper of unorthodox belief.[44] It was an approach calculated to make heretics – and martyrs – of those whose offences were more disciplinary than doctrinal.

Many of the nobles and lairds who became associated with religious reform did not begin by explicitly allying themselves with Lutheran doctrines. They reached evangelicalism by more roundabout routes. In some cases, the reformers were offering to legitimise practices such as breaking the Lenten fast, which had a particular appeal to the wealthy. Lent-breaking seems to have become endemic during the 1530s. One did not need to be a heretic to break Lent, but breaking Lent was an easy way into heresy: George Buchanan later confessed that it was through Lent-breaking in the 1530s that 'I received the first taint of evil and my earliest intercourse with Lutherans'. Lent-breaking was a principal charge against the five heretics executed at Scotland's largest public burning in 1539.[45] Those five had broken Lent when celebrating the marriage of a priest; and the prospect of clerical marriage was also attractive to some, including those noble and lairdly younger sons who wished both to hold lucrative ecclesiastical appointments and to have legitimate children.[46]

Most importantly, though, the landed classes were drawn towards heresy through the widespread culture of contempt for the clergy. Graduation from anticlericalism to heresy was not automatic, but nor was it difficult. The Church's uneven pursuit of evangelicals seems to have alarmed lairds and nobles. Some shared the seemingly widespread distaste for the cruelty of the executions, but this was reinforced by alarm at the arbitrariness of anti-heresy proceedings. According to Buchanan, when the hierarchy responded to heresy 'by abuse rather than by argument', he and others saw this as a concession that the Church could not win such an argument.[47] The Church's insistence on lumping anticlericalism together with heresy became a self-fulfilling prophecy, and lent credibility to the heretics. Alexander Cunningham's anticlerical poem explained, in the words of a corrupt cleric, why he favoured the new religion:

> I dread this doctrine, if it last,
> Shall either cause us work or fast.[48]

For some, the reformers' Gospel meant scales falling from their eyes and conversion of life. For others, it provided an opportunity to kick the clergy while they were down.

REPRESSION AND REFORM AT JAMES V'S COURT

King James V has never enjoyed a good reputation. If some of his subjects called him a 'good poor man's King', it was his supposed rapaciousness which was emphasised after his death, and his reputation amongst historians has been little better. Jamie Cameron's recent political biography has helped to provide a more level-headed assessment of Catholic Scotland's last King.[49] Cameron, however, had little to say on James's religious policy – in part because of his own untimely death, but also because religious policy in general and the heresy problem in particular were not particularly pressing matters for James V. Like environmental issues in the modern world, religious issues in the 1520s and 1530s were universally acknowledged to be of surpassing importance, but were rarely treated as urgent. The more immediate political problems faced by the Stewart kings – finance, law and order, diplomacy and above all relations with the leading nobility – usually crowded religious questions from the field. The religious dissidence which would be convulsing the country within twenty years of James V's death was, during his lifetime, a cloud little bigger than a man's hand. His attention to it was at best intermittent, and filtered through other concerns.

When James V did pay attention to the Church, his policy – on the traditional reading, broadly endorsed by Cameron – amounted to something like a protection racket. The German Reformation; England's schism from the Roman Church under Henry VIII; and the threat of heresy at home opened up diplomatic and financial opportunities for the King of Scots, opportunities which he exploited with some skill. In his dealings with the papacy, James made it clear that he expected substantial rewards for maintaining the loyal Catholicism which had been automatic for his predecessors. The result was a tax income from the Church of some £10,000 per year. James received roughly as much again from the benefices in which he had been permitted to place his illegitimate sons. At the same time, he used the possibility that he might emulate his English uncle's schism both to maintain peace with England for almost the whole of his reign, and to extract two astonishingly good marriages from the king of France. Indeed, it is possible that, as Cameron suggested, James really entertained a schism; that if the ecclesiastical goose had stopped laying golden eggs, he would have been ready to follow Henry VIII and wring its neck.[50]

James was certainly happy to use religious policy to strengthen both his revenue and his international position. His correspondence with Rome was filled with stirring declarations of his loyalty to the faith of his fathers, and with dreadful warnings of the threat of heresy. Such passages were almost always joined to requests for favours. The link was not subtle. When asking for wealthy benefices for his underage sons, he stressed the danger of heretical activity in the relevant areas, and, in the case of the Border abbey of Kelso, the need for a strong royal presence to protect it from the depredations of the schismatic English. When asking for his own rights of patronage within the Church to be extended, he harped on Scotland's ancient orthodoxy and his own personal efforts against heresy. Even when wishing to annex bene-fices to his chapel royal, the King claimed that this was in order to help him 'banish the foul Lutheran sect'.[51] When he wanted taxes from the clergy, he could become positively histrionic. The colossal tax which Clement VII per-mitted him to levy in 1532, to fund his new Court of Session, led to the King's declaration to parliament the same year that all kings of Scots had always 'been most obedient sons to our holy fathers the popes of Rome and the authority apostolic', and that he too intended to 'keep, observe, maintain and defend the authority liberty and freedom of the seat of Rome and Holy Church'. Even the Catholic historian John Leslie, who commended James V's piety, admitted that this declaration of loyalty had been bought.[52] A decade later, the lease on Scotland's loyalty was up for renewal. In 1541, James wrote to Paul III extolling his own efforts against the spread of heresy, describing Lutheranism as a disease which had swept Scotland's neighbours, and against which Scotland had no defences aside from the faith and valour of the King himself. He was duly granted a extraordinary tax on the clerical estate in order to finance his war with England. Of course, these financial exactions made the Church's existing money problems considerably worse.[53]

James V wanted more from Rome than mere money, however. The King's professed loyalty to the Apostolic See did not prevent James from taking a view of the Pope's powers over the Scottish Church which was always jealous and often positively Tudor. Scots who appealed to Rome over the King's head or against his wishes were a recurring annoyance. The practice was legislated against during James's minority, and he confirmed the act in 1541, in the same parliament that passed a barrage of anti-heresy legislation.[54] Another of James's particular bugbears was the recurrent problem of Scots in Rome persuading the Curia to grant them benefices or pardons against the King's wishes. In some cases, James feared that inopportune papal pardons might allow criminals to escape justice, or weaken his own moves against heresy, but he was far more genuinely roused by Paul III's attempt to grant Dryburgh Abbey to the theologian Robert Wauchope in 1540. James was furious at this infringement of his own rights of patronage. In a stream of letters pro-testing against the appointment he made his contempt for Wauchope clear. He wanted Dryburgh for Sir Thomas Erskine, a royal servant who had been instrumental in helping him wring money out of the Church. He had no interest in supporting Wauchope, a blind Highlander whose 'inopportune and Hibernic clamour' irritated James far more than any scholarly brilliance could ever impress him. And eventually, James got his way.[55]

These concerns explain why the most persistent theme of James's relations with the Pope was his repeated (and repeatedly refused) request for a legate *a latere* to be appointed: a papal representative to whom most of the authority of the Apostolic See would be delegated. If such a legate were not under royal control, he would be a distinct and immediate threat to royal power; legislation against receiving legates without royal permission was passed in 1526 and re-enacted in 1541.[56] If, however, the legate was a cleric who was amenable to or, better, nominated by the King, then James V would acquire a similar level of control over the Church to that exercised by Henry VIII, without all the troublesome business of schism. This was not quite how James put it in his petitions to Rome. When trying to secure a legatine commission for Archbishop Gavin Dunbar of Glasgow in 1530, or for Archbishop David Beaton of St Andrews from 1538 onwards, he made shameless play of the threat of heresy. This was not wholly spurious. Constant appeals to Rome could, as James said, make it difficult to impose renewed discipline on the monasteries. However, this argument would have carried more weight if the King himself had treated the monasteries more as religious institutions and less as milch cows. More regularly, James simply waxed melodramatic about the dangerous influences from his schismatic neighbours, and warned that 'the storm of heresy is raging'. When Beaton did indeed show himself to be a vigorous opponent of heresy, James was quick to emphasise this to Rome. And if successive popes would not abrogate their own authority quite as James wished, they did make concessions. Dunbar was not made a legate, but in 1531 James was granted extended rights to act against any clergy suspected of treason. And Beaton was granted a cardinal's hat instead of a legatine commission; a decision which delighted James, both as an earnest of further grants to come and also for the considerable prestige it conferred on the kingdom.[57]

Indeed, one of the most enjoyable aspects of James's new-found international role as a bulwark against heresy was the attention it attracted. Especially after the English schism, European princes were forced to acknowledge the potential importance of the King of Scots. Henry VIII made a treaty of perpetual peace with Scotland in 1534, only the second such treaty in two centuries, and granted his nephew the Order of the Garter in the following year. The Holy Roman Emperor, Charles V, had already granted James V the Order of the Golden Fleece. When attempting to win him as an ally against England in 1534, Charles emphasised James's own blood rights to the English throne and offered to support a marriage between James and Henry VIII's daughter Mary.[58] The most bankable assets which this prestige secured were two lucrative French marriages and the alliance which went with them. Politely rejecting English diplomatic advances in 1540, James could say with almost justified confidence: 'There is a good old man in France, my good-father

[father-in-law] the king of France . . . that will not see me want any thing.'[59] It was even rumoured that Pope Paul III planned to strip Henry VIII of his coveted title, Defender of the Faith, and award it to the King of Scots. Instead, in 1537 the Pope gave James perhaps Christendom's most notable honour: the papal gift of the Blessed Sword and Hat. The gift was explicitly linked to James's efforts against heresy. It was a prestigious symbol. If (as was reported) the English King was daunted by what it signified, it was not without reason.[60]

For if Rome did well out of its relations with Scotland, the same cannot be said of Henry VIII. James strung his uncle along, maintaining friendly relations and hinting – but never more than hinting – that he would follow his example. The Anglo-Scottish peace was broken only in 1542, by Henry VIII's fixation on war with France. In the meantime, James V had played host to fifty or more English refugees, ranging from elderly friars to James Gruffydd ap Hywel, a kind of Welsh Rob Roy who spent much of the 1530s stirring up opposition to Henry VIII in Wales, Ireland and Scotland. James's readiness to shelter such fugitives infuriated Henry, but he could do little about it.[61] It was a symptom of England's broader vulnerability. For most of the 1530s, it was the English who feared an attack by the Scots, not the other way round. An invasion did not materialise, but subversive pamphlets were spread south across the Border.[62] Henry VIII's ideal solution to this problem was to persuade James to follow him into schism, and he worked hard to spread the gospel of royal supremacy over the Church. The ambassadors he chose to deal with Scotland, men such as Bishop William Barlow and Sir Ralph Sadler, were themselves committed reformers. One Catholic chronicler believed that Barlow came 'to infect this realm with heresy'; but James stood firm, especially on the issue of the refugees, 'and so this heretic with his company passed home confusedly'.[63]

Sadler's embassy, in 1540, shows how badly England misunderstood the Scottish situation and James's political achievement. Sadler was sent to Edinburgh with a carrot and a stick to offer the King of Scots. The carrot was the opportunity to seize the Scottish monasteries to augment his revenue, as Henry VIII had done; the stick, a warning that Cardinal Beaton was plotting to usurp James's authority. James listened to the English diplomat carefully: 'somewhile looked very steadily on me, and with grave countenance; somewhile he bit the lip, and bowed his head.' However, both issues looked very different from James's side of the table. On the monasteries, he answered that quite aside from questions of law and conscience, he had no great financial need. Even if he did, he added pointedly 'what need I to take them to increase my livelihood, when I may have any thing that I can require of them? . . . There is not an abbey in Scotland at this hour, but if we need any thing, we may have of them whatsoever we will desire that they have; and so what needs us to spoil them?'. Sadler continued to press him, stressing the supposed immorality of the religious orders; finally James 'interrupted me, and laughed', saying that he would punish those monks who deserved it, and ended the interview. Sadler's warnings about Beaton likewise fell flat. The English had seized a letter – now triumphantly laid before James – in which Beaton expressed his continued ambition to be made a papal legate. It was something of a disappointment for Sadler when James made it clear that he knew of and was actively supporting this ambition. In the passage which the English hoped would be most inflammatory, Beaton had warned that nothing should be done to 'irritate' James against the Church. James, however, saw this not as a plot but as a compliment. Reading the letter aloud to himself in Sadler's presence, when he came to this section he commented audibly, 'By God . . . they dread me'.[64] He had as much control over the Church as he needed, without having to run the risk of schism.

The political advantages of James V's religious policy, then, are plain. However, there was more than *realpolitik* at work here. James was as unsentimental as any of the Stewarts, but he was a man of his time and was devoid neither of belief nor of piety. 'It is impossible', Jenny Wormald has concluded, 'to understand James's own religious position', but it is at least clear that he had one.[65] His fulsome protestations of loyalty to the old Church may have been self-serving, but were also sincere. His conscience was more than an excuse to dismiss unwelcome English advances. He gave some real support to the reform of the religious orders – although only where such reform did not imperil his own income. In 1532 he sought papal permission to merge two impoverished Trinitarian monasteries, on the grounds that one owned a relic to which he professed devotion. In 1535 he gave the hospital of St Lawrence at Haddington to another convent which had impressed him with its holiness. He threw his weight behind internal reform efforts in the Cistercian and Carmelite orders. The Dominican friars received a series of grants of land from their King.[66] Like his father, however, James's greatest affection was reserved for the Observant Franciscans: 'men given to the most devoted service of God'. He solicited papal support for their quarrels with their Conventual brethren, and showed particular concern about the damage which apostate Observants could cause. When the Observants were expelled from Denmark, James wrote in almost idealistic terms to his Lutheran cousin King Frederick I, lamenting the treatment of the 'poor and irreproachable' friars and urging Frederick both to restore them and to defend them against any adversaries. A few years later, when the English Observants were likewise forced to flee, James gave many of them refuge in Scotland and defended them against English attempts to have them repatriated.[67]

James V's piety extended to more than a fondness for friars. He was also genuinely disturbed by heresy. If it served his worldly interests to denounce heretics to the Pope, it was positively undiplomatic to tell the Danish King that he found Luther's doctrines repellent and to denounce the reformers' iconoclasm. He enthusiastically supported Charles V's proposal for a general council to resolve the Luther problem, promising to send Scottish representatives.[68] Within Scotland, James took a personal interest in heresy trials. When James Hamilton of Kincavil was condemned in 1534, the King was present, and when Henry VIII petitioned for him to be pardoned, James refused to do so until Hamilton was reconciled to the Pope.[69] He also presided at the high-profile heresy trial of Norman Gourlay and David Stratoun of Lauriston in 1534. James's presence at these set-piece events was widely noticed.[70] John Knox and John Leslie, from their opposing religious perspectives, broadly agreed on James's role in prosecuting heresy. For Knox, James was 'that blinded and most vicious man', who had made 'a solemn vow, that none should be spared that was suspect of heresy, yea, although it were his own son'. Leslie described him as crushing heresy like a hydra, and claimed that he was 'so commended of his diligence' that 'all his honour and commend, he thought, might be put in cutting off heresy and amplifying the religion'.[71]

This was an exaggeration. Religious persecution during the Scottish Reformation was sporadic. Indeed, Knox was embarrassed by the scarcity of Scottish martyrs. We know of only twenty-one heresy executions in the whole period 1528–58, although there were doubtless a few others.[72] Fourteen of these deaths, however, fell in James V's reign, and nine of them in 1538 and 1539. If we are seeking an index of the regime's energy in hunting heretics, we should also consider those who fled into exile; in a decentralised state such as Scotland, plenty of suspects were always likely to escape arrest. We know of more than thirty Scottish reformers who went into internal or, more usually, foreign exile during James V's reign and, again, these cases are concentrated in the period 1538–40. In the late 1530s, in other words, intermittent persecution developed into a major drive against heresy. Renewed prosecutions were bolstered by fresh legislation. The initial parliamentary act against Lutheranism was renewed in 1535, and in 1541 a detailed package of anti-heresy measures was enacted. This defended the doctrine of the sacraments, devotion to the Virgin Mary, the use of images in worship, and the authority of the Pope. Fresh penalties were laid on those who had abjured heresy and on fugitives; fresh incentives were created for informants.[73] According to one account, in 1540 the King appointed a secular judge to spearhead heresy trials, although this arrangement – and the judge himself – proved short-lived.[74]

The King himself was, of course, only indirectly responsible for much of this activity. Patrick Hamilton's execution was the work of Archbishop James Beaton of St Andrews. The surge of prosecutions during 1538–40, and the 1541 legislation, are linked to the elevation of his nephew David Beaton to the same office. Beaton himself paid for a stage to be built in Holyrood for the show trials of 1539. The tailing-off of prosecutions after 1540 fits neatly with Beaton's absence in France during 1541–42.[75] However, the anti-heresy drive reached well beyond the diocese of St Andrews. Beaton's own emissaries certainly helped to spread the word, but if, as Knox claimed, Archbishop Dunbar of Glasgow resented this, it merely reflected his well-known personal dislike of Beaton. The King believed that Dunbar, too, was an energetic opponent of Lutheranism.[76] Likewise, while Beaton was more single-minded than his king in the pursuit of heretics, the difference between them was one of degree. If Beaton met some of the costs of the anti-heresy drive in the late 1530s, James paid his share too – as well he might, given the profits which he stood to make from the forfeited property of heretics.[77] When heresy was prosecuted in 1530s Scotland, it was with the implicit or explicit approval of the King, and his support was as much a matter of conviction as of convenience.

The traditional portrait of a king who cynically exploited the opportunities which the European Reformation offered him is true, but incomplete. Of the exploitation there can be no doubt, but there is also no reason to doubt James's sincerity. He could be touchy about papal jurisdiction over Scotland, but his affection for aspects of the old Church seems plain enough and his distaste for heresy is unmistakable. He was in the happy position of being able to use his own sincerely held beliefs to substantial political advantage.

However, even this is not a complete picture. Alongside James the politicker and James the persecutor is a third James V, James the reformer. When it suited James, he could seem positively warm towards evangelical reform. The most famous such incident is also the most slippery. In January 1540 a play was performed before the King – apparently, an early version of Sir David Lindsay's *Ane Satyre of the Thrie Estatis*. Unfortunately, we have neither the text of the play nor an eyewitness account of the King's involvement with it. Rather, we have a letter written by the English courtier William Eure in which he summarised the account given to him by the evangelical Scottish lawyer and courtier Sir Thomas Bellenden. Worse, Bellenden himself had not been present either. He did give Eure a summary of the play itself, written by another evangelical Scot who had been there, and this describes a drama which is recognisably akin to Lindsay's later text. It presented the woes of the commonwealth, oppressed by taxation, the exactions of the Church courts and the rapacity of the bishops. At one provocative moment, the character Experience produced a New Testament to measure the bishops against the standards it set: Alexander Seton had been accused of heresy for doing the same thing. This part of the account is probably reliable enough, although our evangelical eyewitness no doubt emphasised the parts of the play he found most congenial.[78]

The mere fact of this performance, however, is less important than what Bellenden told Eure about the King's involvement. He claimed that James knew the contents of the play in advance and was privy to the planning of its performance. And at the end of the play, Bellenden claimed, James turned to the bishops who were present, 'exhorting them to reform their fashions and manners of living, saying that unless they so did, he would send six of the proudest of them unto his uncle of England, and as those were ordered, so he would order all the rest that would not amend'.

Archbishop Dunbar tried to soothe the King with talk of obedience, but James snapped back that abuses were not so easily put right. As if to give substance to this, Bellenden asked Eure for copies of the English statutes by which the monasteries had been suppressed, which he promised James wished to read. He added that James was 'fully minded' to expel all clergy from positions of secular authority, and 'daily studieth and deviseth for that intent'.[79]

It is a striking narrative, but in places obviously unreliable. It is suffused with Bellenden's wishful thinking. As Greg Walker has commented, the request for the English legislation was clearly Bellenden's initiative, and his promise that James would study it seems groundless. Eure had been pressing for intelligence on James's views on 'the reformation of the spirituality'. Bellenden, anxious to give him some good news, could come up only with the account of the play – and it would be only natural for him to exaggerate it. His claim that James intended to expel the clergy from positions of authority is demonstrably false. Less than a month later, Ralph Sadler's attempts to lure James into a more pro-English stance were politely but firmly rebuffed.

Yet this account is not entirely worthless. Some elements of it have parallels elsewhere: in particular, in Knox's problematic tale that Cardinal Beaton drew up a lengthy hit-list of highly placed heresy suspects for the King. This story appears to be a conflation of two separate episodes. The claim that such a list was found in James V's pocket after his death, and that it included hundreds of names, with the Earl of Arran at its head, is most likely simply untrue: Arran himself probably invented it in 1543.[80] Knox also writes, however, of an earlier list of heretics presented by Beaton to the King in the autumn of 1540, on James's return from a voyage to the Western Isles. A closely parallel but not verbally identical account of the incident is also found in the memoirs of James Melville of Halhill. If these accounts are to be trusted, the clergy presented James with a list of lords and lairds who were favourers of heresy, in the hope of tempting the King to seize their lands. Melville claimed that their purpose was to prevent any possible alliance with England. However, Sir James Kirkcaldy of Grange intervened: he was royal treasurer, an evangelical sympathiser, and Knox's most likely source for this story. He persuaded James to reject this list and to concentrate on reforming the clergy themselves. Both accounts describe James berating his bishops for their impertinence.

He declared that he and his predecessors had not given lands to the Church in order to sustain priests in whoredom and idleness. Brandishing a knife, he said: 'I shall reform you, not as the King of Denmark by imprisonment does, neither yet as the King of England does, by hanging and heading; but I shall reform you by sharp daggers.'[81] This is plausible, especially given the two independent accounts. Beaton's determination to keep up the pressure on heresy is well known, and it is likely enough that the King should feel the need to reassert his own control after a three-month absence. If it is true, however, it provides some important corroboration for the Eure/Bellenden account. It shows that in 1540 James's concern about the heresy which he had been prosecuting so fiercely for the previous few years was matched with a concern for the reform of the clergy. And it shows that in pursuit of such reform, he was ready to use Henry VIII as a bogeyman with whom to threaten his bishops.

It is no great surprise that James V should be sincerely interested in reforming the Church. As we have seen, a degree of contempt for the clergy was widespread amongst Scotland's landed classes, the social group to which the King belonged. He gave his backing to reform efforts such as the general provincial council of the Church in 1536, a meeting which may have been more effective than is usually acknowledged. The anti-heresy legislation of 1541 also included a call for reform of the clergy.[82] Moreover, there are numerous hints that James was sceptical towards some traditional pieties and ready to poke fun at the clergy. Around 1530, a Franciscan named John Scot returned to Scotland after travels which had taken him as far as the Holy Land. Rumour claimed that while on his travels, he had fasted from all food and drink for forty days. The King's response to this was not to pay court to the holy man, but rather to have him arrested and held without food or water for another forty days, to see if he survived (which, remarkably, he did).[83] Similarly, when Ralph Sadler was in Scotland in 1540, James defused a potential row over the ambassador's partial observance of the Lenten fast. Sadler was willing to compromise; he merely asked to be allowed to eat dairy products, because he had no stomach for fish ('I am an evil fishman'). The King, however, sent word that the ambassador could eat whatever he liked, and made sure that the message was carried by a herald who could be relied on to give the right impression. When Sadler commented on the priests' dislike of him, the herald replied 'Know ye not our priests? A mischief on them all! I trust . . . the world will amend here once'.[84] It was a hope which the King was willing to encourage, if not to act upon.

Indeed, as on this occasion, James was generally more willing to allow others to promote the evangelical cause than to do so himself. Like the use of drama for political or religious purposes – another favourite technique of James's[85] – this indirect approach to reform had the virtue of deniability. The buck could be made to stop somewhere else. Nevertheless, James's support for evangelical reformers is sufficiently widespread that an unmistakable pattern emerges. The pattern is that of a typical Renaissance monarch. Like his uncle, Henry VIII, James found it expedient, or agreeable, to include in his court men and women whose religious views went beyond his own. The closer parallel, perhaps, is with the 'good old man in France', James's father-in-law, Francis I, who in the early 1530s had willingly nourished a group of evangelical reformers at his court.[86] In some cases – such as James's physician, Michael Durham, his master of the household, James Learmouth, and his treasurer's clerk, Henry Balnaves – it is likely to be mere coincidence that men whom James valued for practical reasons had evangelical sympathies.[87] But James also seems genuinely to have respected the piety and spirituality of some evangelicals. When Alexander Seton was preaching justification by faith and denouncing clerical corruption in the early 1530s, he was also James's confessor. When charged with heresy, Seton was allowed to escape to England, perhaps with James's connivance, and wrote a letter to his old master from Berwick, warning that the clergy were usurping his authority. James did not allow Seton to return, but he did not demand his extradition either (as Henry VIII would have done), and he allowed the letter denouncing the clergy to circulate. Likewise, George Buchanan, who was tutor to James's illegitimate sons, fled into exile when accused of heresy in 1539, and he too claimed that the King had arranged his escape.[88]

James's employment of Buchanan is one of many signs that he had a good Renaissance king's taste for fashionable scholarship. When Erasmus wrote to James in 1534, and commended his messenger as an eminent scholar, the King wrote back in warm terms and sent the messenger on his way with £50 in his pocket. When Giovanni Ferrerio, a second-rank Italian humanist scholar, found his way to Scotland in 1528, he was fêted at court, and remained there for three years. James gave a fair degree of shelter and patronage to Scottish scholars as well. It was useful to have such people on hand for important state occasions. In 1537 Sir David Lindsay produced a formal – and carefully politically calibrated – poem mourning the death of the short-lived Queen Madeleine. The following year, he was joined by Sir James Foulis, the King's Secretary, and Adam Otterburn, the King's Advocate, in producing formal Latin orations to greet her replacement, Mary of Guise.[89]

Renaissance scholarship was not, of course, necessarily heretical. However, James wanted his scholars to be more than ornaments. Like James IV, he encouraged a lively culture of court 'flyting': verbal tournaments, sometimes heated, in which poets exchanged barbed invectives. James V commissioned Buchanan to write a satirical poem against the Franciscan friars, and even rejected Buchanan's first draft of it as too conciliatory, demanding 'a keen satire that would sting to the quick'. Buchanan was chosen for this because he was already disputing with certain friars, 'with hatred and abuse . . . many insults were bandied to and fro'. Such an exchange of insults made, at the least, a good spectator sport. James also patronised the sharpest satirist of the age, Lindsay himself. Lindsay's reward for the play which had so excited the English in January 1540 was a gift worth over £600.[90] Like Buchanan, Lindsay was aware that this was a dangerous way to make a living. The King's sense of humour was unpredictable, and he would not always protect his satirists. One of Lindsay's poems took two of James's favourite hunting dogs as examples of how the King could enjoy boisterous, provocative and even malicious behaviour from his courtiers for a time, but would throw such men over in favour of more reliable types when they became too arrogant.[91]

Even so, the existence of a limited licence to mock and provoke for scholars at James's court was a fact of some importance. It created a certain fluidity and freedom at the court; principally for the King himself, but also for those vying for his favour. It meant that when some of the more zealous clergy mistakenly concluded that Ralph Sadler's embassy included apostate monks, they were 'well laughed at' at court, since their error had been based on a misreading of a Greek badge.[92] Laughing at clerical ignorance was good politics at James V's court. It implied learning, it showed a certain daring wit and it was – usually – quite safe. It could even be an effective way of defusing more dangerous situations. Some accused heretics apparently answered their accusers not with evidence but with sarcastic counter-accusations, and tried to turn their trials into farces. Given the norms of behaviour at the royal court, this may have been a shrewd tactic.[93]

The reformers, scholars and satirists with whom the King surrounded himself were not necessarily evangelicals. Many of them were and remained of unimpeachable Catholic orthodoxy. James was not deliberately nurturing a nest of heretics. If real heresy threatened to emerge from satire and anti-clericalism, he gave it no quarter. However, his willingness to make this distinction – unlike many of his clergy – created space for religious dissidence. His support for reform of the clergy and his enjoyment of anticlerical satire were corrosive to a Church which equated anticlericalism with heresy. His support for humanism gave shelter to evangelicals such as Buchanan as well as to unswerving Catholics such as Ferrerio. And his willingness to foster disagreements – indeed, to play both sides of arguments – meant that the heresy which was acquiring a foothold amongst his nobles could also find a place at his court. With hindsight, it seems dangerously inconsistent to promote and protect such people, and at the same time to burn heretics. James's own perspective would have been different. Heresy was rarely more than an irritant, to be stressed only when it was politically useful to do so. For other reasons, it suited both his policy and his piety to shelter some critics of the old Church, especially when those criticisms were made with scholarly or satirical precision. It helped to keep state, Church, court and nobility under his own restless control. However, it also ensured that on his unexpected death, he bequeathed a political culture in which a degree of dissent had been legitimised. The steadfast defence of the old Church had once been a universally professed value. It was now the policy of a faction.

NOTES

1 *APS*, 295; James V, *Letters*, 130.

2 *Extracts from the Council Register of Aberdeen*, 110.

3 *LP*, IV(ii), 2903.

4 *APS*, 295.

5 Gotthelf Wiedermann, 'Martin Luther versus John Fisher: some ideas concerning the debate on Lutheran theology at the University of St Andrews, 1525–30', *RSCHS*, 22 (1984), 16–19, 22–3.

6 *ALC*, 423.

7 Christiern Pedersen, *The Richt Vay to the Kingdome of Heuine is Techit Heir*, trans. John Gau (RSTC 19525: Malmö, 1533).

8 John Johnsone, *An Confortable Exhortation: of Oure Moost Holy Christen Faith, and Her Frutes* (RSTC 14667: Malmö or Antwerp, 1535); James K. Cameron, 'John Johnsone's *An Confortable Exhortation* . . . : an early example of Scots Lutheran piety' in Derek Baker (ed.), *Reform and Reformation: England and the Continent c. 1500–c. 1750* (Studies in Church History Subsidia 2: Oxford, 1979), esp. 141–2. The book apparently came from the same press as Gau's *The Richt Vay*, so the printers were clearly capable of producing a Scots-language text. Possibly the experience of trying to sell the earlier text had made it clear that the Scots were more ready to buy English works than the English were to buy Scots ones.

9 James V, *Letters*, 241, 273–4.

10 *ALC*, 422.

11 William Tyndale?, *The Examinacion of Master William Thorpe Preste Accused of Heresye* (RSTC 24045: Antwerp, 1530), sig. A2v.

12 *RSS*, II, 2396.

13 Simon Fish, *A Supplicacyon for the Beggers* (RSTC 10883: Antwerp?, 1529?); Donaldson, *St Andrews Formulare*, II, 370; John Row, *The History of the Kirk of Scotland* (Edinburgh, 1842), 6. On the Beggars, Summons, see below, 124–5, 157.

14 *AM*, 1046.

15 Aitken, *Trial of George Buchanan*, 35–7.

16 Ludovic Lalanne (ed.), *Journal d'un bourgeois de Paris sous le règne de François Premier* (Paris, 1854, repr. New York, 1965), 327; Hay Fleming, *Reformation in Scotland*, 173–4.

17 James V, *Letters*, 174, 424; Knox, I, 55–6, 61.

18 *ALC*, 423–4.

19 ALC, 426; James V, *Letters*, 276, 287, 315–6; John Durkan, 'Heresy in Scotland: the second phase, 1546–58', *RSCHS*, 24 (1992), 321–3.

20 ALC, 426–7, 437.

21 Leslie, *Historie*, II, 215; *ODNB*.

22 Dotterweich, 'Emergence of Evangelical Theology', 147. The 'good English books of . . . Frith's translation' which Dundee evangelicals requested from their English occupiers in 1547 can only refer to *Patrick's Places*. NA SP 50/2 fo. 78r (*CSP Scotland*, 74).

23 Knox, I, 15–18; Robert Lindsay of Pitscottie, *The Historie and Cronicles of Scotland*, ed. Æ. J. G. Mackay, 3 vols (Scottish Text Society 42–3, 60: Edinburgh, 1899–1911), I, 310–11; Leslie, *Historie*, II, 215–6; Johnsone, *An confortable exhortation*, sig. E1v; Jane Dawson, 'The Scottish Reformation and the theatre of martyrdom' in Diana Wood (ed.), *Martyrs and Martyrologies* (Studies in Church History 30: Oxford, 1993), 264–5.

24 Knox, I, 36, 42; Johnsone, *An Confortable Exhortation*, sigs E1v–2r; James V, *Letters*, 241.

25 AM, 975; Knox, I, 18–19.

26 James V, *Letters*, 274–5, 307–8, 330; *LP*, VII, 1184; VIII, 734; XI, 248–9.

27 Calderwood, *History*, I, 104; *RSS*, II, 2420, 2797 (Donaldson, *St Andrews Formulare*, II, 367 may refer to the same case); *Diurnal of Occurents*, 18–19; *ALC*, 426–8; Knox, I, 59, 62–3; Yellowlees, 'Dunkeld and the Reformation', 178; Robert Pitcairn, *Ancient Criminal Trials in Scotland*, 3 vols (Edinburgh, 1833), I, 216; BL Cotton MS Caligula B.vii fo. 236v (*LP*, XIV(i), 625). On Stratoun of Lauriston, see also above, 23–4.

28 RSS, II, 3396; Margaret H. B. Sanderson, *Cardinal of Scotland: David Beaton, c. 1494–1546* (Edinburgh, 1986), 282.

29 Knox, I, 72–5; *HP*, I, 337; *RSS*, II, 2952. On Douchtie, see above, 20.

30 Jane Dawson, *The Politics of Religion in the Age of Mary, Queen of Scots* (Cambridge, 2002), 17; Wormald, *Court, Kirk and Community*, 33–5, 112. In 1543–44, however, the Highlander John Eldar claimed that Argyll had been 'ravished' from pro-English opinions by 'the Cardinal and his bishops': BL Royal MS 18.A.xxxviii, fo. 2v.

31 LP, XII(i), 496; Carol Edington, *Court and Culture in Renaissance Scotland: Sir David Lindsay of the Mount* (Amherst, MA, 1994), 48–9; Sanderson, *Cardinal of Scotland*, 271–2; *CSP Scotland*, 567.

32 Lynch, *Edinburgh*, esp. 82–5; Allan White, 'The impact of the Reformation on a burgh community: the case of Aberdeen' in Michael Lynch (ed.), *The Early Modern Town in Scotland* (London, 1987); Verschuur, 'Perth and the Reformation', esp. 330–3.

33 ALC, 372; James V, *Letters*, 261. On Dundee's priority in the Scottish Reformation, see below, 76–7, 79.

34 RPC, 63; APS, 371; James Kirk, 'The religion of early Scottish Protestants' in *Humanism and Reform: the Church in Europe, England and Scotland 1400–1643* (Studies in Church History Subsidia 8: Oxford, 1991), 377.

35 James V, *Letters*, 274–5.

36 NLS MS 1746 fo. 122r–v.

37 Knox, I, 45–6.

38 NLS Adv. MS 10.1.9, 3; Aitken, *Trial of George Buchanan*, 19–21, 119; Calderwood, *History*, I, 127.

39 BL Cotton MS Caligula B.vii fo. 236v (*LP*, XIV(i), 625); *ASP*, 370; Knox, I, 73.

40 Knox, I, 52–3.

41 James V, *Letters*, 241; Dotterweich, 'Emergence of Evangelical Theology', 177–80.

42 *TA*, VI, 307; Donaldson, *St Andrews Formulare*, II, 367; see below, ch. 6.

43 Knox, I, 46–7, 62–3; Calderwood, *History*, I, 113–14.

44 Aitken, *Trial of George Buchanan*, xvii; Knox, I, 36–41, 43–4.

45 Donaldson, *St Andrews Formulare*, II, 401; Aitken, *Trial of George Buchanan*, 5–7, 23, 119; *AM*, 1266; Knox, I, 62.

46 As Mark Dilworth points out, this dilemma was impossible to avoid before 1560 even for the most well-connected commendators: Dilworth, *Scottish Monasteries*, 21.

47 Aitken, *Trial of George Buchanan*, 33.

48 Knox, I, 74.

49 Jamie Cameron, *James V: The Personal Rule 1528–42* (East Linton, 1998), esp. 1–6, 328–335; Knox, I, 93.

50 Cameron, *James V*, 260–2, 289–91.

51 James V, *Letters*, 161, 167, 174–5, 279, 327–8, 343; A. Thomson, *Coldingham Parish and Priory* (Galashiels, 1908), 131.

52 *APS*, 335; Leslie, *Historie*, II, 226–7.

53 James V, *Letters*, 424; Robert Kerr Hannay and J. H. Pollen (eds), 'Letters of the papal legate in Scotland, 1543', *SHR*, 11 (1914), 2; Wormald, *Court, Kirk and Community*, 96–8.

54 *APS*, 294, 306, 377.

55 James V, Letters, 200, 202–3, 206–7, 287, 307, 308, 315–16, 392–3, 398–400, 405–6, 410–11, 421; Roger Mason, *Kingship and the Commonweal: Political Thought in Renaissance and Reformation Scotland* (East Linton, 1998), 121–2.

56 *APS*, 306, 377–8.

57 James V, *Letters*, 174–5, 183, 201–2, 349, 351–2, 353, 359, 422.

58 *Ibid.*, 264–7, 271.

59 *Sadler SP*, I, 30.

60 Charles Burns, 'Papal gifts to Scottish monarchs: the Golden Rose and the Blessed Sword', *IR*, 20 (1969), esp. 181–2; James V, *Letters*, 328; *LP*, XII(i), 665.

61 Clare Kellar, *Scotland, England and the Reformation 1534–1561* (Oxford, 2003), 16–20, 71–2; Peter Marshall, 'Catholic exiles' in his *Religious Identities in Henry VIII's England* (Aldershot, 2005).

62 *LP*, VI, 975; VII, 847; X, 1205; XIV(i), 625; James V, *Letters*, 365.

63 NLS MS 1746 fo. 124r; *Diurnal of Occurents*, 19; NLS Adv. MS 10.1.9, 5; Andrew J. Brown, *Robert Ferrar: Yorkshire Monk, Reformation Bishop and Martyr in Wales (c. 1500–1555)* (London, 1997), 27, 33.

64 *Sadler SP*, I, 26–8, 30–2, 42–4.

65 Wormald, *Court, Kirk and Community*, 84.

66 James V, *Letters*, 204–5, 286–7, 301, 339; Foggie, *Renaissance Religion*, 42.

67 P. Hume Brown (ed.), *Early Travellers in Scotland* (Edinburgh, 1891), 40; James V, *Letters*, 213, 231–2, 275–6, 315–16; *LP*, VII, 1607.

68 James V, *Letters*, 231, 278.

69 James V, *Letters*, 274–5, 307; *Diurnal of Occurents*, 18; *LP*, VIII, 734.

70 Leslie, *Historie*, II, 231–2, 244; NLS MS 1746 fo. 122r.

71 Knox, I, 66–7; Leslie, *Historie*, II, 244.

72 Knox I, 4; Dawson, 'Scottish Reformation', 259–60; Sanderson, *Cardinal of Scotland*, 277.

73 *APS*, 341–2, 370–1.

74 Lindsay of Pitscottie, *Historie*, I, 387–91; Edington, *Court and Culture*, 54–5.

75 Sanderson, *Cardinal of Scotland*, 149–50; Robert Kerr Hannay (ed.), *Rentale Sancti Andree: Being the Chamberlain and Granitar Accounts of the Archbishopric in the Time of Cardinal Beaton, 1538–46* (Scottish History Society 2nd series 4: Edinburgh, 1913), 93.

76 Knox, I, 64–5; James V, *Letters*, 388–9.

77 For example, *TA*, VI, 313, 430; VII, 153.

78 BL Royal MS 7.C.xvi fos 137r–138v.

79 *Ibid.* On this episode, see Greg Walker, 'Sir David Lindsay's *Ane Satire of the Three Estaitis* and the politics of the Reformation', *Scottish Literary Journal*, 16:2 (1989), 5–17.

80 Cameron, *James V*, 295.

81 James Melville of Halhill, *Memoirs of his own life . . . MDXLIX–MDXCIII*, ed. T. Thomson (Edinburgh, 1827), 60–4; Knox, I, 82–3.

82 *APS*, 342, 370; Foggie, *Renaissance Religion*, 41.

83 Leslie, *Historie*, 220; Buchanan, *History*, II, 304–5; Knox, I, 96; *AM*, 1274.

84 *Sadler SP*, I, 47–8.

85 Sarah Carpenter, 'David Lindsay and James V: court literature as current event' in Jennifer Britnell and Richard Britnell (eds), *Vernacular Literature and Current Affairs in the Early Sixteenth Century: France, England and Scotland* (Aldershot, 2000), 151.

86 David Nicholls, 'France' in Andrew Pettegree (ed.), *The Early Reformation in Europe* (Cambridge, 1992), 123–6.

87 Kellar, *Scotland, England and the Reformation*, 98; Edington, *Court and Culture*, 48.

88 Knox, I, 47–52; Aitken, *Trial of George Buchanan*, 7–9.

89 Knox, I, 71; James V, *Letters*, 252, 271; John Durkan, 'The beginnings of humanism in Scotland', *IR*, 4 (1953), 10; John Durkan, 'Giovanni Ferrerio, humanist: his influence in sixteenth-century Scotland' in Keith Robbins (ed.), *Religion and Humanism* (Studies in Church History 17: Oxford, 1981); Edington, *Court and Culture*, 46–7; Carpenter, 'David Lindsay and James V', 143–7.

90 Aitken, *Trial of George Buchanan*, xix, 3–5; NLS Adv. MS 10.1.9 p. 4; *ALC*, 488.

91 Carpenter, 'David Lindsay and James V', 141–3.

92 *Sadler SP*, I, 48–9.

93 Dawson, 'Scottish Reformation', 266–7.

Chapter 3

The crisis of 1543

ARRAN'S 'GODLY FIT'

On 14 December 1542, James V died, unexpectedly, after a short illness. He was thirty years old. His only surviving child, who succeeded to the Crown, was a baby. It was a disaster but, for the Scots, a familiar one. Not since 1390 had an adult succeeded to the Scottish throne, although even by these standards James V cut it alarmingly fine – his heir was only six days old. The novelty of this particular disaster was that the new monarch was worse than an infant: she was a girl.

Female monarchy as such was uncontroversial in Scotland. When the new Queen was in her teens, John Knox was to denounce her, her French mother and her English cousin in the book with the most memorable title of the sixteenth century: *The First Blast of the Trumpet Against the Monstruous Regiment of Women*. Knox's view was that the 'regiment', the rule, of women over men was, literally, monstrous: a violation of nature. Knox, however, was a lone voice, on this as on much else. In 1542–43 no Scots challenged the young Mary Stewart's right to succeed, even those with obvious motives for doing so. Her sovereignty was unquestioned. The problem – and there was widely acknowledged to be a problem – was more practical. It was best summed up by her dying father. On being told that his wife had borne him, and his kingdom, a daughter, he is said to have lamented: 'It came with a lass, it will pass with a lass.'[1] The Stewart dynasty had inherited Scotland in the fourteenth century through the female line. Now that the last Stewart was a woman, surely the Crown would pass into another family in the same way.

If Knox's wild language appears darkly comic to modern eyes, we should not dismiss James V's concerns so lightly. In a patriarchal, patrilinear monarchy, the difficulties confronting a ruling queen were formidable. The problem was not her immediate authority. Queens regnant, and female regents, were frequently able to wield real power in early modern Europe. The difficulty lay in those sinews of monarchy, marriage and succession. The intractability of these problems for queens regnant is neatly demonstrated by the various solutions to them attempted by Mary Stewart, Mary Tudor and Elizabeth Tudor. The most prestigious option – marriage to a foreign prince – risked ceding sovereignty to that prince and his family in perpetuity. Mary Stewart openly courted this risk in her marriage to Francis of Valois, Dauphin and subsequently King of France; yet even Mary Tudor's much more carefully negotiated marriage to Philip II of Spain caused her grave political problems. Marriage to a lesser man risked his attempting to assert authority over his wife and her kingdom – risks which came horribly to fruition in Mary Stewart's second and third marriages, to the Anglo-Scottish princeling Henry, Lord Darnley, and to the Earl of Bothwell. The path which Elizabeth eventually chose, of remaining single, may appear more successful, but its political cost was high. As well as entailing the extinction of her dynasty – a calamity, in most early modern minds – this also subjected her realm to forty years of nail-biting political uncertainty about the succession. There was, in fact, no good solution to the problem of how to be a queen regnant in sixteenth-century Europe.

The accession of a baby girl was therefore one of the proximate causes of the Scottish Reformation. It was deeply destabilising, because it raised the prospect that not only the Stewart dynasty, but the kingdom as a whole, might be absorbed by whoever managed to secure the marriage of the infant queen. Scotland was abuzz with gossip about the different possible matches, and every dynast in Western Europe hurried to calculate the potential matches. However, it was immediately clear who would be the main contender. Edward Tudor, Prince of Wales, who would in 1547 succeed his father Henry VIII and become King Edward VI, was five years old in December 1542. If he were to marry the young Scottish Queen, and they were to have children, the English and Scottish Crowns would be permanently united. The potential gains for England were obvious, and on hearing of James V's death, English agents did not even wait for their King's permission before beginning to pursue Edward's candidacy.[2] From the beginning, therefore, the political stakes of this new reign were alarmingly high.

This contest over Mary, Queen of Scots's marriage would dominate the next decade or more. It began by tipping Scotland into a year of frightening and (for some) exhilarating political turbulence. 1543 was a bewildering year for those who lived through it, and it has not been much less confusing for historians. This is partly because, on one level, very little actually happened. When the dust cleared at the end of the year the political landscape looked very much the same as it had done twelve months earlier. Yet the evaporation of the year's grand hopes – particularly England's grand hopes – left a poisonous residue. The dramatic religious changes during 1543 were also quickly reversed, but again, that religious turmoil had enduring consequences.[3]

The political chaos was all the worse because of another disaster which had befallen Scotland shortly before James V's death. In 1542, Henry VIII had finally broken the long peace with Scotland, as a prelude to his hoped-for Continental war.[4] An inconclusive autumn of campaigning ended with an unexpected confrontation on 24 November. The military encounter – it scarcely deserves the name of 'battle' – at Solway Moss in Cumberland may have been farcical, but its consequences were important enough.[5] Traditionally, James V is supposed to have died from shock at the news of the defeat, and while a more mundane medical explanation is more likely, it was an understandable mistake. Some rumour-mongers put two and two together and concluded that the King had been killed in battle.[6] More importantly, the 'battle' delivered dozens of senior Scots nobles into English custody. This gave Henry VIII an early lead in the contest for the young Queen.

In Scotland itself, the King's death prompted an unedifying, and obscure, scramble for power. The two main contenders were Cardinal David Beaton, the Archbishop of St Andrews and an able and ruthless political operator; and James Hamilton, the Earl of Arran. Arran was the natural candidate for the regency, since he was widely (not universally) acknowledged to be the heir to the throne; however, he lacked Beaton's political talents. The two men were related, and an alliance, pairing Arran's legitimacy with Beaton's authority, would have been natural. In fact, however, Arran was initially excluded from the regency government. Arran himself, supported by later Protestant conspiracy theorists, blamed this exclusion on Cardinal Beaton, who had (he claimed) forged the dying King's will in an attempt to exclude the Earl from power. This allegation was effectively demolished in 1906 by Andrew Lang, but it remains unclear quite what did happen. It may be that James V himself was to blame: for if, as Lang has argued, the notarial instrument drawn up by the King to regulate the regency is genuine, it was James who took the decision to exclude Arran. Perhaps he feared placing a newborn baby into the care of a man who would stand to profit should she die. In any case, the arrangement quickly unravelled. The instrument named a regency council of four, headed by Beaton. Within days, Arran had joined this council. His claim was legitimate and could not be ignored; and he was probably more dangerous outside the government than in it. Yet Arran was soon openly quarrelling with Beaton. The new council was clearly unstable, and in the first week of January, the dead King's instrument was abandoned completely. Arran was now accepted as sole governor. Beaton was made Chancellor, a valuable consolation prize. The other members of the short-lived council were bought off more cheaply. Arran would retain his new status for eleven years. The unprecedented factional spirit which these events heralded in Scottish politics would persist for decades.[7]

The truce between Arran and Beaton was temporary, however. Each man quickly came to represent a political faction. Arran led a group which favoured making peace with England and pledging the young Queen in marriage to Edward Tudor. This faction also showed some signs of favouring the evangelical cause. Arran's principal allies were the Scots nobles whom the English had captured at Solway Moss, and who returned home in January 1543, having promised Henry VIII that they would work to unite the two countries. Some of these 'assured Scots' may even have been sincere. Alongside the captives, several magnates returned from English exile, finally safe from James V's wrath: the Earl of Bothwell, the Earl of Angus, and Angus' brother, Sir George Douglas, perhaps the most cunning and mendacious politician of his generation. The Douglases had long been advocates of an English alliance, albeit for entirely self-serving reasons. Against this pro-English faction stood Beaton and his allies, violently opposed to any reconciliation with England or to any dilution of the old faith. Beaton was joined by the senior clergy, much of the old nobility, and by James V's widow, Mary of Guise, who quickly emerged as a shrewd tactician in her own right. Another returned exile also allied himself with Beaton, more for loathing of Arran than love of the Cardinal: Matthew Stewart, Earl of Lennox. Lennox was Arran's rival for the succession to the Scottish Crown. If – as was arguable – Arran's parents' marriage was invalid, Lennox would be the heir in his place. As a result, the guiding principle of Lennox's political life was that he would always oppose Arran and the Hamiltons, a principle which made him one of the most faithless and duplicitous politicians in an age when the competition was fierce.

Arran was ill prepared to rule this vipers' nest. He was a young and inexperienced man, and both contemporaries and historians have dismissed him as indecisive, impressionable and greedy. Mary of Guise, his rival for nearly two decades, claimed he was 'the most inconstant man in the world; for whatsoever he determineth today, he changeth tomorrow'. According to an English spy, the common view of him was that he was 'a man nothing dreaded . . . of small wit or policy to compass, conduce, or bring to effect a matter of any importance'. George Douglas thought he was of 'weak spirit, and faint hearted'. The English ambassador thought much of what he said was mere bluster.[8] These views should not be swallowed whole. Arran was, like most Scottish politicians, constant enough when pursuing his own dynastic interest. He showed some mettle as a military commander,[9] and he also had a remarkable talent for political survival. It was a talent which he needed in 1543. For the first few months of the year events moved his way. In March he secured parliamentary approval for his negotiations with England.

In June, a marriage treaty was actually agreed, at Greenwich, but by now the weight of the political forces arranged against Arran was beginning to tell. The assembly which ratified the Greenwich treaty was hastily convened and partisan. Early in September, recognising that he had been outmanoeuvred, Arran executed a sudden political about-turn. He was reconciled to Beaton, abandoned his pro-English stance and repudiated the treaty. This was humiliating, but he was able to retain the title of Governor and at least some of the authority that went with it. His former allies, in particular Henry VIII, were outraged; and one of his former opponents, Lennox, inevitably performed a screeching U-turn of his own. The new arrangements themselves proved unstable, but from now until the Cardinal's death in 1546, the underlying theme was that Beaton would rule in Arran's name.

For our purposes, this politicking matters not so much for itself as for its religious consequences. Arran not only pursued an alliance with England; he briefly pursued a policy of evangelical reform. The episode is commonly described as Arran's 'godly fit' ('fit' meaning an interval of time, not a seizure). Yet this was more than a passing phase, and it had enduring consequences. The purpose of this chapter is to examine Arran's godly fit: to ask what he did, why he did it and what effect it had.

Within days of Arran's elevation as Governor, rumours were reaching the English that he was 'a great favourer of the scripture', and 'a good soft God's man [who] loveth well to look on the scripture'.[10] Soon Arran himself declared to the English agent in the north, Lord Lisle, that he intended 'to put some reformation in the state of Church of this realm to the high honour of God [and] forth-setting of his true word'.[11] He sponsored two evangelical friars, Thomas Gwilliam and John Rough, to preach in Edinburgh, and by mid-February they were doing so daily, deprecating the use of traditional prayers and urging Bible reading and spontaneity in prayer. Rough in particular was 'vehement against all impiety'. Preaching was heard beyond Edinburgh, too. In February Gwilliam and another friar went on a preaching tour, and in May the town council of conservative Aberdeen decided it was politic to hire two friars for 'preaching and teaching of the true word of God'.[12] Maybe more significant was Arran's decision in January to place Cardinal Beaton under arrest. This precipitated a crisis in the Church. After the arrest, 'there was no due service done in no diocese, nor to no manner of great men nor small', except where Arran himself compelled it to be done. It was an established legal principle that if a bishop was imprisoned without papal permission, his diocese was thereby placed under interdict, a form of collective excommunication which meant that no sacraments could be celebrated.[13] This was, in other words, a kind of strike by the clergy. The stand-off lasted for nearly two months, until Easter. In order to resolve the matter, Arran allowed Beaton's imprisonment to turn into a house arrest which was soon abandoned altogether.[14] It was an unnerving episode. However, from an evangelical point of view, the effective suspension of the Mass and its replacement with reformist preaching was hardly a cause for grief. It was a dramatic statement of the sudden change of religious direction.

Meanwhile, in March, a parliament confirmed Arran as Governor and authorised negotiations with England. In addition, the parliament relaxed some of Beaton's new-minted heresy laws and, importantly, allowed the Governor to dispense with the ban on abjured heretics holding public office. Arran proceeded to bestow his patronage on reformers and their sympathisers at many levels, even paying for a gown for Patrick Hamilton's orphaned daughter. Most importantly, though, the parliament voted to permit the use of vernacular translations of Scripture, in the teeth of fierce opposition from the bishops. It was, as Knox said, 'no small victory'. Arran personally made sure that this particular law was proclaimed from the market cross in Edinburgh. He had already written to England to urge printed vernacular Bibles to be sent north for the Scottish market, a request he continued to press. And his ambitions went further: he spoke to the English ambassador of the dissolution of religious orders, the rejection of the papacy and the suppression of prayer for the dead. It was said that he was reading Protestant controversial works. 'All men', John Knox later commented, 'esteemed the Governor to have been the most fervent Protestant that was in Europe'. It began a trend. Knox claimed, sourly, that an English Bible suddenly became a fashion accessory around the court, with those who had scarcely opened it claiming to have been reading it secretly for ten years.[15]

However, there were limits to Arran's reformism. In April, his two preachers were dismissed. This decision was widely ascribed to the influence of Arran's half-brother, John Hamilton, Abbot of Paisley, who had recently returned from France.[16] Yet Hamilton's arrival did not mark a sharp change of direction. If the two friars were sent on their way, Arran continued to sponsor other reformist preachers. Moreover, Gwilliam at least was given a substantial fee before his departure, at Arran's personal request. Their dismissal was, however, a sign that the reformers were not simply pushing at an open door. The legislation which permitted the use of vernacular scripture also insisted that it was still illegal to 'dispute or hold opinions' about the Bible. Despite his own reading habits, in April Arran reaffirmed that vernacular works of religious controversy were to remain banned. In June, the Court of Session was made to issue a formal decree against 'slanderous bills, writings, ballads and books'. This had anti-reformist religious tracts in its sights as well as evangelical writings, but the latter were plainly the principal targets. The decree went on to condemn those heretics who doubted Christ's real presence in the Mass, 'which tends plainly to the enervation of the faith catholic'. These shifts in policy, particularly the last, have usually been taken as early warnings that Arran's 'godly fit' was passing and that normal service would soon be resumed.[17]

How are we to explain this set of policies: a decisive, but neither whole-hearted nor permanent, shift towards supporting evangelical religion? There are, of course, several possibilities. The Earl of Arran's own personal religious views must be a part of the story. However, real evidence for his beliefs is very scanty indeed. He seems happily to have changed religious sides through-out his life, according to his political interests. The most we can sensibly say is that he was not averse to adopting a reformist stance if it suited him.[18] The views of his political backers, and of his enemies, were probably more influ-ential. Several members of James V's court who had been sympathetic towards evangelical reform found themselves at the heart of Arran's regime. Some even claimed that reformers such as James Kirkcaldy of Grange or Henry Balnaves had helped to manoeuvre Arran into power, although there is little sign of this in the contemporaneous evidence.[19] More importantly, some of Arran's noble supporters – most notably the Earls of Glencairn and Cassillis, both of whom had fallen into English hands at Solway Moss – made no secret of their own evangelical views. Equally, his opponent Cardinal Beaton was an aggressive supporter of the old Church. The religious fault line was beginning to be a factor in Scottish politics, and arguably Arran's political position made evangelicalism the rational policy for him. However, this can be only a minor theme. Arran would have been naïve indeed to imagine that evangelical policies would win more friends than they would alienate.

The decisive influence, surely, was England. Only Arran's hope for an English alliance, and for an English alliance on his own terms rather than Henry VIII's, can explain why he adopted evangelical policies, and why he adopted the specific evangelical policies that he did. For Henry VIII's hopes for the alliance were different from Arran's. The English aims were nakedly expansionist and imperialistic. The old English claim to feudal suzerainty over Scotland had been revived in 1542, and during 1543 Henry never allowed it to recede too far into the background. He wanted a marriage treaty, and one which would deliver the infant Queen of Scots into his own custody. He also wanted the title of Governor of Scotland for himself. He was ready, if necessary, to send an English army into Scotland to secure these objectives. And he did not want to make any guarantees regarding Scotland's laws and liberties, or regarding what might happen if either Prince Edward or Queen Mary died before the marriage could be solemnised. The marriage was, for Henry, a form of conquest, and his patience with the Scots was vanishingly short. His first personal letter to the infant Queen's regents showed him at his most conciliatory. 'We . . . hate no one of you', he wrote, 'further than your particular practices and doings shall deserve'. Yet he kept suspicious watch for practices and doings that might deserve his hatred, and had difficulty containing his anger when he found them.[20]

Arran's goals are less plain, but he certainly had a very different vision of the marriage. He, of course, wanted to be Governor of Scotland himself, and to protect his own position as heir to the Scottish throne. He also hoped for a royal marriage for his own family – there was talk of marrying his eldest son to Henry VIII's daughter Elizabeth, a marriage proposal which would be revived equally fruitlessly in the 1560s. He wanted financial, but not military, support from Henry VIII; he knew that to use English troops in Scotland would damn him as an English stooge. For the same reason, he refused to give Beaton into English custody.[21] Above all, he wanted the young Queen to remain in Scotland under his own protection until she was of an age to marry, or at least for several more years. This would keep his options open, including the option of the young Queen's marrying someone else – such as, for example, Arran's own son. It would also safeguard his own right to succeed were she to die. If the English marriage did eventually go ahead, Arran wanted to ensure that Scotland would retain its distinctive political identity in a united monarchy. He seems to have envisaged that he and his descendants would be the permanent representatives of their absent monarchs.[22] Many Scots were, it seems, willing to contemplate an arrangement of this kind. Almost none would have been willing to accept what Henry VIII was proposing. It is in this gap between Henry's and Arran's ambitions that the religious policies of that year flourished.

Arran's dilemma was uncomfortably clear. He needed the English alliance, because without it he was not strong enough to maintain his independence from Beaton and Guise. At the least, he needed to placate English aggression for as long as he could. But he would not and could not give the English everything they wanted. He therefore needed to find some other means to bolster the alliance, or at least to spin out the negotiations. The most plausible way to do so was through pursuing, or appearing to pursue, a religious policy which aligned Scotland with Henry VIII's England. This was, after all, what Henry had been pressing on James V for years. Arran would not offer England a humiliating marriage treaty, but he was prepared to offer the flattery of imitating Henry VIII's religious settlement.

From the beginning Arran presented his commitment to religious reform to England as a guarantee of his good faith and as one of his motives for supporting the alliance. He needed a secure peace with England, he claimed, if he was to reform the Scottish Church as he wished. His slippery ally George Douglas assured the English of Arran's hope 'to reform the whole Church of Scotland in to the same sort that the King's majesty has reformed England' – a hope which, Douglas again emphasised, was conditional on a secure peace.[23] Arran also drew attention to the political risks that he was taking for England's sake by opposing the bishops and their allies. With Ralph Sadler, the English ambassador, he was free with his anticlerical talk, scorning the papal legate who was then en route to Scotland and openly affirming his hatred for Beaton. He also claimed, implausibly, that he had long ago been accused by Cardinal Beaton of being 'the greatest heretic in the world'.[24] Similarly, he took care to ensure that the men he sent as emissaries to England were evangelical or at least fashionably Erasmian. The diplomats sent to negotiate the marriage treaty included the Earl of Glencairn and the fiercely committed Protestant Sir Henry Balnaves. The anticlerical satirist Sir David Lindsay was sent to return James V's Order of the Garter to England. Likewise, when a Scottish evangelical who had been in exile in France and England arrived at the court with Henry VIII's recommendation, Arran took care not only to hear him preach and to promise him a benefice, but also to make sure that news of this favour reached England.[25]

Aside from such general demonstrations of his earnest reformism, Arran also did his best to imitate the idiosyncratic detail of Henry VIII's religious settlement. In February, an English messenger visiting the Scottish court was made to sit through a sermon delivered by one of Arran's evangelical friars. The sermon's burden was a lengthy denunciation of 'the abuses of the Church'; the only substantial reform urged was the setting forth of vernacular scripture. These were very English themes. After the sermon, Arran called the English messenger over and 'asked him how he liked the same'.[26] Arran's own letters south were full of the same generalised anticlericalism, and of vague promises that most Scots were 'as well minded as we to set forth the word of God'.[27] In March, Arran insisted to Sadler that he had long regarded the Pope as no more than a bishop, 'and that a very evil bishop'. It was a slightly unusual sentiment for a Protestant, but it meshed precisely with the rhetoric of an English regime which was fond of dismissing the Pope as merely the Bishop of Rome. He begged to be sent copies of the English religious legislation and royal injunctions. One of his heralds asked the English emissaries not merely to send them copies of Henry VIII's approved English translation of the Bible, but also English primers and Psalters. It was also being said that Arran intended to suppress the monasteries in Scotland, as part of a general plan to 'make alterations in the state of the Church, following such injunctions as in like case have been set forth in England'.[28]

In early 1543, however, to try to emulate Henry VIII's Reformation was to strike at a moving target. Henry VIII's religious policy was never wholly stable, and these months saw a dramatic lurch in a more conservative direction. Henry's regime was rounding up evangelical preachers and printers, restricting access to the English Bible, and approving a distinctly conservative doctrinal statement, the *King's Book*.[29] The Scots could be forgiven for being confused. Through the spring and early summer Arran's regime was trying to align itself with the newly conservative signals coming from south of the border. This may be why he dismissed the two friars in mid-April. There is no direct evidence for this, but the chronology fits very neatly, coming a few weeks after a wave of arrests in England. On the matter of books and censorship, the evidence is plainer. The ban on disputing about Scripture or reading controversial books in the March 1543 legislation might have been lifted directly from English formulations – a point which Arran emphasised to Sadler. When told of the forthcoming *King's Book*, Arran asked to be sent a copy as soon as possible, and said that 'he will not fail to publish it here, desiring, with all his heart, that the two realms may concur'.[30] By the time it did arrive, matters had gone too far for Arran to make any effective use of it, but the decree in June against radical heretics was also in keeping with the new mood coming from south of the Border. Such policies were not a change of direction, although some Scots reformers were dismayed by them. They were entirely consistent with Arran's attempt to align himself with England. As Martin Dotterweich has suggested, this period is not so much a 'godly fit' as a 'Henrician experiment'.[31]

The most remarkable feature of this policy is that it worked. Immediately after James V's death, the English regime was focused almost exclusively on the hoped-for marriage. In January 1543, the English agent Lord Lisle was exasperated by Arran's insistence on talking about religion. 'As touching the Earl of Arran's letters, me think they sound altogether upon Church matters and toucheth no part of the King's purposes.'[32] Yet the English came to place steadily more importance on Arran's plans for religious reform, for several reasons. On a cynical level, driving Arran into the reformist camp deepened the rift between him and the bishops, so forcing him to rely on English assistance. The English repeatedly urged Arran to beware Beaton's treachery, and reminded him that Henry was his best ally against the Scottish clergy.[33] Yet English enthusiasm for Scottish reformism was more than tactical. It helped that several of those entrusted by Henry VIII with implementing his Scottish policy were themselves evangelicals. Ralph Sadler enthusiastically endorsed Arran's request for evangelical books to be sent from England, and encouraged Arran's ambitions for religious reform.[34] But the King himself also seems to have been tempted by the prospect of exporting his Reformation to Scotland. England provided books and preachers to support Arran's reformist project. Indeed, the English regime spent a surprising amount of effort winkling one Scottish exile out of a French prison so that he might be sent home to preach.[35]

English advice to Arran on religious matters also became more detailed and involved as the year went on. This advice always took the English experience of religious reform as normative, urging Arran to follow the English example both in principle and in detail. In February, Lord Lisle wrote to Arran recommending that Beaton should be kept in prison, and that 'some learned man well addicted to the truth' be installed as commissary of the archbishopric of St Andrews: a man who might play the same role in Scotland as Archbishop Cranmer had in England. Lisle also warned Arran 'not to attempt too many things at once'. 'As well time and policy must be used in the demeaning of these affairs, as force, and all three tempered together.' This could hardly be a neater description of the mixture of 'hard' and 'soft' power with which Henry VIII's own Reformation had been implemented. More positively, Lisle urged Arran to legalise vernacular scripture – not to increase godliness, but so that the people may 'know the better how to eschew sedition'. The peculiar belief that vernacular scripture would have this effect had been Henry VIII's principal justification for permitting it.[36] Sadler, likewise, warned Arran against allowing Beaton to escape to France, lest he stir up international feeling against Scotland: a warning which surely reflected England's bitter experience with its own exiled Cardinal, Reginald Pole.[37] Henry himself sent the newly published *King's Book* to Arran during the summer, and pestered the Governor to give his opinion of it.[38]

Most remarkably, Henry sent Arran detailed advice on religious policy in a letter of April 1543 which the King corrected in his own hand. Henry was in the midst of one of his periodic bouts of theological activism, and was almost as keen to impose his views on the Scots as on his own subjects. In this letter, he recommended that the provision of vernacular scripture should be balanced by a crackdown on unauthorised books, and then laid out a plan for the dissolution of the Scottish monasteries. He suggested that a smokescreen of moral reform and a judicious distribution of bribes would allow the bulk of the monasteries' wealth to fall into Arran's lap.[39] This is not only an embarrassingly clear statement of Henry's own policy; it showed no understanding of Scotland's very different legal and financial situation. Yet if the advice was bad, the enthusiasm with which it was offered shows how successfully Arran had muddied the diplomatic waters. After some initial puzzlement, the English undoubtedly became convinced that Arran's commitment to Henrician reform was genuine. They assumed that this meant he was committed to his pro-English policy and had burned his bridges with the bishops. When Arran did change sides in September 1543, the bitterness and surprise of the English in general and of Sadler in particular underlines how far they had been deceived.[40]

Arran's purpose may not have been to deceive, or even to distract; but this was the effect of what he did, and he certainly did not regret it, especially once it became clear how eagerly the English were taking the bait. This does cast Arran's policy during 1543 in a new light. If his 'godly fit' was more of a political ploy than a principled stand, it can be seen as a success of sorts. By the time the policy unravelled in the late summer, the danger of an English invasion that year had passed. If not a political mastermind, Arran does emerge as a wilier politician than is usually allowed. The most obviously incompetent player in the dramas of the year was not Arran, but Henry VIII. By the end of 1543 Arran was still Governor, and his rival Lennox was as far from power as ever. He had also successfully outmanoeuvred the English, and so had at least postponed the war which they had been prosecuting the previous year. This policy, however, had its price.

SCOTLAND'S WONDERYEAR

Playing politics with heresy is a dangerous game. James V had dabbled in it, but Arran committed himself much more deeply. If it was principally a political move for him, it was a providential opportunity for Scottish evangelicals. What impact did these few months of comparative freedom and official patronage have on the Protestant movement in Scotland?

Our evidence for the impact of Arran's policies is inevitably sketchy, but three patterns emerge. Most tantalisingly, some Scottish evangelicals may have seen James V's death as an opportunity to put their heads above the parapet, even before Arran's policy became clear. This is at least plausible. Regents are always less powerful than adult kings, and reformers who had fled James V might sensibly have hoped that they would be safer after his death. Knox claimed that reformers rejoiced at the King's death. The evangelical John Wedderburn is said to have returned from his German exile as soon as James V was dead, only to flee again before the end of the year. Knox and Sadler both testify to a genuine hunger for vernacular scripture in Scotland before it was legalised, although neither was a neutral witness. Arran did not invent the Protestant movement in 1543: he used it. As Gordon Donaldson pointed out, the mere fact that it was possible for Arran to adopt pro-English, evangelical policies demonstrates that those policies already had some support by the time of James V's death.[41] So there are hints that Scotland's heresy problem would have taken a turn for the worse during 1543 even without Arran's intervention.

Second, of course, is the direct impact of Arran's policies. The legalisation of vernacular scripture and the spread of evangelical preaching made the evangelical message newly available to substantial audiences. The English martyrologist John Foxe, whose informant was the shrewd Scottish cleric John Winram, wrote that thanks to the legalisation of scripture 'in sundry parts of Scotland . . . were opened the eyes of the elect of God to see the truth, and abhor the Papistical abominations'. One such convert, it seems, was John Knox himself. In June 1544 a number of distinguished lairds and nobles were pardoned for disputing on scripture and reading forbidden books. Edinburgh and Aberdeen had evangelical preachers; one of those at Aberdeen,

John Roger, also preached in Glamis and perhaps much of the rest of Angus. George Wishart, the most powerful reformist preacher of the decade, may also have returned from English exile in 1543.[42] Perth's craftsmen later claimed that many of them had been persecuted for reading the Bible after Arran licensed it. One burgess was later pardoned for holding conventicles and disputing about scripture. By July the people of Edinburgh's port of Leith were, Sadler claimed, 'noted all to be good Christians'. In November, the papal legate, Marco Grimani, agreed that Leith was being brought back into conformity with some difficulty. Bibles and heretical books had been widely circulated. There were not only imports from England, but Scots-language works pouring abuse on the Pope, presumably circulating in manuscript. That month an 'immense number' of heretical books had been publicly burned in Edinburgh. In October, Mary of Guise told Grimani that Scotland was 'divided on account of the Lutherans, whose errors had become disseminated throughout almost the whole country since the death of the King'.[43] The decree against heretical books in June 1543 may have been in tune with English policy, but it surely also reflects events in the parishes in some parts of Scotland. The seed which Arran had permitted to be sown was sprouting, and in some places growing with more vigour than the Governor liked.

This leads to the third feature of Scottish reformism in 1543: violence against the established Church. Arran did not sanction this, but it was clearly made possible by the contraction of Crown authority following James V's death and by the new regime's hostility to the old Church. In June the Court of Session recognised that there was an epidemic of assaults on churches and monasteries. Some attacks had nothing to do with theology. In November 1543, when the Countess of Atholl's men seized Dunkeld Cathedral, forced the steeple and attacked the Bishop's palace with siege artillery, the sole motive seems to have been her (robust) defence of her property rights. Likewise, the expulsion of the Laird of Arnot's son from the Franciscan house at Scotlandwell in Fife led to an armed attack on the house in June 1543. Arnot and his allies, having briefly secured official backing for their actions, flung out the friars and reinstalled not only his son but himself and the rest of his family. The dispute was not finally resolved until 1546.[44] Neither Atholl nor Arnot had any discernible religious purpose, but Arran's policy had made the Church vulnerable to attacks of all kinds. In some cases, Arran had actively encouraged this kind of behaviour. In March 1543, he offered the profits of Scotland's premier monastery, the Charterhouse at Perth, to James Gordon, parson of Crieff. Gordon marched into the Charterhouse with twenty-four armed men, made off with as many valuables as he and his men could carry, and threatened to close down the house entirely unless he received the income to which he insisted he was due.[45] Such attacks can only have weakened the Church's ministry and authority. Moreover, some of these attacks did have more explicitly religious motives. A month before Gordon's attack on the Charterhouse, Perth's Dominican friary was ransacked by townspeople who made off with £6 worth of goods, principally from the kitchen. This arose from a dispute over rents, not iconoclastic zeal, but it was a sign of the times. It is no coincidence that this dispute had blown up at this moment, nor that in the same year the burgh council chose to withhold its regular annual payment to the Dominicans. Moreover, four of the seven ringleaders of the raid had evangelical connections.[46] Anyone with a grievance against the Church, whether secular or religious, would find 1543 a good time to pursue it.

Significantly, however, the most alarming acts of violence took place after it had become clear that Arran's 'godly fit' was coming to an end. There was a well-documented case of defiant iconoclasm in Perth in October and November. It had been a year of political unrest in the town, which may have provoked Arran and Beaton to make an example of the vandals: five of them were executed in January 1544, the only evangelical martyrs of this period, and the executions were policed by a substantial armed force.[47] The most dramatic set of events, however, took place early in September 1543. As it became clear that Arran was going to abandon the reformist cause, iconoclastic riots broke out in a number of East Coast towns, possibly with Arran's own connivance. Lindores Abbey, Arbroath Abbey and perhaps also the Aberdeen Dominican house were attacked. In Edinburgh, some of Arran's own footsoldiers participated in an assault on that town's Dominican friary, although the people of the town turned out to protect the friars and successfully saw off the attackers. Dundee's Franciscan and Dominican houses were both destroyed in a substantial riot, and several of the town's churches were damaged too. The Dundee riots in particular became notorious. No-one had any doubt that they were inspired by heresy rather than mere anticlericalism.[48] Arran had released forces which neither he nor his successors were able adequately to control.

However, none of this means that there was a Protestant wave which Arran could have ridden. His religious innovations stirred up much more opposition than support. A ballad written against them, and Arran, was so popular that it nearly cost the author his neck. John Scot, the friar whose prodigious feats of fasting had made him famous in James V's reign, publicly opposed the reformers. When another friar, John Routh, denounced the innovations in Ayr and was summoned to Edinburgh to face trial, the burgh council not only supported him but paid handsomely for an escort to accompany him.[49] By contrast, when Arran's evangelical protégés preached in Edinburgh, armed guards were needed to prevent the crowd from tearing them to pieces. The same Edinburgh crowd was to fight off the attack on the town's friaries in September. Arran's imprisonment of Beaton caused particular outrage. The interdict was widely supported, and when parliament met in March, the first and most pressing petition that was put to it was for the Cardinal to be freed.[50]

If religious innovation was unpopular, however, it was made much more so by association with England. Some Scottish magnates favoured the marriage, for even religious conservatives could see that they might personally benefit from it.[51] Most of the rest of the country, however, seems to have reacted to the idea with raw hostility. Arran was derided as 'a heretic, and a good Englishman' – alluding to his partially English ancestry. His supporters were 'commonly hated . . . and throughout the realm called the English lords'. Songs were being sung of how English gold had corrupted them. And by July, even some of those allies were balking at the proposed alliance, declaring 'that they be Scotsmen, and true Scots they will be in heart and deed against England'. This was particularly so if they suspected – rightly – that when Henry VIII spoke of union, he meant conquest. George Douglas warned that the Scots would rather 'die rather all in a day, than they would be made thrall and subject to England'. Sadler doubted whether Arran could even rely on his own servants to be loyal to him if he went too far down the English road.[52] An English ship bearing diplomatic messages which anchored at Leith in June was promptly seized as a prize of war by the townsmen, who grudgingly returned it on orders from the regime. Yet, Sadler wrote, the seizure of several Scots ships in England in early September brought Edinburgh 'in to such a rage and fury, that the whole town is commoved against me, and swore great oaths, if their ships were not restored, that they would have their amends of me and mine, and that they would set my house here afire over my head, so that one of us should not escape alive'. Sadler was shaken by the visceral hostility which he met throughout his mission in Scotland. His men were jeered in the street, and once someone even fired a gun at them. During the chaos of early September he was effectively besieged in his house. 'Under the sun', he concluded, 'live not more beastly and unreasonable people than here be of all degrees'. The antipathy was clearly mutual.[53]

So, far from precipitating a mass conversion, Arran's Henrician experiment had stirred up a hornet's nest of opposition. It had, as Sadler observed, divided the political nation into distinct factions. One group, the 'heretics, and the English lords', who favoured both religious reform and an English marriage, were opposed by those 'which be called Scribes and Pharisees and of the cast of France'.[54] In 1543, there could be no doubt that the pro-French, pro-Catholic party was the stronger. Yet perhaps the lasting importance of the year's events was not so much that immediate victory as the solidification of those factions. The evangelical and the English causes were now inseparable. In the short term, the two causes probably damaged each other more than they supported each other, but their alliance was to be pivotal in Scottish politics for most of the rest of the century.

What, then, are we to make of the crisis of 1543? It was not unique. Other European countries experienced similar crises, of which perhaps the best known is the event known in the Netherlands as the 'Wonderyear'. In 1566, the Netherlands saw a sudden explosion of public evangelical preaching, followed by a wave of iconoclastic destruction which was then violently suppressed.[55] However, 'Wonderyears' were a more general phenomenon of the European Reformation. A similar set of events took place over a longer period in France in 1560–62. Even England had a Wonderyear, albeit a more sedate one: the burst of scarcely regulated evangelical activity in 1547–48, early in Edward VI's reign, when censorship was abandoned and unofficial iconoclasm ran ahead of the government's own programme. The events of 1543 in Scotland can be seen in the same light. All of these episodes shared some common characteristics. In all four cases, a former regime had suppressed evangelical heresy with vigour and some brutality. In all four cases, those regimes and their repression ended abruptly – following the deaths of strong adult monarchs who were succeeded by minority regimes in England, France and Scotland, and through the collapse of the authority of Philip II's absentee government in the Netherlands. In all four cases, the sudden removal of firm pressure produced an explosion of evangelical ideas – or rather, an explosion of public *interest* in such ideas, manifested in a willingness to read books and to give the new preachers a hearing. In each case religious conservatives were temporarily disorientated by the speed of events. In each case the evangelical movement was not wholly under anyone's control, neither governments nor reformist leaders; but in each case this phase of chaotic expansion proved short-lived, as politics caught up with the changes. Governments reigned the evangelical movement in, ostracised it and brutally suppressed it in England, Scotland and the Netherlands respectively, and in France there was civil war. But in each case the brief moment was massively influential for the subsequent history of the Reformation in that country.

The 'Wonderyear', in Scotland as elsewhere, was a moment of coming up for air, from which the later Protestant movement could draw both numerical strength and heightened hopes. It was also a point of radicalisation, as the dashing of newly raised hopes engendered a more confrontational approach than before. During James V's reign, Scottish Protestantism was a collection of scholars, courtiers and anticlerical nobles. It was 'a state of mind',[56] with little cohesion and no programme. In 1543, it came briefly into the open and tasted power. A political means by which it might gain power permanently – the English alliance – became imaginable. It would, in fact, be a bitter decade and a half before the reformers regained any kind of political power. However, those years would be shaped by the ambitions which Scottish Protestantism had learned in 1543.

NOTES

1 Lindsay of Pitscottie, *Historie*, I, 407; Knox, I, 91.

2 *HP*, I, 261, 267, 268, 272.

3 On the events of 1543 generally, see Marcus Merriman, *The Rough Wooings: Mary Queen of Scots, 1542–1551* (East Linton, 2000), 111–36.

4 Elizabeth Bonner, 'The genesis of Henry VIII's "Rough Wooing" of the Scots', *Northern History*, 33 (1997), 36–53.

5 Merriman, *Rough Wooings*, 77–82.

6 Cameron, *James V*, 325; Hastings Robinson (ed.), *Original Letters Relative to the English Reformation* (Cambridge, 1846), 240.

7 Andrew Lang, 'The cardinal and the king's will', *SHR*, 3 (1906), 410–22; *HP*, I, 259.

8 Sadler *SP*, I, 115 (*HP*, I, 346), 180–1 (*HP*, I, 367); *HP*, I, 397; II, 2. For a kinder assessment of Arran, see Merriman, *Rough Wooings*, 89, 350–1.

9 Elizabeth Bonner, 'The recovery of St Andrews Castle in 1547: French naval policy and diplomacy in the British Isles', *English Historical Review*, III (1996), 596.

10 NA SP 1/175 fos 10v, 17r (*LP*, XVIII(i), 26.1, 27).

11 *HP*, I, 282.

12 *HP*, I, 301; Leslie, *Historie*, II, 266; Knox, I, 95–6; *TA*, VIII, 170; *Extracts from the Council Register of Aberdeen*, 189; White, 'Impact of the Reformation', 85.

13 *Diurnal of Occurents*, 26; *LP*, XVIII(i), 105; Leslie, *Historie*, II, 266; *ALC*, 401.

14 Sadler *SP*, I, 110–11 (*HP*, I, 345).

15 *ASP*, 415, 425; Marcus Merriman, 'James Henrisoun and "Great Britain": British union and the Scottish commonweal' in Roger Mason (ed.), *Scotland and England 1285–1815* (Edinburgh, 1987), 88; *LP*, XVIII(ii), 176; *TA*, VIII, 183; Knox, I, 98–101; *HP*, I, 303; Sadler *SP*, I, 108, 128 (*HP*, I, 345, 351); Calderwood, *History*, I, 156.

16 Sadler *SP*, I, 158 (*HP*, I, 362); Knox, I, 105–6.

17 Sadler *SP*, I, 128, 210 (*HP*, I, 351, 375), 217; *TA*, VIII, 183; *APS*, 415; NAS CS7/1 fo. 368r; *ALC*, 528; Knox, I, 97; Merriman, *Rough Wooings*, 122–3.

18 Sanderson, *Cardinal of Scotland*, 161; Wormald, *Court, Kirk and Community*, 105.

19 Melville of Halhill, *Memoirs*, 71; Knox, I, 95.

20 *HP*, I, 269, 343; *LP*, XVIII(i), 402.1; Sadler *SP*, I, 101.

21 Sadler *SP*, I, 110 (*HP*, I, 345), 259.

22 *ASP*, 412–13, 426; Sadler *SP*, I, 86 (*HP*, I, 338).

23 *HP*, I, 282, 289.

24 Sadler *SP*, I, 92 (*HP*, I, 341); Sadler *SP*, I, 200.

25 *LP*, XVIII(i), 307, 591, 804.18; Sadler *SP*, I, 210, 217 (*HP*, I, 375).

26 *HP*, I, 298.

27 *Ibid.*, 303.

28 *Sadler SP*, I, 92, 108 (*HP*, I, 341, 345); BL Additional MS 32649 fo. 196v (*HP*, I, 316); *HP*, I, 452; Gladys Dickinson (ed.), *Two Missions of Jacques de la Brosse: An Account of the Affairs of Scotland in the Year 1543 and the Journal of the Siege of Leith, 1560* (Scottish History Society 3rd series 36: Edinburgh, 1942), 23.

29 Alec Ryrie, *The Gospel and Henry VIII* (Cambridge, 2003), 44–51.

30 *Sadler SP*, I, 128 (*HP*, I, 351)

31 *Sadler SP*, I, 264–5; Dotterweich, 'Emergence of Evangelical Theology', 231.

32 *HP*, I, 289.

33 *HP*, I, 298.1, 299.1, 356, 364, 435; *LP*, XVIII(i), 402.1.

34 BL Additional MS 32649 fo. 196v (*HP*, I, 316); *Sadler SP*, I, 94 (*HP*, I, 341). On Sadler, see Ryrie, *Gospel and Henry VIII*, 200, 202.

35 *LP*, XVIII(i), 354.2, 358, 361, 389, 390; *Sadler SP*, I, 210, 217 (*HP*, I, 375).

36 *HP*, I, 299.1; Richard Rex, 'The crisis of obedience: God's Word and Henry's Reformation', *Historical Journal*, 39 (1996), 863–94.

37 *Sadler SP*, I, 207.

38 *HP*, I, 450, 457; *Sadler SP*, I, 264–5, 282 (*HP*, I, 469).

39 BL Additional MS 32650 fos 123r–126v, 131r (*LP*, XVIII (i)364; *HP*, I, 348).

40 *Sadler SP*, I, 262; *HP*, II, 2, 27, 51, 55.

41 Knox, I, 92–4, 100–1; Calderwood, *History*, I, 142–3; BL Additional MS 32649 fo. 196v (*HP*, I, 316); Donaldson, *All the Queen's Men*, 15.

42 *AM*, 1267; *RSS*, III, 820; Hannay, *Rentale Sancti Andree*, 200; Knox, I, 119, 125; Calderwood, *History*, I, 156. Knox – who knew Wishart well – claimed that he returned 'in company of the Commissioners . . . in the year of God 1544'. However, the commissioners were those who negotiated the 1543 treaty; no commissioners travelled to Scotland in 1544. The matter is unclear, but the normal assumption that Wishart did return in 1543 probably needs to be questioned.

43 Perth Museum and Art Gallery papers no. 34 fo. iv; *RSS*, III, 612; *TA*, VIII, 219; *Sadler SP*, I, 242 (*HP*, I, 436); Hannay, 'Letters of the papal legate', 19, 21; Knox, I, 101.

44 *ALC*, 527, 531, 535–6, 538, 545, 553, 558, 560–1.

45 *ALC*, 528–9; Verschuur, 'Perth and the Reformation', 340–1.

46 *Ibid.*, 341–6; Foggie, *Renaissance Religion*, 44–5.

47 *AM*, 1267; *TA*, VIII, 252; Verschuur, 'Perth and the Reformation', 354. On this case, see below, 123–4.

48 *HP*, II, 11, 14, 30; Dickinson, *Two Missions*, 23, 37; *Diurnal of Occurents*, 29; *Extracts from the Council Register of Aberdeen*, 206; *RSS*, IV, 2580.

49 Knox, I, 96–7; Pryde, *Ayr Burgh Accounts*, 90; Bryce, *Scottish Grey Friars*, 80.

50 *HP*, I, 301, 332; *HP*, II, 14; *LP*, XVIII(i), 286.

51 *HP*, I, 334; *LP*, XVIII(i), 325; *Sadler SP*, I, 170 (*HP*, I, 367); Donaldson, *All the Queen's Men*, 20.

52 *Sadler SP*, I, 162–3, 165–6, 216 (*HP*, I, 380), 234 (*HP*, I, 408), 259; *ALC*, 527; *HP*, I, 337, 350, 397; II, 85.

53 *ALC*, 527; *HP*, II, 2, 27; *Sadler SP*, I, 237 (*HP*, I, 409).

54 *Sadler SP*, I, 216 (*HP*, I, 380).

55 Andrew Pettegree, *Emden and the Dutch Revolt: Exile and the Development of Reformed Protestantism* (Oxford, 1992), 109–46.

56 Maurice Lee, *James Stewart, Earl of Moray* (New York, 1953), 15.

Chapter 4

———————◆———————

1544–50: imperial Reformation

THE ROUGH WOOINGS

As the young Mary, Queen of Scots reached her first birthday in December 1543, it was becoming clear that she was likely to live. She had survived a bout of smallpox in August; Ralph Sadler saw her later in the summer, and declared that 'she is a right fair and goodly child, as any that I have seen, for her age'.[1] The question of whom she might eventually marry was becoming more urgent. The English regime of Henry VIII still favoured pledging her to her cousin Edward Tudor, the Prince of Wales. The Scottish political establishment was now clearly opposed to this, and had repudiated the treaty in which the Tudor marriage had been agreed. The battle-lines were firmly drawn.

However, some Scots continued to favour the English marriage. Often this was out of hope for personal or political gain, but there was also an ideological factor. Some – not all – of those Scots with evangelical inclinations supported an English alliance. Henry VIII's England was not in any meaningful sense Protestant, but reformers could reasonably hope that it was moving in their direction; a hope which was fulfilled when the old King died in 1547, and his son's regime pursued much more decisively Protestant policies. Religion aside, there was a well-established tradition in late medieval Scotland of favouring an English alliance and of seeing Scotland as part of a 'British' polity. This tradition received a powerful boost from the circumstances of the early 1540s. For there to be a Scottish queen so close in age to the heir to the English throne genuinely seemed providential to many on both sides of the Border. It was God's will, apparently, that the two realms should be united.

For the rest of the decade, England pursued that union by force. The marriage negotiations turned into the most intense period of Anglo-Scottish warfare for two centuries, as England tried to hold the Scots to the treaty of

1543 and to require the marriage at swordpoint. The Earl of Huntly's bitter joke on this incongruous episode has given it its common name: the 'Rough Wooings'.[2] This struggle has recently been discussed in Marcus Merriman's masterly study, and the grim details of its military and diplomatic history are not our concern. But the Rough Wooings inescapably also belong to the story of the Scottish Reformation's origins.

The wars fell into four phases. The first was the short but large-scale English invasion led by Edward Seymour, the Earl of Hertford, in the spring of 1544. This was a formidable operation. Seymour's large sea-borne army appeared silently and without warning off the Lothian coast one foggy morning.[3] This force quickly occupied Edinburgh and Leith, doing considerable damage to both towns. Equally quickly, however, it abandoned them, and marched home overland, devastating the countryside on its way. The second phase of the war was cross-border raiding of the kind which had characterised Anglo-Scottish warfare for generations. This went on at an intensified rate throughout the wars, steadily laying waste both sides of the Border, although the Scots fared considerably worse.[4] During 1545 this was the main theatre of war. In February of that year it provided the Scots with their first battle victory of the wars, at Ancrum Moor, and in September Seymour led another major incursion into the eastern Borders.

The third episode of the wars is the oddest. In May 1546, a gaggle of Scots lairds assassinated Cardinal Beaton in his castle. Then, astonishingly, they fortified themselves within St Andrews Castle for more than a year. These 'castilians' held out against a rather half-hearted siege, and turned St Andrews into a Protestant and pro-English enclave. Their timing, however, was unlucky. Only nine days after Beaton's murder, England and France concluded a peace treaty which put a temporary stop to English activities in Scotland. This made the English hesitant about giving open support to the castilians. Indeed, it has recently been argued that English carelessness about naval intelligence was decisive in the eventual outcome of the siege.[5] In July 1547, a French naval expedition arrived and, in one of the most remarkable small engagements of the period, reduced the castle within hours. Surprisingly, the castilians managed to negotiate a surrender by which their lives were spared, but they were taken prisoner by the French and St Andrews was safely back in Catholic hands.

The last phase of the wars was the longest and bloodiest. In 1547, with Henry VIII dead and Edward Seymour (now Duke of Somerset) Lord Protector to the new King Edward VI, England launched a full-scale invasion. Seymour's commitment to the Scottish war and to the marriage was much more whole-hearted than his old master's had ever been. For a while it looked as if this invasion might succeed. A crushing English victory at the battle of Pinkie in September 1547 was followed by the military occupation of large parts of southern and eastern Scotland. In the event, however, the victory succeeded only in pushing the Scots into the arms of their old ally, France. Some rather ineffectual French help had reached Scotland in 1545, but the new French King Henry II was much more willing to commit himself to protecting Scotland. This was partly because the Scots were now willing to pay the necessary price, by pledging Queen Mary in marriage to Henry's eldest son, the Dauphin Francis. French troops arrived in Scotland in June 1548. A treaty was concluded the following month, and the five-year-old Queen was shipped off to France. Any kind of English victory now seemed impossible, and indeed the English were quickly besieged in their Scottish strongholds, notably Haddington. By the end of 1549 the military defeat was total. In March 1550 a treaty was concluded which confirmed the rout of the pro-English and pro-evangelical party in Scotland. The French sealed the renewed alliance by showering Scots magnates with favours. In particular, in 1548 Governor Arran was given the lucrative title of Duke of Châtelherault. This politely concealed the fact that France itself, and in particular the Queen Mother, Mary of Guise, was now the real political power in Scotland. That reality was formally accepted in 1554, when Châtelherault finally resigned as Governor and Guise became Queen Regent.

In one sense this Franco-Scottish victory was no surprise. As Merriman has argued, conquering Scotland by force was never a realistic ambition for any English regime. Not only could France be guaranteed to intervene if its old ally's situation became too perilous; Scotland itself posed formidable obstacles. Invading Scotland was easy enough for its richer and better-armed neighbour, and winning battles was always possible although never certain. Subduing the country, however, was a different matter. Scotland was a decentralised state which, unlike England, could not have been taken in a single decisive battle. Its geography and the sparseness of its settlements were not kind to invaders. And as Merriman points out, Edinburgh and Stirling castles were two of the finest defensive strongholds in Western Europe. When Seymour occupied Edinburgh in 1544, his Italian engineers, the best in the world, told him that the castle was all but impossible to assault.[6] Moreover, anti-English feeling ran deep in Scotland, and an English invasion could unite the country as little else could. It was a proverb in England that 'in Scotland is nought to win, but strokes'.[7]

However, the Rough Wooings were not simply a war of conquest. From the beginning, England hoped to mobilise support for the English cause within Scotland. For most of the wars, some Scots magnates were at least neutral, hedging their bets to an extent which alarmed and worried the Scottish regime.[8] There was low bribery and intimidation, and there was high-minded nationalist and internationalist propaganda. In addition, the English tried to stir up religious controversies within Scotland, on the grounds that a Protestant party would be a pro-English party. This was a period when a different kind of Scottish Reformation beckoned, or threatened: an imperial Reformation, imposed on the country from outside as it was 'liberated' from the French and Catholic yoke. This was, perhaps, the only means by which the Rough Wooings might have succeeded: if they had become a Scottish civil war in which one party had English support, rather than an international slugging match. It did not happen. In the event, the pro-English Scots were too few and too unreliable. This chapter's purpose is to consider why this part of England's war effort failed; and to ask, nevertheless, what lasting impact it had on Scotland's religious and political life.

In military terms, the propaganda war was a side-show. At most, it was a possibility which England never succeeded in exploiting. The English did produce some printed propaganda, and sponsored some preachers, especially after 1547. They also made some effort to ensure that the propaganda they produced was actually distributed in Scotland.[9] Little came of it. Merriman's survey of the subject concludes by quoting the Scottish polemicist Robert Wedderburn, who wrote that 'realms are not conquered by books, but rather by blood'. However, that claim is of course not a statement of fact, but itself a piece of propaganda. Wedderburn justified writing his book with a classical allusion: 'The Romans were more reinforced in courageous enterprises by the virtue of the pen, and by the persuasions of orators, than they were reinforced by the swords of men of war.'[10] The issue in the propaganda war was the Scots' willingness to defy the English. Books and blood, belief and action, are the sinews of war, and cannot neatly be separated. The English regimes' failure to understand this did as much as anything to ensure their defeat.

'THE FAITH AND OPINION OF ENGLAND'

The most tantalising section of the propaganda front is its explicitly religious face. For much of the 1540s, England was sending preachers and books into Scotland in order to build a pro-evangelical (and thus pro-English) party there, but we do not know much about this campaign. We do know that Lord Methven was worried in 1548 that 'part of the lieges has taken new opinions of the Scripture and has done against the law and ordinance of Holy Church', and that these people were supporting England's cause.[11] We have John Knox's testimony that English evangelical books were being imported in large numbers, and some hints in the English military correspondence that this was indeed the case.[12] We know that Scots looking for English patronage went out of their way to fill their correspondence with evangelical catchphrases.[13] We also know that when the English were negotiating with the Earl of Huntly, in 1548, in an attempt to win him to their side – which would have been a spectacular coup, had it succeeded – they insisted that he promise to protect those in Scotland who had renounced the Pope.[14] Indeed, when other Scottish magnates pledged their allegiance to the English cause – or 'assured' – they were frequently made to promise that they would 'cause the word of God to be truly taught and preached among them and in their countries'. Even the Bishop of Caithness assured with the English on these terms, but this was less impressive than it looks: he was the brother of England's only truly reliable Scottish ally, the Earl of Lennox, and spent much of the 1540s in England, even holding a benefice in Canterbury. The impact of these 'assured' Scots on the country's religious life was probably fairly limited. Clare Kellar has recently argued that the act of 'assurance' itself had religious overtones, but if so, this was probably scarcely apparent to Scots who were used to conducting politics through personal bonds. The English did, however, use religion as a shibboleth, deliberately including a commitment to evangelical reform in some pledges of assurance so as to separate fair-weather friends from the truly committed.[15]

Plainly, some were committed. Some Scots chose English exile and fully supported the war effort, often from religious motives. Lennox's brother seems to have been genuine enough in his Protestantism. Another nobleman, Lord Somerville's brother-in-law, fled south in 1544 because he had been 'troubled for the using of the New Testament'. John, Lord Borthwick, in exile for heresy since 1540, found himself hosting something of a Scottish evangelical clique in London. Other exiles were drawn from humbler stock. James Harryson was an Edinburgh merchant of long-standing evangelical convictions. He attached himself to Seymour's army when Edinburgh was occupied in 1544, returning to England with the invaders. He remained in England for the duration of the war, although it was only after Henry VIII's death that the regime made any use of him. Thomas Schort, an Edinburgh armourer, moved to Holy Island in Northumberland with his sister during the wars, and died there 'at the faith and opinion of England'. An Orcadian priest named James Skea fled to England in late 1547 'for fear of burning for the word of God', offering his services to the war effort. When the Scots retook Dundee in January 1548 after a brief English occupation, one wealthy townsman and his family left on the English ships. In a few cases, it seems, religious loyalties could trump national ones.[16]

The English did more than attract a few exiles, however. Their support for Protestantism also helped them to strengthen their hand militarily. In September 1547 the captain of the castle of Broughty Crag, some two miles from Dundee, betrayed it to the English. He acted, he said later, 'for the good mind and favour I bore both unto the true setting forth and knowledge of the Gospel, and unto the king's majesty of England, maintainer and defender of the same'.

During the winter of 1547–48, Andrew Dudley, the English commander at Broughty Crag, recognised the possibility of using religion to divide the Dundonians from their countrymen. The articles of 'assurance' that he granted them in October 1547 were headed by their pledge to be 'favourers of God's word [and] faithful and earnest setters forth of the same'. Days later, Dudley was urging Seymour to send him English Bibles and Protestant tracts on as large a scale as possible. He renewed the plea in December and in January 1548. It was not, he insisted, his own idea, but a request which was pressed on him urgently by the Dundonians themselves. He was also certain, however, that it would 'do very much good in all the country'.[17] Similarly, the English commander at Haddington in 1548 urged Seymour that preachers should be sent to him, who would 'be right willingly received amongst the greatest number, and both stay such as be already won, to continue, and win also many others to that purpose'. In the same year John Rough, formerly one of Arran's protégés, was sent to preach in the hinterland of English-occupied Dumfries.[18] Rough had also participated in the most dramatic outbreak of reformist preaching during the wars. In early 1547, a truce at St Andrews temporarily allowed the reformers who had sheltered in the castle – Rough and John Knox amongst them – to preach in the town and beyond. The most influential preacher of this period, however, was George Wishart, who spent much of 1544 and 1545 preaching in Angus, Ayrshire and Lothian, and became a major political headache for the regime.[19] There were real military benefits to be had for the English from such reformist activities. In 1546, five members of Perth's town guard (a body which numbered only forty) refused to join the siege of St Andrews, apparently because of their reformist sympathies.[20] It was reasonable for English commanders to hope, as Andrew Dudley did, that 'a good preacher and good books . . . would do more good than fire or sword'.[21]

Remarkably, Wishart was able to preach openly for as much as two years before Cardinal Beaton had him arrested and executed. This was one of the most obvious symptoms of a general collapse in the Church's authority during the wars. The regime was divided; Wishart had friends in high places. The Archbishop of Glasgow had avoided confronting him, and Governor Arran may also have wanted him to be spared. Under such circumstances it was, as Lord Methven commented, 'doubtsome to punish [heresy] by the law as the same requires'. Beaton took no chances. Both at the trial and at the execution, he put on a fearsome display of military force. But it was a symptom of Beaton's weakness that one heretic should require such excessive security, and of course, the contrast between the warlike cardinal and the humble martyr only played into the reformers' hands.[22] Beaton's subsequent murder forced the regime to confront a widespread crisis of lawlessness. It seems likely that propaganda against the regime was even being printed in Scotland. In March 1547, Arran issued a series of decrees against theft, murder and criminality of all kinds, but he focused his attention on attacks on the Church. Heretics were openly teaching, he declared, 'without any fear'. Bishops' officers who tried to enforce the law faced violence – 'dinging, handling, striking, boasting [and] menacing'. In some cases they were even made to eat the letters of summons or excommunication which they carried.[23] The Church's authority was disintegrating under the strain of war.

This was partly because war was a direct drain on the Church's resources. In 1544 some were urging that for the duration of the war, the Crown should hold all vacant abbacies and bishoprics 'to sustain men of war'. Cardinal Beaton himself promised to 'cause all the chalices, silver gear, and bells in churches be sold' to support the war effort. Later in the war, the Church's resources were plundered more systematically in a series of swingeing taxes.[24] In a war being fought partly to defend the Church, it was predictable that it should be asked to pay its way; but the cure might not be much better than the disease.

However, the wars also did direct and immediate harm to the old Church. English forces intimidated, and in some cases perhaps murdered, Catholic clergy.[25] They also damaged churches and abbey buildings, and the paraphernalia of traditional worship. These acts of military iconoclasm stripped the Church of much of what had made its piety live. The precise extent of the physical damage is hard to reconstruct, and written accounts on all sides tend to exaggerate it,[26] but it was impressive on any account. Seymour did not burn the whole of Edinburgh to the ground in 1544, as he claimed to his bloodthirsty sovereign. The high church of St Giles was too close to the castle for his men to approach it safely. However, Holyrood Abbey and the Dominican friary were certainly gutted. During the occupation of St Andrews in 1546–47 some of the town's churches and friaries were burned, and during the siege of Haddington in 1548 the parish church was actually dismantled. The shrine of Our Lady of Loretto at Musselburgh was attacked. The Border towns suffered badly. Coldingham, Jedburgh, Melrose and Kelso Abbeys were devastated; the friary at Roxburgh was first unroofed, and then used by the English as a stable. English raids also targeted religious houses in Angus and Perthshire.[27] Lawlessness within Scotland exacerbated these problems. In 1544, the Bishop of Aberdeen evacuated his cathedral's treasures, fearing a possible attack, only to have them stolen in transit by a local laird who demanded a hefty ransom. The following year, the Laird of Tullibardine ambushed Cardinal Beaton's baggage train, seizing valuables worth nearly £3,000.[28] After the end of the wars, there were real efforts at rebuilding, but there was a great deal to be done. Ten years on, large numbers of places of worship remained ruinous as a direct result of the wars.[29]

The worst-hit town of all was Dundee. The entire town was devastated as it was fought over during 1548, but at least to begin with, the English forces targeted 'the idols in the church'. In the 1550s, a single aisle of the parish church was re-roofed, but much of the rest remained in ruins and the rebuilding was painfully slow. The other burgh churches were abandoned completely. Charitable donations from the townspeople for the upkeep of the churches dried up at the same time.[30] The impact of this destruction is impossible to gauge, but across Europe, iconoclasm of this kind gravely undermined traditional religion. The destruction was a brutal political drama, a demonstration that something perceived as sacred could be defiled with impunity. Moreover, the long-running theatre of traditional religion was being forcibly changed. It was easy to read material impoverishment as spiritual impoverishment. It is perhaps the impact of war, as much as trade with the Protestant states of northern Europe, which accounts for Dundee's consistent status as the most radically reforming town in Scotland.

This destruction was more than collateral damage. It was deliberate English policy to try to damage the Scottish Church and to alienate the population from the bishops – in particular from Beaton, the leading opponent of the English marriage. Henry VIII ordered that the invasion forces in 1544 should post notices at churches and villages they devastated, reading 'You may thank your Cardinal of this; for if he had not been, you might have been in quiet and rest, for the contrary whereof he hath travailed as much as can be, to bring you to sorrow and trouble'.[31] It was not the snappiest slogan, perhaps, but the point is clear enough, and these proclamations may have had some effect. Seymour reported that as Edinburgh was burning in April 1544, the women of the town could be heard crying bitterly against Beaton, who had withdrawn his forces from Edinburgh and thus abandoned the town to the English.[32] There is some evidence, indeed, of a more widespread willingness amongst the Scottish population to blame the war on the clergy. In Fife, fishermen protesting at being conscripted as naval reserves said that they would gladly use their boats to ferry the priests and friars to the battle-front.[33]

As well as trying to demonise Beaton, the English also explored the possibility of assassinating him. This is a murky subject. The idea was first floated in April 1544, but nothing came of it. In May, Beaton was rumoured (falsely) to be planning a covert voyage to France. When the rumour reached Seymour, he immediately saw it as an opportunity to seize the cardinal. Another plan for assassinating Beaton was put to Henry VIII by an enterprising Scot in May 1545, and the King's response was coy: 'his majesty will not seem to have to do in it', but, he said, he did not mislike the offer. Henry made a show of distancing himself from this plan, but he instructed Sadler to tell the plotters, as if it were his own idea, that if he were a Scot he would kill the Cardinal anyway, because Henry would probably be pleased. Sadler carried out this convoluted plan, writing enthusiastically that if Beaton were killed, Scotland would 'soon flourish with God's word and his truth'.[34] When Beaton was eventually murdered, it was natural to assume that England was responsible, but this does not in fact seem to have been the case.[35] Beaton had plenty of enemies, and in any case, anyone who was trying to court favour with England would not need specific instructions to realise that killing the Cardinal would win applause. And indeed, the murder damaged traditional religion in Scotland more than any other single action during the wars. Even aside from the occupation of the castle, it removed Scotland's most aggressive and well-resourced opponent of heresy. When news of the murder reached Edinburgh, there was public disorder and, for a time, no Masses or daily offices were said in the town. This time, it felt less like an interdict than like chaos, 'the people all running wild'.[36]

This attack on the old Church in general, and on Beaton in particular, was also reflected in the propaganda produced by the English regimes and their Scottish allies. John Eldar, an unctuous Highlander looking for Henry VIII's patronage, blamed the wars on 'the Devil's convocation, and the father of mischief, David Beaton their Cardinal'.[37] James Harryson likewise claimed that the clergy were traitors who had abused both nobility and commonalty: 'pretending religion', he wrote, they 'persuade rebellion, preaching obedience, procure all disobedience, seeming to forsake all thing, possess all thing, calling themselves spiritual, are indeed most carnal, and reputed heads of the Church, be the only shame and slander of the Church'.[38]

In an unpublished manifesto for a united realm, Harryson described a godly unity as the first aim of the war.[39] Likewise, the English polemicist William Patten claimed that England's chief war aim was to free Scotland from 'the most servile thraldom and bondage under that hideous monster, that venomous asp and very Antichrist, the Bishop of Rome'. Expounding the advantages that that freedom would bring, he observed that England was now free from papal taxes and administrative meddling, and that 'our consciences [are] now quite unclogged' from papal cursings, pardons, fasts, pilgrimages and 'a thousand toys else of his devilish devising'. In place of all these burdens, Scotland would have the free use of the Scriptures. A proclamation issued by Seymour in 1547 promised to advance the glory and the word of God, and to abolish 'the Bishop of Rome's usurped jurisdiction'. The most widely circulated English propaganda pamphlet blamed Scotland's woes on clergy who were content to beggar their homeland in defence of the papacy, because they derived their own incomes from overseas – the bulk of Beaton's income had derived not from St Andrews, but from his French bishopric of Mirepoix.[40]

The Scottish response to this propaganda is ill documented, but the little that we have is instructive. Two substantial pieces of anti-English polemic penned by Scots survive from the period of the Rough Wooings, which take very different approaches to the religious issues. The lawyer William Lamb attacked Henry VIII as a lustful tyrant 'severed from society of Christian men', and denounced Edward VI similarly:

> God will not suffer such bastard seed to reign, and what his father was I trust the walls of every good town will tell where abbeys stood. I will not your lords and ladies rehearse, which for the truth were miserably murdered, their heirs disinherited; the spoiling of your churches; the extortion of the yeomanry and gentleman; as concerning the faith and religion, their acts and proclamations yearly one against another will speak when we be gone.[41]

Lamb's treatise, however, was never published. The only printed reply to the English propaganda effort, Wedderburn's *Complaynt of Scotland*, took a very different tack. Remarkably, Wedderburn entirely ignored the religious dimension to the wars; but at the same time he used Scripture copiously, and actually agreed with the English in blaming the clergy for Scotland's troubles. As we shall see, this text can be linked with the wider sense in late 1540s Scotland that criticism of the old Church was eminently justified.[42] Wedderburn did not even call the English heretics, although he showered them with every other insult his fertile imagination could find.[43]

Between them, these two tracts suggest that it was valuable, even necessary, for the English to emphasise their godly purpose. If Lamb's tract is any guide, it was a truism in Scotland that the English were murderous heretics. It was worth the English regime's while to rebut this charge. The silence of Wedderburn's *Complaynt* suggests that such rebuttals might have been effective. He was, apparently, reluctant to let the war be defined as a war of religion. Such a war might have divided the Scots more than it unified them. We know of several prominent Scots who were sympathetic to the reformist cause, but who remained staunchly opposed to England – the most prominent being the Earl of Argyll, in military terms Scotland's most powerful nobleman.[44] Convincing such men of England's godly intentions might have had a dramatic military effect. It might even have tested Wedderburn's own loyalties. His evasion of this issue points to England's opportunity.

In the event, however, religion was never more than a minor theme of English propaganda. For all that he loathed Beaton, Henry VIII was no crusader. John Eldar was pensioned by Henry, but neither his diatribe against the bishops nor a propaganda pamphlet he wrote in 1545 was used.[45] Even Seymour's more openly Protestant regime after 1547 did not make much of its religious purpose in Scotland. Harryson was the only propagandist to dwell on the religious or even the anticlerical arguments at any length. It was, perhaps, a missed opportunity. A more full-hearted campaign for Scots' souls might have divided Scotland, and blunted some Scottish fear of English motives. Yet such a campaign would have required a different set of priorities from the English regimes, whose religious ambitions were easily trumped by issues of politics and nationalism.

'THE GOOD SCOTTISH ENGLISHMAN'

Why did England not present the Rough Wooings as a religious war? Simply, because they did not themselves see it in those terms. Especially under Henry VIII, but also under Edward VI, the English were principally fighting nationalistic battles which, even at their most idealistic, played into the Scots' hands.

The idealism is plain enough. If there was not much about the Gospel in England's propaganda, there were genuine appeals for Scottish support on other grounds, especially after Edward VI's accession. The heart of this propaganda was the idea of Britain. The constant theme was that the wars were civil wars; that the English and Scottish monarchies both derived from a united, pre-Roman British monarchy, and that the opportunity to reunite the sundered realms by marriage was a divine providence; that peoples of one blood, speaking one language, and sharing the same island should naturally be united. A bidding prayer circulated for use in English churches begged for the English and Scots to be 'knit into one nation', and scrupulously avoided assigning any blame for the war. These were old ideas, but the circumstances of the 1540s gave them new strength. So did an evangelical twist. Harryson quoted the Gospel text: 'every kingdom divided in itself shall be brought to desolation.'[46] (By contrast, the idea of Britishness was one of which Roman Catholics remained profoundly sceptical until deep into the seventeenth century.[47]) Seymour, as Lord Protector, held out the positively Shakespearean vision that 'we two . . . having the sea for wall, the mutual love for garrison, and God for defence, should make so noble and well agreeing [a] monarchy, that neither in peace we may be ashamed, nor in war afraid, of any worldly or foreign power'.[48]

Conquest, this propaganda declared, was not England's purpose. Seymour stressed that Scotland's laws and customs would not be affected by a union. Indeed, he repeatedly claimed that so far from turning Scotland into an English fiefdom, his aim was to abolish the name of England entirely, as well as that of Scotland, and to unite both realms under 'the indifferent old name of Britons again'.[49]

The Scots engaged with this British propaganda with some vigour, both by obstructing its distribution[50] and by answering its claims. William Lamb mocked the dubious historical arguments for English sovereignty. They were, he said, like claiming that Rome had been founded by Robin Hood. He also pointed out that if England and Scotland should be united because they shared the same land-mass, the same logic required that all Europe, Asia and Africa should be under a single Crown.[51] Robert Wedderburn confronted head on the claim that the two peoples were kin:

> There are not two nations under the firmament that are more contrary and different from others, than are Englishmen and Scotsmen, howbeit that they be within one isle and neighbours, and of one language: for Englishmen are subtle and Scotsmen are facile; . . . Englishmen are humble when they are subjected by force and violence, and Scotsmen are furious when they are violently subjected; Englishmen are cruel when they get victory, and Scotsmen are merciful when they get victory. And to conclude, it is impossible that Scotsmen and Englishmen can remain in concord under one monarch or one prince, because their natures and conditions are as different as are the natures of sheep and wolves.[52]

This was stirring, but a little outlandish even in wartime. The English propagandists' arguments were strong. Seymour stressed that the Scots were being offered an honourable union of equals. In the place of ongoing war, an increasingly suffocating French alliance and subjection to clerical greed, the English marriage promised peace and prosperity. The prosperity, in the form of open access to English ports for Scottish merchants, was not an insignificant lure.[53] However, there were also more idealistic grounds for favouring a union, even for religious conservatives. James Stewart, Earl of Moray, an illegitimate son of James IV, was robustly traditional in his religion, but in 1543 he was reportedly saying that a united Britain 'should be strong enough to pluck the Great Turk out of his den' – perhaps remembering his father's crusading dreams. John Mair had argued earlier in the century that alliance with England was a prize worth pursuing – if, and only if, it was a free union of equals. Hard-headed English observers reckoned that powerful Scottish nobles could be won round, 'if they had thought the King's majesty had demanded no further but the marriage and peace'.[54]

In speaking of union in these idealistic terms, the pro-English propagandists were not necessarily being mendacious. Many of them clearly believed in this delightful vision, some passionately so. Yet holding to such a belief required at least a good deal of naïveté, if not wilful disregard of the main thrust of English sentiment and policy. The English spoke peace and union, but conquest and subjugation rumbled on scarcely beneath the surface. When he first declared war on Scotland in 1542, Henry VIII had revived the old claim that he was the rightful overlord of all Scotland, and that the Scottish Crown itself was illegitimate. During 1543 that claim was downplayed, but when war resumed it was taken up again, and English legislation reasserted it in 1544.[55] Whenever they met opposition, English authors and negotiators were liable to fall back on this claim. In 1543, Ralph Sadler used this threat as a counterpoint to his promises of free union. If the infant Queen married Prince Edward, he said, she might 'be made a queen of two realms by a just and rightful title, where she had now scant a good title to one'.[56] Even Sadler, Henry VIII's most trusted Scottish diplomat, apparently had little sense of how provocative this kind of language was to Scots. But then, Sadler's private opinion of the Scots was that they were 'such a malicious sort of people [that] I had rather be amongst the Turks'.[57]

It was a common English sentiment. Publications on the war written primarily for an English audience have a markedly different flavour from Seymour's scrupulously evenhanded pamphlets, and the spies whom we know that the Scots maintained in England will certainly have sent such imprints home.[58] These books scolded the Scots as a people who 'sought war for the love of war only', as 'rebellious children' consumed with malice towards their rightful English overlords. (Even Seymour compared England's relationship with Scotland to that of a 'loving physician' with a 'mistrustful and ignorant patient'.) If these authors spoke of Britain, they emphasised that England was 'the only supreme seat of the empire of Great Britain'. Rather than guaranteeing Scottish laws and customs, they mocked them as barbarous.[59] Even those who spoke of the natural affinity of the Scots and English clearly saw the unionist project as one of English absorption of the Scots. John Hooper looked forward to the appearance of a creature he called 'the good Scottish Englishman'. John Eldar wrote that Scotland is 'a part of your highness's empire of England'.[60] Even when trying to be equitable and reasonable, English authors could not, it seems, avoid falling into nationalistic patterns. Simple frustration that the Scots would not do the reasonable thing and conform to English hopes repeatedly breaks through. William Patten's account of the bloody English victory at Pinkie, written for an English readership, regretted that the battle had had to be fought, and addressed the Scots as 'my countrymen'. Yet he also gloried in a battle which displayed 'the ancient English courage and prowess'. Indeed, his attempt to be moderate is chilling:

> Yet seek we not the mastership of you, but the fellowship; for if we did, we have ye know a way of persuasion of the rigorous rhetoric so vengeably vehement (as I think ye have felt by an oration or two) that if we would use the extremity of argument, we were soon able so to beat reason into your heads, or about your heads, that I doubt not ye would quickly find what fondness it were to stand in strife for the mastery with more than your match.[61]

Or, as Seymour himself put it in a similar outbreak of frustration at Scottish obtuseness: 'You will not have peace, you will not have alliance, you will not have concord: and conquest cometh upon you whether you will or no.' If that was how matters fell out, he warned, 'the stubborn overcomed must suffer the victor's pleasure'.[62] If persuasion seemed to be failing, the English were always ready to speak the language of force.

This is even clearer if we look at the actual conduct of the war. Several pro-English Scots offered detailed advice on how the English should pursue their campaigns, in particular Sir George Douglas, the younger brother of the Earl of Angus (and, as such, Henry VIII's brother-in-law). Douglas probably did incline both towards evangelicalism and the English alliance, but he was also playing a very complicated set of games and, as the English slowly realised, almost nothing he said could be taken at face value. However, his analysis of the Scottish situation remains powerful. He recommended patience, persuasion, and propaganda, 'fair means and gentle handling', backed up with the discreet but decisive use of force, acting through Scottish intermediaries whenever possible. 'That that is so won in time with love shall remain for ever', he wrote, 'for . . . ye have often won with force, which hath engendered hatred'. However, if England attempted open conquest, he warned that 'there is not so little a boy but he will hurl stones against it, the wives will come out with their distaffs, and the commons universally will rather die in it'. He urged that English force should be concentrated on specific, limited objectives, such as removing Beaton and preventing French troops from reaching Scotland. Above all, he recommended that everything possible should be done to persuade individual Scottish nobles and lairds to join with the English cause. In particular, the English must defend those individuals against reprisals from the Scottish Crown, by establishing a series of strongholds within Scotland. These would serve as rallying-points for pro-English Scots, and, by indicating that the English were planning to stay, would encourage waverers to come over to the English side. At the very least, English raiding parties must try not to devastate the lands of pro-English magnates. Indeed, Douglas argued that destruction and devastation must be kept to a minimum if the battle for the Scots' allegiance was to be won. Indiscriminate destruction was a propaganda gift to the pro-French party in Scotland, he wrote, and this at least was undoubtedly true.[63]

Douglas's own agenda is clear enough: he did not want his own lands devastated, and he much preferred the idea of a negotiated settlement which the Douglases might broker to that of a conquest in which the Tudors would hold all the cards. But his analysis remains persuasive, and was backed up by others. In 1544 a collection of Lothian gentry told Henry VIII that they would come over to his service if a permanent garrison was put in place to defend them, but that if the English simply carried out destructive raids and then left, 'it shall be a means to lose the hearts of all the people of this realm, and to put them in utter desperation of your majesty's favour and clemency'. By the end of that year some Scottish nobles – men who were not opposed to the marriage as such – had come to believe that the English aim was to 'destroy and put away all the noblemen and the old blood of Scotland'.[64] In 1545, the Protestant Earl of Cassillis warned that Henry was being seen not only as rapacious to his enemies, but unable to protect his friends.[65] The Laird of Buccleuch, in the Borders, was more colourful than most in his response to English raids: 'Jesus! what ails you thus to overrun us.' He favoured the marriage, he said, but 'he would not be constrained thereto . . . if all Teviotdale were burnt in ashes to the bottom of Hell!'.[66] And while these Scots all shared an interest in keeping the war as civilised as possible, some English observers agreed. In 1547, the English commanders at Broughty Crag believed that Dundee would come over to their allegiance if they could guarantee to protect them against reprisals.[67] The Duke of Suffolk, an old warhorse who was hardly squeamish, recommended garrisoning Scottish strongholds to bring support out. Mere punitive raids would mean, he warned, that 'your highness shall have nothing in Scotland but by the sword and conquest'.[68] Sadler had warned back in 1543 that the Scots 'had rather suffer extremity than be subject to England, for they will have their realm free and their own laws and customs'.[69]

However, these voices were rarely listened to, and acted on more rarely still. After Arran's about-face in 1543, Henry VIII was no longer willing to play the patient game which was being urged on him. 'It was told us', he wrote furiously that September, 'that if we would bear a little with them at the first, all should succeed after as we would have it'.[70] From then on he, at least, had little interest in wooing the Scots except by the roughest of means. And indeed, English conduct of the war was not significantly shaped by the need to win Scottish support at any point. The pattern was set in the first campaign of the wars, Seymour's attack on Edinburgh in 1544. Seymour's initial plan, agreed with the King, was to garrison and fortify the port of Leith as a rallying point for disaffected Scots. It was a sensible plan. The logistics of resupplying Leith would be tricky, but not impossible, and it was a strong position, as the French were to realise fifteen years later. In 1544, however, as soon as Seymour had left for the North, Henry began to change his mind. The problem began when Seymour drew up a draft proclamation declaring Henry to be Protector of Scotland during the Queen's minority, and pro-mising succour to the pro-English party. Its hope was that 'both realms might by united perpetually to live in peace and quietness'. However, Henry spotted the flaw in this plan. Seymour could not 'afterward burn and spoil the country with his majesty's honour, having once proclaimed his majesty to be . . . protector of the realm'. And Henry was insistent that he should have his burning and spoliation. So the order was changed. Rather than occupying Leith, Seymour should land his sea-borne army there, burn the town, take Edinburgh and burn it too, and then march back to Newcastle overland, destroying everything in his wake. Henry even hoped, quite un-realistically, that Seymour might cross to Fife and burn indiscriminately there. If he met any resistance, he was to slaughter entire populations: men, women and children.[71]

The letter carrying these instructions has become infamous. Its threats could never have been fully implemented, but it does read like an order to commit war crimes. Seymour was very unhappy with these orders. He repeatedly protested, arguing for the original plan, and indeed spending a sleepless night after receiving the instructions from London, but Henry was adamant. He was also clear as to why he had changed his mind. Henry's principal aim was not to subdue Scotland at all, but 'to invade France this summer in his most royal person'. Therefore, 'the chief respect of this enter-prise into Scotland . . . is this, so to diminish the Scots' strength as they may not be able to assemble themselves and to make any force to annoy this realm in the King's majesty's absence'. In other words, what had begun as an attempt to woo the Scots into a union of the realms had been turned by Henry VIII's wish for French conquests into the roughest of pre-emptive strikes, in which large-scale destruction was being used as an instrument of policy. A new proclamation was drawn up, giving more prominence than before to Henry's claim to sovereignty over Scotland, and describing the attack as a punishment for the Scots' faithlessness in reneging on the mar-riage treaty. The call for allies to rally to the English was reduced to a vague promise of future mercy for those who showed themselves conformable. Seymour was specifically forbidden to spare any in Scotland on the grounds of professed English allegiance. He obeyed his orders, although even when on campaign he continued to tell his king that they were folly, and to urge the establishment of more permanent strongholds.[72]

In its limited way, Henry's plan worked. Scotland was indeed prevented from attacking England that autumn, and, after a colossal effort, the English captured Boulogne. But the lie was given to English claims of benevolent overlordship. Subsequent Scottish campaigns avoided the worst of the excesses of 1544, but the pattern had been set, not least in the Scots' own minds. The pro-English party in Scotland was dissolving in the face of rumours that Henry's ambition was simply to devastate the country and to strip the Scottish nobility of their titles and authority.[73] Sir George Douglas wrote in February 1545 that the English had been 'so cruel . . . that the whole people believes that if ye be masters there is nothing but death to them all, man, woman and child'. But Henry was by now sufficiently disillusioned with Douglas's two-step that he had put a price on his head.[74] Scottish Protestants who did make their way south were more liable to be arrested as spies than welcomed as brother Britons.[75]

Seymour himself made some effort to break this pattern. In the autumn of 1545 he tried to establish fortified strongholds in the Borders. However, he was unable to do so, and the raid's only real achievement was, again, destroying villages and crops. 'There was not so much hurt done in Scotland with fire at one raid this hundred years.' This did little more than give some of the English commanders reputations as butchers. As one English observer commented ruefully, the population in the ravaged area had been reduced to a wretched condition, but remained stubborn.[76] Likewise, when Cardinal Beaton's murderers seized St Andrews Castle, they expected the English to use it to bring Fife under their protection. The English certainly saw the opportunity, but nothing came of it, in part because even Seymour, as Lord Protector, was unwilling to cede any meaningful control over the operation to the castilians themselves. When provisions ran short in November 1546, it was the castilians' local friends, not the English, who resupplied them. The English instead carried out destructive raids on the surrounding countryside. Even so, some local lairds did openly side with the castilians; after the castle fell to a French assault, they found themselves defenceless, and faced outlawry or forfeiture of their property. An unrepeatable opportunity to exploit Scotland's political divisions was frittered away. In January 1548, another English commander in a valuable but exposed posting was (justifiably) worried by the precedent: 'I pray God I be not . . . served as St Andrews was.'[77]

In the final and most ambitious phase of the wars – Seymour's invasions in 1547–49 – there was a renewed and genuine attempt to appeal to potential Scottish support. Seymour set about establishing a protected zone to which Scots who had 'assured' with England could withdraw in safety, as well as compensating them for losses which they had incurred in English service. This was, in effect, George Douglas's policy. Seymour could not prevent his army from living off the country, but he did at least apologise for the damage. Scottish exiles were given a far warmer welcome than before. Seymour also used propaganda much more systematically than Henry VIII, attending not only to the printing but also the distribution of several pamphlets. One was even translated into Latin, for an international readership. 'Great Britain' was adopted as an English slogan; honourable union was a theme which Seymour pressed on those, such as the Earls of Argyll and of Huntly, whom he hoped to win over. This 'Edwardian moment' of British unionism is eye-catching, but was probably less important than it appears.[78] The rhetoric was not matched by English behaviour on the ground. Rumours that the English planned to massacre the Scottish ruling classes still circulated. While some commanders worked to win over local populations, others continued to wreak indiscriminate destruction. In November 1548, an English soldier at Berwick-upon-Tweed wrote: 'The countries be so wasted, that there is nothing to destroy. . . . The bareness of the country, want of lodging, scarcity of victuals, wet, and cold, maketh the war here more hard and painful than in other places.'

Trust between the English and their nominal allies in Scotland was equally threadbare. In April 1547 George Douglas defended his treasonable negotiations with England to the Earl of Arran by claiming that he was acting as a double agent, and would 'sow a division in England which is not able to be laid for seven years'. However, his days of sowing divisions were over. Seymour was warning his commanders that Douglas 'means nothing else but utterly to deceive you'. Scots who offered themselves to English service met with intense suspicion, and were required to wear visible identification at all times. When, despite the humiliations imposed on them, some proved their courage and loyalty, their English commander could only explain this by commenting that they 'have of late received English hearts'.[79] There was no more talk of 'Britons'. The nationalist lines had been drawn; few Scots and fewer Englishmen showed any inclination to break away from them.

Those Scots who had made the leap and chosen English exile found themselves doubting whether they could, in conscience, support what looked ever more like a war of conquest.[80] James Harryson angrily asked Seymour 'whether it were better to conquer hearts without charges, or burn, and build forts to great charges, which without hearts will never conquer Scotland?'. He already knew that the attempt to conquer hearts had failed. As he observed, even those English authors who tried to speak of reconciliation between the two realms only 'lay on the brands to feed the flame'. As the war turned sour, the exiles were cast adrift by a regime which was no longer interested in the spurious legitimacy which they could confer, and their Catholic countrymen mocked their discomfort.[81] The slaughter at Pinkie did not convince Scots of the virtues of English overlordship, but rather made them turn on Protestants as fifth-columnists. In 1548, the French believed that Scottish morale had never been higher.[82] The ambitious cleric Alexander Gordon, the Earl of Huntly's brother, was sympathetic both to the English and to the evangelical causes, but in 1548 he was appalled by England's conduct of the war. Prisoners were being murdered, he had heard. 'If they think to have heartiness', he told his brother, 'they should treat us more tenderly'.[83] William Lamb depicted a frustrated Englishman exclaiming that the Scots would never surrender 'while one of you is alive'; it was almost true.[84] One of the less subtle English propagandists, Nicholas Bodrugan, wrote in 1548 that concord between neighbours was an estimable jewel. A printer's error, however, meant that the book as published proclaimed 'what an estimable evil concord is'.[85] For once, most Scots would have agreed. They had become unpersuadable on the subject of the English alliance. Perhaps they had always been so.

What, then, is the legacy of England's imperial ambitions in Scotland in the 1540s, and of its abortive imperial Reformation? The defeat of Scottish Protestant hopes is obvious. The English decisively lost the wars, and their Scottish allies were disheartened and discredited by their ham-fisted aggression. Scotland's French–Catholic alignment was reconfirmed. Hindsight might suggest that this arrangement was fragile, and France's embrace suffocating, but in 1550 its eventual collapse was neither inevitable nor even particularly plausible. The English defeat was a defeat. Scottish Catholics could reasonably believe that the English and Protestant threats had been seen off, and indeed had been weakened by association with each other.

English policy in Scotland in the 1540s is an object lesson in how to lose a war fought in the name of high principle. The aims that the English regimes professed – spreading the Gospel and peaceful union – were controversial, but they were not ignoble and were capable of winning real support in Scotland. However, neither Henry VIII nor even Edward Seymour was able to act as if these aims mattered to his policy. Their ambitions were, transparently, the old English aims of conquest and strategic dominance. The Earl of Argyll, perhaps a reformist sympathiser himself, reviled England's 'pretence of godliness' as a cloak for mere theft: 'it was not by God's word to take away our neighbours' goods'.[86] England's conduct of the wars belied its proclaimed higher purposes and tainted it with hypocrisy as well as cruelty. Indeed, its conduct tainted those higher purposes themselves. Ten years later, Knox still worried that Protestantism was seen in Scotland as 'the cause of all calamity'.[87] Those who had hoped in 1543 that peace might be sealed by godly unity were unlikely to forget the bitter lessons the 1540s had taught them. The old truism of English treachery was now coupled with a new precept about the hollowness of Protestant promises.

Yet any Catholic triumphalism in 1550 was, of course, premature. If it is perverse to try to find grains of comfort for the Protestants amidst the wreckage of their military hopes, in simply religious terms they had given a fair account of themselves during the wars. For several years they had enjoyed *de facto* toleration in parts of the country. To reassert the Catholic status quo after the end of the wars would not be easy. The wounds in the body of the old Church had been held open long enough for a serious infection of heresy to become established in them. Worse, the wounds of war were themselves severe, and not easily healed. The physical destruction, the financial plundering and the loss of authority endured by the Church during the war did it real harm. And of course, these injuries were sustained by a Church already weakened by systemic financial difficulties and whose moral authority was already compromised. It was reasonable for Catholics to hope that a corner had been turned in 1550, but the problems which remained were daunting.

As we shall see, it was in a bold attempt to remedy these problems that the Church contracted its most fatal disease.

NOTES

1 *Sadler SP*, I, 253, 263.

2 Merriman, *Rough Wooings*, 8–10.

3 Knox, I, 119–20.

4 *LP*, XXI(i), 1279.

5 Bonner, 'Recovery of St Andrews castle', 581–5, 598.

6 Merriman, *Rough Wooings*, 14–15; *HP*, II, 233; *CSP Scotland*, 10.

7 NA SP 1/27 fo. 207r (*LP*, III(ii), 2958).

8 Marcus Merriman, 'The assured Scots: Scottish collaborators with England during the Rough Wooing', *SHR*, 47 (1968), 10–34; *RPC*, 16–7, 23; Wedderburn, *Complaynt*, 58, 142–3.

9 *CSP Scotland*, 34, 41.1, 168.

10 Wedderburn, *Complaynt*, 8, 64; Merriman, *Rough Wooings*, 291.

11 Annie I. Cameron (ed.), *The Scottish Correspondence of Mary of Lorraine* (Scottish History Society 3rd series 10: Edinburgh, 1927), 241.

12 Knox, I, 101; *CSP Scotland*, 156.

13 *LP*, XX(ii), 40.

14 Odet de Selve, *Correspondance Politique de Odet de Selve, ambassadeur de France en Angleterre (1546–1549)*, ed. Germain Lefèvre-Pontalis (Paris, 1888), 269.

15 NA SP 49/7 fos 14v–15r, 49v (*LP*, XIX(i), 243, 522); Gordon Donaldson, 'The Scottish episcopate at the Reformation', *English Historical Review*, 60 (1945), 357; Kellar, *Scotland, England and the Reformation*, 96–100.

16 LPL MS 3192, p. 113 (*LP*, XIX(i) 1021); John Durkan, 'Scottish "evangelicals" in the patronage of Thomas Cromwell', *RSCHS*, 21 (1982), 153; Merriman, 'James Henrisoun'; *RSS*, III, 1461; NA SP 50/3 nos 25, 81 (*CSP Scotland*, 142, 206).

17 NA SP 50/2 fos 69r, 78r, 149r; 50/3 no. 82 (*CSP Scotland*, 71, 74, 107, 207); *CSP Scotland*, 129.

18 NA SP 50/4 no. 21 (*CSP Scotland*, 239); Kellar, *Scotland, England and the Reformation*, 107.

19 On preaching during the wars, see below, 128–9.

20 Verschuur, 'Perth and the Reformation', 373–4.

21 NA SP 50/2 fo. 149r (*CSP Scotland*, 107).

22 *AM*, 1268–9; Lindsay of Pitscottie, *Historie*, II, 54–6; Knox, I, 148; Sanderson, *Cardinal of Scotland*, 207–9; Cameron, *Scottish Correspondence*, 133.

23 *RPC*, 59–65, 69–70.

24 *HP*, II, 347; LPL MS 3192, 186 (*LP*, XIX(ii), 709.1); *RPC*, 83; *APS*, 472.

25 *CSP Scotland*, 170.

26 Dilworth, *Scottish Monasteries*, 27; David McRoberts, 'Material destruction caused by the Scottish Reformation' in McRoberts (ed.), *Essays*, esp. 421.

27 *RSS*, III, 2368, 2955; *CSP Scotland*, 115, 119, 233, 253; McRoberts, 'Material destruction', 422; Foggie, *Renaissance Religion*, 45–6; Kellar, *Scotland, England and the Reformation*, 92; Bryce, *Scottish Grey Friars*, I, 84.

28 McLennan, 'Reformation in Aberdeen', 126; *ALC*, 539.

29 McRoberts, 'Material destruction', 425; Pollen, *Papal Negotiations*, 529; Patrick, *Statutes*, 168; Dr Gunn, *The Book of Peebles Church: St Andrews Collegiate Parish Church, AD 1195–1560* (Galashiels, 1908), 137, 144, 146–7, 150.

30 NA SP 50/3 no. 25 (*CSP Scotland*, 142); *CSP Scotland*, 132; Alexander Maxwell, *Old Dundee Prior to the Reformation* (Edinburgh and Dundee, 1891), 123–31; Iain E. F. Flett, 'The Conflict of the Reformation and Democracy in the Geneva of Scotland, 1443–1610' (MPhil dissertation, University of St Andrews, 1981), 12.

31 *LP*, XIX(i), 188.

32 *HP*, II, 233.

33 NA SP 50/2 no. 25.1 (*CSP Scotland*, 73.1); *CSP Scotland*, 34.

34 *LP*, XIX(i), 404; XX(i), 857, 1177, 1178; BL Additional MS 32654 fo. 137r (*LP*, XIX(i), 350); NA SP 49/8 fos 67r, 90r–91r (*LP*, XX(i), 834, 1178); *HP*, II, 250. The 'Wysshert' who first proposed murdering Beaton is certainly John Wishart, the Laird of Pittarrow, not the preacher George Wishart. Sanderson, *Cardinal of Scotland*, 193; Dotterweich, 'Emergence of Evangelical Theology', 285.

35 *LP*, XXI(i), 1070.1.

36 NA SP 49/9 fo. 2r (*LP*, XXI(i), 958).

37 BL Royal MS 18.A.xxxviii fos 3v, 15r–v.

38 James Harryson, *An Exhortacion to the Scottes, to Conforme to the Vnion, betwene Englande and Scotlande* (RSTC 12857: London, 1547), sigs A4v–A5r.

39 NA SP 50/4, 130.

40 William Patten, *The Expedicion into Scotlande of Edward, Duke of Soomerset* (RSTC 19476.5: London, 1548), sigs b8r–c6v; Annie I. Camevon (ed.), *The Warrender Papers* (Scottish History Society 3rd series 18–19: Edinburgh, 1931), 26 (Merriman, *Rough Wooings*, 275); Edward Seymour, *An Epistle or Exhortaction, to Unitie & Peace* (RSTC 22268: London, 1548), sig. B8r–v; cf. Mason, 'Scotching the Brut', 67.

41 William Lamb, *Ane Resonyng of ane Scottis and Inglis Merchand betuix Rowand and Lionis*, ed. Roderick J. Lyall (Aberdeen, 1985), 35, 39–41, 169–71.

42 See below, 107.

43 Wedderburn, *Complaynt*.

44 On Argyll's reformism, see above, 33.

45 *LP*, XIX(i), 278.71, 1035.10; XX(ii), 533.

46 Harryson, *Exhortacion*, esp. sig. B2v; NA SP 10/2 fo. 11r–v (C. S. Knighton (ed.), *Calendar of State Papers Domestic Series of the reign of Edward VI: revised edition* (London, 1992), 49); cf. BL Royal MS 18.A. xxxviii fos 6r–7v; NA SP 50/4, 128; Seymour, *Epistle*, sigs A4r–5v; John Hooper, *A Declaration of Christe and of his Offyce* (RSTC 13745: Zürich, 1547), sigs A2r–4r; Mason, 'Scotching the Brut', 68–70.

47 Christopher Highley, '"The lost British lamb": English Catholic exiles and the problem of Britain' in David J. Baker and Willy Maley (eds), *British Identities and English Renaissance Literature* (Cambridge, 2002), 45–8.

48 Somerset, *Epistle*, sig. C1r.

49 *Ibid.*, sigs B1v, B3v; Cameron, *Warrender Papers*, 26 (Merriman, *Rough Wooings*, 275); *CSP Scotland*, 177.

50 *TA*, IX, 110.

51 Lamb, *Ane Resonyng*, 65, 71–3.

52 Wedderburn, *Complaynt*, 83–4.

53 Donaldson, *All the Queen's Men*, 20–1; Seymour, *Epistle*, sigs C2v–3v.

54 *HP*, I, 298, II, 119; Roger Mason, 'The Scottish Reformation and the origins of Anglo–British imperialism' in Roger Mason (ed.), *Scots and Britons: Scottish Political Thought and the Union of 1603* (Cambridge, 1994), 162–7; Sadler *SP*, I, 170 (*HP*, I, 367); *CSP Scotland*, 192.

55 *A Declaration, Conteynyng the Iust Causes and Considerations, of this Present Warre with the Scottis* (RSTC 9179: London, 1542); Merriman, *Rough Wooings*, 140.

56 Sadler *SP*, I, 155 (*HP*, I, 360).

57 *HP*, II, 120.

58 *CSP Scotland*, 10; NA SP 50/3 no. 25 (*CSP Scotland*, 142); *TA*, VIII, 479; *LP*, XIX(i), 540.

59 Nicholas Bodrugan, *An Epitome of the Title that the Kynges Maiestie of Englande, Hath to the Souereigntie of Scotlande* (RSTC 3196: London, 1548), sigs A5v, D3v, G7r–8r; Seymour, *Epistle*, sig. A3v.

60 Hooper, *Declaration*, sig. A3r; BL Royal MS 18.A.xxxviii, fo. 6r.

61 Patten, *Expedicion into Scotlande*, sigs 5v, b2v, b7r–v, c8v.

62 Seymour, *Epistle*, sigs B5r, B7r.

63 *HP*, I, 337; II, 149, 237; NA SP 49/8 fos 1r–2v (*LP*, XX(i), 202.2); *LP*, XX(i), 265, 1106.2; XX(ii), 414.

64 *HP*, II, 232; *LP*, XIX(ii), 709.2.

65 *LP*, XX(i), 547.

66 *HP*, II, 327.2.

67 *CSP Scotland*, 46, 56.

68 *HP*, II, 171.

69 *LP*, XVIII(i), 325.

70 *HP*, II, 51.

71 *HP*, II, 194, 207; BL Additional MS 32654 fo. 56v (*LP*, XIX(i), 249); *LP*, XIX(i), 319.

72 *HP*, II, 171, 207, 211, 217, 222, 232, 237, 248.

73 *HP*, II, 391; LPL MS 3192, 327 (*LP*, XX(i), 381); *LP*, XX(i), 265. Cf. *LP*, XIX(i), 77.

74 NA SP 49/8 fo. 2r (*LP*, XX(i), 202.2); *LP*, XX(i), 4.

75 LPL MS 3192, 111, 113 (*LP*, XIX(i), 1021).

76 NA SP 49/8 fo. 179r–v (*LP*, XX(ii), 359); *LP*, XX(ii), 96, 130, 169, 216, 328, 347, 400, 456.2; Leslie, *Historie*, II, 285–6; *HP*, II, 418; BL Cotton MS Caligula B.vii fos 323r–v (*LP*, XXI(i), 940).

77 *LP*, XXI(ii), 114, 123.1, 576, 743; Bonner, 'Recovery of St Andrews castle'; Merriman, *Rough Wooings*, 226–7; *RSS*, III, 2515, 2955; *CSP Scotland*, 2, 27, 30; NA SP 50/3 no. 27.1 (*CSP Scotland*, 144.1).

78 Merriman, 'James Henrisoun', 89, 95; Roger Mason, 'The Scottish Reformation and the origins of Anglo–British imperialism' in Roger Mason (ed.), *Scots and Britons: Scottish Political Thought and the Union of 1603* (Cambridge, 1994), 171–80; Merriman, *Rough Wooings*, 263–4, 277–81; Stephen Alford, *The Early Elizabethan Polity: William Cecil and the British Succession Crisis, 1558–1569* (Cambridge, 1998), 45–6; Cameron, *Warrender Papers*, 26 (Merriman, *Rough Wooings*, 275); Selve, *Correspondance*, 269; *Miscellany of the Spalding Club*, vol. IV (Aberdeen, 1849), 146–50.

79 Wedderburn, *Complaynt*, 81; NA SP 50/1 fo. 32v, SP 50/2 fo. 54v, SP 50/4 nos 4, 119 (*CSP Scotland*, 13, 69, 221, 337); *CSP Scotland*, 114, 115, 168, 233.

80 Ian A. Muirhead, 'M. Robert Lokhart', *IR*, 22 (1971), 93–5.

81 NA SP 50/4 no. 67, SP 50/5 no. 24 (*CSP Scotland*, 285, 357); *CSP Scotland*, 352; Merriman, 'James Henrisoun', 99; Wedderburn, *Complaynt*, 81–2.

82 Herries, *Historical Memoirs*, 21; *CSP Foreign 1547–1553*, 73.

83 Cameron, *Scottish Correspondence*, 213–14.

84 Lamb, *Ane Resonyng*, 3.

85 Bodrugan, *An epitome*, sig. G8v.

86 NA SP 50/3 no. 25 (*CSP Scotland*, 142).

87 Knox, IV, 251.

Chapter 5

1549–59: Catholic Reformation

THE TASK OF REFORM

In the late 1540s, the prospects for Scottish Catholicism looked bright. The war against Protestant England was being won. The damage the Church had suffered was real, but at least this meant that the long-standing call for reform was now impossible to ignore. The Church had lost its most redoubtable defender, Cardinal Beaton, but his aggressive leadership had not been to everyone's taste. In his place was a more supple figure: John Hamilton, Governor Arran's illegitimate half-brother, the Abbot of Paisley and (from 1549) the Archbishop of St Andrews.

Hamilton was not a bishop of any great moral stature. He owed his position to dynastic politics, and he notoriously kept a mistress. He consulted a magician when he was seriously ill in the early 1550s. A Spanish diplomat who visited Scotland in 1551 formed the view that 'he is miserly and covetous, and loves discord better than peace'. He spent much of the early part of his episcopate fighting jurisdictional battles with Rome; he wanted legatine powers for himself, and the archbishopric of Glasgow for another of his and Arran's brothers. He has had a mixed reputation amongst historians.[1] He may seem an unlikely reformer. Yet whatever his personal convictions, it was clear from the time he secured the archbishopric that he intended a vigorous programme of renewal. He pursued this effort through a series of general provincial councils of the Scottish Church, which met in 1549, 1552, 1556 and 1559. The council of 1556 has left no records, and was probably a brief affair concerned with enforcement and implementation, but the other three were ambitious, reforming synods whose legislation was aimed at the suppression of heresy.[2] They are the high points of a reform programme which was wider in its ambitions and more consistent in its methods than has usually been recognised.

In 1559 Hamilton's reform programme was overtaken by events, as the Protestant movement which seemed to have been suppressed reappeared in open rebellion. Some of the leading Catholic reformers joined the rebels. The reform effort's failure is commonly ascribed to one or both of two causes: that reform ran out of time, or that it was insufficiently radical. The first argument is that the tortoise of Catholic reform did not have quite enough time to overtake Protestantism's hare, although it was perhaps 'an extraordinarily close-run thing'.[3] The second argument is that the reform effort was merely 'half-hearted tinkering' which did not begin to address the Church's 'fundamental problems'.[4] This line of criticism argues that little was done about education of the parish clergy, and that the councils were neither able nor wholly willing to tackle the Church's financial woes.[5] In other words, the accepted view of these councils is the cliché: too little, too late.

It was a view which had been formed within a generation of the Reformation. Protestant historians of the Scottish Reformation scarcely noticed the Catholic reformers; they were mere flotsam swept aside by a providential tide. Some limited and confused material on the provincial councils can be found in John Knox's, John Foxe's and Robert Lindsay of Pitscottie's histories.[6] Scottish Catholics integrated the reform effort into their narrative of a Church doomed by its own corruption, but these accounts were scarcely more reliable. Bishop Leslie, writing in the 1570s, gave a garbled account of the first two councils, describing them – misleadingly – as parallel to the international Catholic reform programme which was eventually laid out by the Council of Trent. His account of the 1559 council is fuller and more circumstantial, but here too his polemical purpose colours his description. He claimed that that council precipitated the Reformation crisis, for the threat of real discipline drove the corrupt and loose-living clergy into the arms of the Protestants: 'not so much for conscience's cause, or any way to serve their conscience, as to satisfy their affection and lust of their flesh, when they held up common whores, in the name of wives.'[7] It is a morally satisfying narrative, echoed by one modern Catholic historian, but it too clearly reflects post-Reformation needs rather than pre-Reformation realities.[8]

This chapter argues that these views misunderstand the movement for Catholic reform in 1550s Scotland. Hamilton's reform effort was in fact impressively broad. He and those who worked with him took account of the weaknesses and strengths of their situation and developed a distinctive and imaginative approach to dealing with them. It was a reform programme which might well have blocked the advance of heresy. However, as matters turned out, Hamilton's reform programme was not merely swamped by a rising Protestant tide. It seems likely that, in an attempt to reform the Church, the new Archbishop gravely undermined it – not least because he lacked the political support necessary to finish what he had begun.

As we have seen, the Scottish Church had a number of systemic problems of finance, administration and discipline, but these did not automatically turn it into a seedbed for heresy.[9] For the same reasons, reforming that Church to face the threat of heresy was not simply a matter of addressing those systemic problems. It was Catholics who worried about abuses and corruption in the Church. Protestants had more far-reaching concerns, which were ultimately about theology, not discipline. This theological attack was the focus of Hamilton's reform effort. His central concern was to confirm the laity in the faith: through building an active preaching ministry, through restoring respect for the clergy and, critically, through striving to make that faith palatable to those who might be inclined to doubt it.

Two major strands of reform stand out. First, there was an effort to restore the dignity and distinctiveness of the priesthood. The 1549 council insisted on clerical celibacy, and put in place some shrewdly designed mechanisms to enforce it. It also reaffirmed the traditional requirements that clergy should refrain from secular occupations; that they should be appropriately dressed, clean-shaven and tonsured; and that they should keep sober households and austere tables. The stated purpose of these reforms was both to deflect mockery of the clergy and to ensure 'that they as clergymen may be distinguishable from laymen'. Similarly, the need carefully to examine prospective ordinands was re-emphasised. The 1559 council reiterated many of these points, creating tighter and more detailed mechanisms for their enforcement. In addition, some of the worst financial flash-points between the clergy and laity were addressed. In other words, the reformers were aiming to disarm the most common criticisms of the clergy, and to reassert the distinct and austere status of the clerical estate. This was essential if the message which those clergy preached was to be heard. The 1549 council warned that clergy who were seen to be corrupt in life and morals at the same time as they were correcting the morals of others were the cause of 'the greatest scandal to the laity, and the largest proportion of the heresy'.[10]

Yet clerical discipline was merely a beginning. The reformers' second main priority was to equip and mobilise these newly respectable clergy to preach. The 1549 council drew on the work of the Council of Trent, which was then suspended and which was to remain so for most of the 1550s. The council adopted Trent's draft decrees which established lectureships in theology at cathedrals and collegiate churches, affirmed the priority of preaching and granted bishops sweeping powers to control suspect preaching. The councils also reaffirmed the traditional requirement that all parishes receive four sermons a year, ordering that such preaching be centred on Scripture and on the exposition of basic Christian doctrine. Monasteries and cathedrals were to become centres of preaching, and monasteries were required to send men to the universities to study theology. The avowed

97

purpose of this preaching effort was the confutation of heresy. The 1559 council even provided a list of specified controversial doctrines which preachers were to defend.[11]

The Catholic reformers recognised that discipline was not enough. It was a means to an end, a necessary but not sufficient condition for regaining the ground lost to heresy. The actual battle had to be centred on the preacher, and on doctrine and theology, for it was this which made the heretics dangerous. Provincial councils had very limited scope to fight this battle. They had no authority to pronounce on doctrinal matters, but were restricted to reforming and enforcing discipline. Yet doctrine was the key battleground; and inevitably the Catholic reformers were drawn to fight there, whether or not they had the formal authority to do so.

CATECHISM AND COMPROMISE

The impact of the provincial councils is almost impossible to gauge. Scraps of records tell us that some parishes and dioceses put some measures into effect. The Bishops of Aberdeen and of Glasgow acted to implement the decrees of the 1559 council in their dioceses. The burgh council of Peebles tried during the later 1550s to stamp out non-residence amongst the prebendaries of their collegiate church. Archbishop Hamilton himself is said to have embarked on a preaching tour of Fife immediately after the 1559 council.[12] However, the paucity of evidence is severe. Even the councils' decrees themselves only survive by chance, in a single copy in the Glasgow diocesan archives. Later Protestants had little interest in preserving the records of the popish Church.

One reform, however – arguably the centrepiece of the entire reform programme – was certainly put into effect, and crossed explicitly from disciplinary into doctrinal territory. This was the vernacular catechism whose commissioning was the main business of the 1552 council. It is a weighty but accessible statement of the Church's beliefs, closely modelled on similar documents which had been produced in Germany and England in the previous fifteen years.[13] Its 400 pages lead the reader through discussions of the Ten Commandments, the Apostles' Creed, the seven sacraments and of prayer. It was, the council decreed, to be circulated to the clergy alone, 'as much for the instruction of themselves as of the Christian people committed to their care'. It was not to be lent to the laity, except perhaps a few folk of exceptional gravity and piety. However, every Sunday and holy day, for half an hour, every curate was to read from the catechism to his people. Swingeing fines were imposed on clergy who failed to do so.[14] We cannot know how far this order was observed, but the 1559 council was petitioned to ensure all parish clergy were 'sufficiently qualified . . . distinctly and plainly [to] read the Catechism'. This suggests that any problems were of competence, not compliance. It is certainly possible that the catechism was used very widely. We do not know how many copies were printed, but a single full-size print run of some 1300 copies would have provided easily enough for every parish in Scotland to have one. It was probably the most easily implemented, cost-effective and far-reaching reform that the councils introduced. Like the official homilies which English churches had been using for five years, the catechism bypassed the sloth or incompetence of the parish clergy to broadcast officially approved doctrine directly to the people.

The project was impeccably orthodox: the doctrine, however, less so. It never explicitly challenged accepted orthodoxies, but its emphases were not what we would expect from a Catholic formulary. For example, it made only one explicit mention of the papacy – in the preface, where Archbishop Hamilton was described as a legate of the 'see Apostolic'. Elsewhere, the so-called 'power of the keys' – normally claimed by the Pope – was said to have been given to the apostles collectively. The catechism's declared yardstick of authority was Scripture itself, as interpreted by general councils. The book is a tissue of Biblical quotation, with texts always given first in Latin and then in Scots. The traditional doctrine of 'unwritten verities' (the claim that the Church's tradition had preserved authoritative doctrines which were not grounded in Scripture) was evaded, if not actually denied.[15] Likewise, the catechism's discussion of the sacraments went out of its way to respect evangelical sensibilities. The word 'Mass' was avoided; the benefits which the sacrament bestows were discussed but the touchstone Catholic belief that it is beneficial as a sacrifice was scarcely mentioned.[16] Or again, the catechism's discussion of justification and the role of faith was soaked in Protestant language. It spoke of the believer's being 'clad with the righteousness of Jesus Christ'. It distinguished between what it called a dead faith – mere assent to the facts of Christian doctrine – and a living faith, consisting of trust in God's mercy, 'the faith that justifies a Christian man'. It even insisted that this faith was inseparable from hope and charity, a view which had been condemned as heretical when Patrick Hamilton had advanced it.[17] These are only the most striking of a number of significant silences or flirtations with evangelical ideas. For example, there was some doubt cast on the use of images in worship, and, although the sacrament of matrimony and the commandment not to commit adultery were discussed at length, no mention was made of clerical celibacy.[18] Moreover, the text was forthright throughout in its criticism of laxity amongst the clergy.

These oddities are well known. Some historians have minimised them, pointing out that the document remained fundamentally Catholic. Catholic historians, by contrast, have been disturbed by them. Others scholars have concluded that the catechism was crippled, and that flirting with evangelical ideas in this way was reckless. Ian Cowan has even suggested that the catechism is a crypto-evangelical cuckoo in the nest of the Scottish Church, placed there by English exiles.[19] This last idea seems unlikely. It is true that the man normally named as its author is an English Dominican friar, Richard Marshall: we know this because a friend of his later described the text as 'friar Marshall's Catechism'.[20] Yet even if a Catholic exile such as Marshall can be suspected of closet Protestant sympathies, he cannot be seen as the text's author in any simple way. It is most unlikely that Marshall would have written such fluent, idiomatic Scots, much less referred to the language he was using as 'our Scots speech'. Indeed, the catechism itself refers to its authors in the plural.[21] Marshall was probably not so much its author as its research editor. This seems particularly likely given the extraordinary mixture of sources on which the catechism drew. The most important of these were catechisms and formularies produced in Germany, in particular the *Enchiridion* of Johannes Gropper of Cologne. Some, but not all, of the Scottish text's oddities can be traced to these sources. However, the Scottish compilers also drew on Henry VIII's 1543 summary of doctrine, the *King's Book*; on the Scottish Lutheran John Gau; and on Luther himself. Remarkably, they seem even to have consulted the work of the radical Reformed theologian John Hooper. What they did not do was simply assemble the catechism with scissors and paste. None of these sources was absorbed uncritically, nor can its theological flavour be blamed wholly on them. In particular, the omission of the sacrifice of the Mass is not paralleled in any of the sources.[22] The sources may have provided raw materials, but deliberate choices were made regarding their selection and use; other, more orthodox sources were neglected. Hamilton and his staff cannot have been unaware of the catechism's studied silences and careful ambiguities. It seems perverse to conclude that they were anything other than deliberate policy.

Moreover, those ambiguities have echoes elsewhere. The provincial councils themselves were far from enthusiastic about papal authority. Most of the few references to the papacy in their decrees viewed it as an administrative menace, which, by granting inappropriate exemptions, hindered bishops' ability to control their dioceses.[23] Or again, the 'short declaration' on the Eucharist authorised by the 1559 council affirmed the Real Presence, but made no mention of the Mass as a sacrifice. Instead, it described the sacrament's benefits as faith and love kindled within the believer. It also warned against ungodly clergy who ministered the sacrament irreverently.[24] The impression is of a Church which was at least as keen to repent of its own faults as it was to confute those of its opponents.

This impression is reinforced by the only piece of vernacular Catholic printed propaganda which survives from 1550s Scotland. Quintin Kennedy, the Abbot of Crossraguell, was the brother of the Protestant Earl of Cassillis and a cousin of the Protestant Earl of Argyll. He was also an articulate Catholic

reformer and a participant in the provincial councils. In 1558, he published
*Ane compendius Tractiue . . . Declaring the Nerrest, and Onlie Way, to Establische
the Conscience of ane Christiane Man.* Its subject was the perennially knotty
question of whether bare Scripture is authoritative, or whether it needs the
Church to interpret it. Kennedy came down emphatically on the side of
the Church, but again, he was oddly respectful of evangelical sensibilities.
The papacy was mentioned only once, in passing. His assertion of the Church's
authority was, again, attached to general councils. And while he insisted that
such councils 'assuredly have never erred', the only such councils whose
rulings he actually discussed were those from the fourth and fifth centuries
AD, whose authority Protestants recognised. Throughout, he carefully used the
Protestant buzzword *congregation* to describe the universal Church.[25] Likewise,
he deplored the use of the heresy laws against honest critics of ecclesiastical
abuses, and he refused to condemn vernacular Scripture. In other words, this
was something like an old-fashioned Renaissance humanist view, an impression reinforced by his praise for Erasmus.[26]

Nothing else published by Scotland's Catholic reformers in this period
survives, but we do know of other texts which seem to have followed a similar
line. Knox referred to a document printed in 1559 which became known as
the 'Two-Penny Faith', and is probably now lost. Apparently, it discussed the
Mass, Purgatory and prayer to saints. Intriguingly, Knox claimed that it was
set forth so that the bishops 'might give some show to the people that they
minded reformation', suggesting that it echoed the moderate tone of the
catechism and of Kennedy's treatise. Given the delicate doctrinal negotiations which the Church was then conducting with the leading Protestants,
it seems likely that this document should also be placed in the context of
that conciliatory effort.[27] John Winram's case is more tantalising. Winram,
the subprior of St Andrews, was one of the more 'advanced' of the Catholic
reformers. In 1559 he was to join the Protestants, who held him in sufficiently high regard that he promptly became Superintendent of Fife. In 1546
he published a catechetical sermon in the vernacular; we may sensibly guess
it tended in the same doctrinal direction. It was a text which Protestants felt
able to use, and (if we may trust his own, later account) in the same year
Winram preached a sermon blaming the spread of heresy on the ignorance
of the clergy.[28]

A few other fragments of evidence do suggest that that direction was
shared more widely. In late 1557 or early 1558, the old Earl of Argyll took the
Protestant preacher John Douglas into his household. By March 1558 the
matter had come to Archbishop Hamilton's ears. Hamilton's letter to the Earl
was cautious, as one might expect, but this seems to have been more than
mere discretion. When pointing out the error of Douglas's doctrine, Hamilton
insisted that his ideas 'are many years past condemned by General Councils

and the whole estate of Christian people' – again stressing the authority of councils, not of the Pope. He also offered to provide Argyll with an orthodox preacher who could instruct him. Argyll rejected this offer with ironic contempt, yet it is fully consistent with the priority which the Catholic reformers had given to preaching.[29] The Church was negotiating in the same careful and constructive way with Protestant petitioners to the regime later the same year.[30]

We also have some more direct testimony to the Catholic reformers' willingness to moderate their rhetoric. During the occupation of St Andrews Castle in 1546–47, university men preached sermons in the town which even Knox admitted set forth Christ and were 'penned to offend no man'. The only criticism he could make was that these men had never preached such sermons before. George Wishart's tour of Ayrshire likewise stirred Archbishop Dunbar of Glasgow to preach a sermon in which he apologised for failing to preach in the past, and promised to improve.[31] Knox also gave a vitriolic account of the preaching of John Sinclair, the future Bishop of Brechin. In the late 1550s, Sinclair managed to persuade some Protestants that he was 'not far from the kingdom of God', even toying with evangelical views of justification. Yet when challenged, he unambiguously affirmed his loyalty to the old Church. Accounting for Knox's jaundiced perspective, this sounds like another manifestation of a cautiously eirenic style of Catholic reform. According to Winram, Sinclair was 'not ungodly in the understanding of the truth', and amongst other things had given 'Christian consolation' to the condemned heretic Adam Wallace in 1550.[32] Or again, John Row's history of the Reformation includes an intriguing tale of a friar who preached 'invectives against the new preachers' in Perth, but who was persuaded to change his mind. This man remained a Catholic, but began to focus his attention on the Church's shortcomings:

> If we had done our duty in calling faithfully, and made you, God's people, to know God's truth, as we should have done, the new teachers had not done as they do; for what shall poor silly sheep do that are pounded in a fold where there is no meat, but break the dyke and go to their meat where they may have it?[33]

In August 1559, Hamilton himself delivered a sermon in Edinburgh in which he apologised for his ineptitude as a preacher.[34] It seems one of the public faces of the Catholic Church in Scotland in the 1540s and 1550s was distinctly non-confrontational and self-critical.

A distinct pattern therefore emerges. Scottish Catholic reformers in the 1550s appear to have been candid to the point of flagellation in their assessment of the Church's shortcomings. They professed a remarkable degree of indifference towards the papacy, taking instead a view of ecclesiastical authority which elevated the authority of the general council; this was the fifteenth-century dream of conciliarism. They would not depart materially from Catholic orthodoxy on issues such as the sacraments, justification and ceremonial, but they were certainly willing to toy with evangelical ideas and language on those subjects. Yet for all this, they gave no quarter to heresy. The 1549 council provided for the appointment of inquisitors against heresy. The 1552 council warned that those who questioned the catechism should be denounced by their parish priests as heretics.[35] The catechism itself denounced 'heretics, who stiffly hold false opinions against the true faith of Holy Church'. It insisted that those who denied the Real Presence of Christ in the Eucharist were guilty of 'great heresy', and denounced those who opposed prayer to saints.[36] One of John Sinclair's purposes in visiting Wallace in prison was to urge him to believe in the Real Presence. The equally reformist Bishop Reid felt that the denial of that doctrine was 'a horrible heresy'.[37] Quintin Kennedy denounced Protestants as 'the Church malignant', and attacked named Protestant theologians at some length, along with all those who would meddle in the doctrine of justification or defame 'the ineffable mystery of the blessed sacrament of the altar'. He also worried that if the laity saw heretical preaching go unpunished, they might believe it. And for all its discretion, Hamilton's letter to Argyll in 1558 contains unmistakable threats.[38] The effort for Catholic reform which took place under his supervision may have brushed with modish doctrines, but it did not drift into crypto-Protestantism. The determination of the reformers to remain true to their principles cannot be doubted; although the prudence of their approach perhaps can.

THE SUPPORTERS OF REFORM

By their nature, none of our sources states why Scotland's Catholic reformers took this stance. It may have been a matter of conscience or of policy. The reformers may have believed that their doctrines were correct, that they were useful, or (more likely) both.

Scottish Catholics were not alone in taking a non-confrontational approach towards evangelical ideas in the mid-sixteenth century. Henry VIII's England had produced some such compromises, on which Scottish Catholic reformers drew. More significant, however, was the evangelical Catholic reform programme of Hermann von Wied, Archbishop of Cologne. Von Wied's *Enchiridion Christianae Institutionis* was one of the sources for the 1552 catechism and had an agenda strikingly similar to that of the Scottish Catholic reformers. It was well known in Scottish academic circles.[39] As James Cameron has demonstrated, the influence of the Cologne reformers went beyond the catechism to underpin the reform of the universities as well.[40] Archbishop Hamilton set about reviving his university at St Andrews with some vigour. He secured a papal refoundation of the new college, St Mary's, and began building work there. In 1554 he established a new constitution for the college, closely modelled on von Wied's plans for the foundation of a school of divinity in Bonn. St Mary's was now clearly a theological establishment intended principally for training clergy. The education which Hamilton envisaged those clergy receiving there was thoroughly grounded in Renaissance humanist principles. Indeed, in this period the Scottish universities seem finally to have embraced humanism: Greek and Hebrew began to be taught at Aberdeen in the 1550s. Hamilton, who himself had a passably distinguished humanist background, made some efforts find staff for his refounded college amongst the best Scottish scholars on the Continent.[41] The new Dean of the Faculty of Arts was David Guild, whose readiness to indulge in theological speculation had seemed heretical a decade earlier. His successor in 1557, John Douglas, was not only a product of several distinguished European universities but also, unprecedentedly, a layman.[42]

The sense that a vanguard of fashionably educated Catholic reformers was being established in the universities is reinforced by John Foxe's story of the disputes in St Andrews in 1551–52 over the Paternoster (the 'Lord's Prayer').[43] The dispute turned on whether the Paternoster might legitimately be prayed to saints, or only to God. Richard Marshall, the editor of the 1552 catechism, took the latter view, and his uncompromising statement of this position sparked 'a dangerous schism' in St Andrews. This was debated at the 1552 council, where Marshall and the reformers won the day with Archbishop Hamilton's support. The catechism itself does not specifically mention the issue, but does nothing to imply that the prayer may be said to anyone other than God.[44] The reformist party in the Church and the universities was determined enough publicly to oppose the doctrine preached by other Catholics, and it was strong enough to succeed when it did so.

This reforming party's convictions and approaches arose not only from continental models, but also from pre-existing Scottish traditions. Much of Quintin Kennedy's argument, in particular his view of the authority of councils, is closely parallel to the position elaborated in the 1480s by John Ireland, James III's confessor. Indeed, conciliarism had a long pedigree in Scotland. In John Mair, St Andrews itself had perhaps the most distinguished of the last generation of European conciliar theorists. Mair died in 1550, and was too infirm to attend the 1549 provincial council, but he was represented there by his proctor, establishing at least a symbolic link. Scepticism towards papal pretensions was well established in both Church and state, and conciliarist texts were widely circulated.[45] On a smaller scale, Hamilton's attention to his university built on the pattern laid down by his episcopal predecessors at St Andrews. Even Beaton had made a contribution, confirming the status of St Leonard's College in 1545, and doing so explicitly so that the college might oppose heresy and protect the faith. Giovanni Ferrerio, the Italian scholar who had helped to turn Kinloss Abbey into something like a university in the 1530s, was uncompromising in his orthodoxy, but had insisted to Beaton that holiness, not repression, was the best means of defeating heresy. Beaton disagreed, as his condemnation of George Wishart showed, but he was already being urged 'to provide better defences than fire and sword' for the Church. Mere force of law was not enough.[46]

Hamilton's alternative solution – preaching – also had its precedents. In 1547 a preaching canon, John Watson, was appointed to the cathedral in Aberdeen, and charged to preach across the diocese. Watson was a conscientious and learned preacher who, again, seems to have placed more weight on Scripture than on the authority of the Church. Likewise, when Bishop Reid of Orkney refounded his cathedral in 1544, regular cycles of lectures and sermons were built into its life.[47] Rather than the slow and uncertain road of trying to rebuild the parish ministry, these reforms tried to bypass the problem by creating cadres of high-quality itinerant preachers. Elsewhere in Europe such policies met with considerable success. The achievements of these earlier reformers had been piecemeal, but principles had been laid down which Hamilton, in more peaceful times, was able to follow.

It is not to doubt the sincerity of those principles, however, to point out that the Catholic reformers' programme was politically motivated. Archbishop Hamilton and his circle do appear to have held conciliarist and Erasmian views, but their pursuit of them was part of a deliberate campaign against heresy. They apparently hoped to present their faith in as inoffensive a light as possible to those who were dissatisfied with the old Church, so as to persuade them to stay on board. This rather obvious possibility has been met with scepticism from many historians,[48] on the twin grounds that the Catholic reformers were not going far enough to forge a doctrinal compromise with Protestantism, and that Scottish Protestants had no interest in such compromises. However, dissatisfaction with the old Church extended well beyond Protestantism *per se*. The humanists, dissidents and satirists at James V's court were not doctrinaire Protestants, and if they had been classed as heretics, it was not through their own choice.[49] There were plenty of Scots whose loyalties were torn and whose dissatisfaction with the rigidities of the old religion was sufficient to make them flirt with the new.

After James's death, the most prominent representative of this pattern of thought in Scottish public life remained Sir David Lindsay of the Mount. Lindsay's commentary on religious controversies was subtle but penetrating.[50] *The Tragedie of the Cardinal*, written in 1547, did not condone Cardinal Beaton's assassination, but nor did it stint in its criticism of him. Lindsay's religious comment was most detailed and far-reaching in his most famous work, *Ane Satyre of the Thrie Estaitis*, first performed in the form we know in

1552; and in his last composition, *Ane Dialoge of Experience and ane Courtier*, usually known as *The Monarche*. These later works, aimed at a wider audience than his earlier, courtly poems, included detailed prescriptions for reform. As well as raising uncontroversial disciplinary issues, he also followed the Catholic reformers onto contentious doctrinal ground. His approach to the papacy was hostile and contemptuous, although he was never willing to discard it or to deny that it could be reformed. He referred to the papacy as a manifestation of the forces of Antichrist, but (except in one early poem of doubtful attribution) only as one Antichrist amongst many. When proposing major ecclesiastical changes in the *Thrie Estaitis*, he made only the swiftest and most contemptuous reference to the need to secure papal approval, and envisaged the ideal Christian king as being virtually free of papal oversight. *The Monarche* included a vitriolic attack on the degeneracy of the court of Rome, and denounced the papacy for defending its doctrines 'by flaming fire'. Yet he continued to see the papacy itself as having been instituted by Christ. He had less to say about the Bible, but he clearly saw it as being central to the life of the Church and came close to endorsing vernacular Scripture. Other dalliances with evangelical ideas include his attacks on indulgences and pilgrimages; his unease about the use of images; and, most radically, his outspoken advocacy of clerical marriage, which went beyond anything in the official reform programme. Yet his exploration of controversial ideas had clear limits. He argued for the use of prayers in the vernacular, but accepted prayer to saints. His view of justification strongly emphasised the place of works, giving much less ground to evangelical ideas on this point than the catechism did.[51]

Lindsay's works were widely circulated, and while we cannot measure their impact it is clear that he was not along in holding such views. Aside from those already discussed, we know of only two other texts touching on religious issues which were printed in Scots in the 1550s. A short verse treatise by William Lauder, *Ane Compendious and Breue Tractate, Concernynge ye Office and Dewtie of Kyngis*, was published in Edinburgh in 1556. Although he was later a Protestant minister, Lauder was no dissident. In the late 1540s and 1550s the regime employed him as a playwright on several occasions. His book was, he insisted grandiosely, written for the edification of 'all Catholic kings and princes'. He accepted the validity of canon law, and the final page of the book bears a thoroughly traditional woodcut of Christ in glory displaying the Five Wounds.[52] Yet his Catholicism was of a strikingly Biblicist and reformist kind. His central requirement for a righteous king was: 'first cause your preachers, all and odd / Truly set forth, the word of God.' He emphasised Scripture's authority but downplayed the Church's power authoritatively to interpret it. Indeed, he claimed, it is the godly preacher who is the 'true successor' of St Peter (and therefore, by implication, not the Pope). He warned against the appointment of timeservers or hypocrites as preachers. In his discussion of the standards to be expected of such preachers, he emphasised many of the same disciplinary requirements as the reforming councils, but made no mention of clerical celibacy. He was also silent on the subject of the sacraments; he clearly saw the ministry of his 'ghostly ministers' as over-whelmingly one of preaching. None of this was heretical (although his suggestion that 'all grace, . . . prosperity, love and peace' depends merely on faith is at least unguarded). Yet his scripturalism, emphasis on a preaching ministry, scepticism towards the clergy and apparent lack of interest in much of the traditional framework of Catholicism suggests that he, like Lindsay, would have been thoroughly in sympathy with the more provocative aspects of Archbishop Hamilton's reform programme.[53]

The other Scots text from this period was Robert Wedderburn's *Complaynt of Scotland*. The *Complaynt* is war propaganda, not a religious treatise, although its emphasis on the regeneration of the Scottish commonwealth was one which both Lindsay and Lauder shared. However, Wedderburn did turn his attention briefly to the clergy. He condemned clerical corruption in unfor-giving (but wholly orthodox) terms; and argued that heresy should be fought by persuasion and virtuous example, not by persecution. Stamping out heresy by force, he argued, was like trying to quench a fire with oil. He also warned it would provoke 'dissent, discord and hatred in the realm', a prospect for which few Scots had the stomach after the Rough Wooings. And again, there was a robust attitude towards authority. When arguing that priests should take up arms and fight the English like all other Scots, he claimed those who disagreed with him were 'more obedient to the canon law than they are to God's law'. It was in this context that he made his only reference to the papacy: he denied that only the Pope had the authority to license clergy to fight. When the papacy impinged on Scottish Catholic consciousness, it did so as an administrative inconvenience.[54]

Lindsay's, Lauder's and Wedderburn's testimony suggests that the eirenic approach taken by Scotland's Catholic reformers was not as quixotic as it seems. The educated voices we can hear from 1550s Scotland, lay and clerical, seem to have been persuaded that matters in the old Church could not go on as before. Beaton's bitter-end orthodoxy had apparently died with him. In 1547, it seemed entirely routine for a schoolboy in Musselburgh to own not only an English New Testament, but also a copy of George Buchanan's satire on the Franciscan friars. Maurice Lee's description of the religion of Sir Richard Maitland of Lethington fits the same pattern. Maitland was largely uninterested in doctrine, but was disgusted by the corruption of the clergy and appalled by religious strife. He was clear that the Church needed to be reformed, but prayed with equal fervour, 'God make us quit of all heresy'. Maitland eventually conformed to the Protestant Church. He was one of many who, as James Kirk has noted, converted in or after 1559, having previously had Erasmian or Catholic-reformist inclinations.[55] But this journey was not predestined, and an attempt by the old Church to appeal to those with such inclinations could have arrested the process.[56] Lord Seton, for example, was sufficiently interested in religious reform to attend the preaching of the Protestant John Willock in 1558; but he was clearly persuaded that reform did not mean schism, for he became the staunchest noble defender of the old Church during 1559–60. Nor was he alone. When the Principal of Glasgow University set himself to refute Quintin Kennedy's book in 1562, he admitted that 'there has been many moved to continue still in their superstition and idolatry, through the reasons contained in the same'.[57]

The Catholic reformers' eirenic approach and measured arguments had some purchase even on convinced Protestants. After John Winram preached in favour of a humbler approach to heresy at George Wishart's trial, Wishart clearly felt that he could trust Winram, and chose to make his final confession to him. Richard Marshall's attack on the practice of addressing the Paternoster to saints picked up on the precise concern which the Protestant Henry Balnaves had raised some four years earlier. In 1557–59 there seems to have been a widespread hope that a workable religious compromise along the lines favoured by some Catholic reformers could be thrashed out. And even once the Reformation rebellion had broken out, when the Queen Regent said 'that the true religion should go forward, and that all abuses should be abolished', there were rebels who were willing to listen.[58]

The Catholic reformers' message was a powerful one. It would not have won over convinced Protestants. However, its compromises, shifting emphases, and evangelical mood music were closely aligned with many educated Scots' concerns, as well as with the Catholic reformers' own convictions. It was a programme which appealed to those who looked for an inclusive, generous reform both of discipline and of doctrine, who were opposed to heresy but not deaf to it: the 'floating voters' of a religiously unsettled country. It was a risky approach but not, perhaps, a foolhardy one. The potential constituency was large and influential. Moreover, it is noticeable how many of the leading figures in the Catholic reform effort came, in 1559–60, to throw their lot in with the Protestants.[59] If those reformers were trying to persuade their people that Scottish Catholicism could be rejuvenated, perhaps many of them were also trying to persuade themselves.

THE FAILURE OF REFORM

Regardless of the potential of Catholic reform, it was defeated. It also seems likely that it was not merely overtaken by events; rather, it contributed to its own destruction. If some Catholic reformers were trying to convince themselves that it was possible to remain in the old Church, they failed. The reforms they had set in train may, so far from strengthening Catholic Scotland against heresy, have fatally weakened its defences. If this is so, however, it does not reflect a misjudgement by the reformers as much as it does the incomplete and unbalanced implementation of their programme.

As we have seen, almost all of the documents which testify to that programme, official and unofficial, include the requirement that the laws against heresy should be maintained and enforced. This was essential. If a greater area of doctrinal freedom was being opened up, it was vital to provide clear and effective boundaries to that area. No moment is more dangerous for a much-criticised regime or institution than the point at which it begins to heed those criticisms and to reform itself. Opponents will naturally tend to interpret any concessions as a sign of weakness, and think that if they have been given an inch they may be able to take a mile. If reform is to be perceived as an act of strength, rather than of weakness, it must be accompanied by intensified repression of those outside the new settlement. If one is going to speak softly, one has to carry a big stick. Reformers who hoped to persuade waverers to rejoin the old Church needed not only to appeal to them directly, but also to do all they could to stifle the contrary arguments of their Protestant opponents. In particular, the Protestant leadership had to be silenced, whether by arrest, exile or execution. It appears, from their repeatedly stated intentions, that Scotland's Catholic reformers understood this.

However, the matter was out of their hands. The Church could pursue reform on its own initiative; for repression, the active co-operation of the secular power was needed. While Archbishop Hamilton's half-brother the Earl of Arran (from 1548, the Duke of Châtelherault) remained Governor, the Catholic reformers retained a degree of support from the Crown. The Archbishop was able to use his position as treasurer to buy books needed for the reform effort in the Governor's name.[60] In February 1552, while the provincial council was still in session, parliament enacted several statutes against religious offenders. The act against blasphemous oaths must surely have remained merely aspirational, for all the careful sliding scale of fines it imposed; yet the act against those who made 'perturbation in the church the time of divine service' was precisely the kind of support from the state which Catholic reform needed. Even better was the same parliament's imposition of a system of censorship for printed books.[61] Yet little was done to enforce these laws, even while Châtelherault remained nominal head of the government.

When he was finally supplanted by Mary of Guise in 1554, political support for the Catholic reform effort ceased altogether. One of Guise's first acts as Regent was to sack Archbishop Hamilton as Royal Treasurer and replace him with the Protestant Earl of Cassillis. Cassillis, rumour had it, also persuaded her to imprison her Chancellor, the Catholic Earl of Huntly, and to strip him of some of his titles and most of his authority. Guise was consistently generous to her Protestant subjects. James Harryson, who had written propaganda for the English in the 1540s, was given a pension by Guise, and secured the office of conservator of Scottish privileges in the Netherlands, which he had coveted for more than a decade. Guise helped the 'castilians' of 1546–47 to be released from French captivity, and came to be on excellent terms with some of them, including the earnest Protestant Henry Balnaves.[62] In so far as she took any interest in religious policy, it seems she was concerned to undercut the primate, rather than to support him. During the long wrangle between Hamilton and the papacy over the bishopric of Dunkeld, the Guise interest consistently backed Hamilton's opponent Robert Crichton, and in 1554 the Archbishop was forced to concede.[63]

Virtually the only evidence for Guise's interest in Catholic reform comes from a letter on the plight of the Scottish Church, written by Cardinal Sermoneta to Pope Paul IV in or around 1556. Sermoneta wrote in the name of the child Queen, Mary, but he can be taken as representing her mother's views. (His first priority, indeed, was to support the Crown's wish to tax the clergy.) Without even hinting that a substantial reform effort was already under way, he insisted that nothing could be done without 'upright and honest prelates'. He named five such who could be trusted as reformers, 'and who are by far the most acceptable to the same most serene sovereign lady'. The five were the Archbishop of Glasgow and the Bishops of Orkney, Moray, Dunblane and Galloway. It is a peculiar list. While Archbishop Beaton and Reid of Orkney deserved the confidence which Sermoneta had been led to place in them, Hepburn of Moray and Durie of Galloway were in no way model bishops. Archbishop Hamilton was, of course, passed over. So were the two prelates who had supporting him during the dispute over the Paternoster in 1552: Robert Stewart of Caithness and Alexander Gordon, titular Archbishop of Athens and (since 1554) Bishop of the Isles.[64] Mary of Guise could perhaps never have been expected to be warm towards a Hamilton, given the dynastic threat which the family represented, but through isolating the Archbishop in this manner, she was potentially sabotaging the entire reform effort.

One result was that Paul IV became more concerned about Guisard empire-building than about reforming the Scottish Church. He was most reluctant to accede to requests for assistance with Scotland's problems. When he responded to Sermoneta's appeal in 1557, he refused to operate through the Scottish bishops at all, instead empowering Cardinal Trivulzio, his legate in France, to visit Scotland. (Trivulzio, unsurprisingly, had not done so by his death in 1559.) Even when rebellion had broken out, the Pope refused to grant the French Crown's request to empower the Bishop of Amiens to visit Scotland. He would not allow France to dictate policy to him.[65] International power politics had neutralised Paris and Rome, as well as Edinburgh, as active participants in Scottish Catholic reform. St Andrews was on its own.

The most obvious sign of this isolation was Guise's persistent reluctance to allow any significant clampdown on heresy. While there had been a steady trickle of heresy executions in the reign of James V, after 1544 only three Protestants were killed for their faith in Scotland: George Wishart in 1546, Adam Wallace in 1550 and Walter Myln in 1558. Again, Châtelherault's regime did give some official support to Archbishop Hamilton – for example, ensuring that if suspected heretics whom he summoned did not appear, they forfeited their goods or their sureties.[66] By contrast, Myln's execution seems to have been entirely Hamilton's initiative, and Guise carefully distanced herself from it.[67] There were few other attempts even to prosecute heretics under her regency. Where she did lend her support to such efforts – as when she ordered the arrest of those using 'certain odious ballads and rhymes lately set forth' in Edinburgh in 1556 – she emphasised her fear of 'misorder', rather than any religious offences. Parliament was silent on the religious question after 1554, excepting a 1555 statute against those who broke the Lenten fast. Guise even personally intervened to allow John Knox to escape to exile after his covert preaching tour in 1555–56, so much so that Knox saw her as a potential honest broker between the Protestants and the bishops.[68] It is hard to see what more she could have done to undermine Hamilton and to leave the Catholic reformers' flank exposed.

This policy of Guise's made sense in its own, somewhat narrow terms. Her consistent aim was to secure her daughter's throne, and to ensure a stable succession through the French marriage and through the eventual union of the Crowns which the marriage promised. In the pursuit of these aims she felt the need of as wide a base of support as possible, and was unwilling to alienate Scottish Protestants. She seems to have been disinclined by temperament to be a persecutor. The temptation to turn a blind eye to heresy became all the stronger after 1553, when Mary Tudor's accession to the English throne returned England to full-blooded Catholicism. This seemed to break the potentially dangerous link between Protestantism and pro-English sentiment. Guise's failure to appreciate the risk that the Protestant movement still posed to her and to her daughter was understandable; even if, with hindsight, it was a disastrous political miscalculation.[69]

The principles of our own age lead us to assume that religious persecution is an evil, and so it is, but we should not therefore assume that it was ineffective. Clare Kellar has argued that the absence of persecution in 1550s Scotland 'avoided a damaging association with brutal Roman repression'.[70] It is not, in fact, clear that such associations were avoided. Yet one of the reasons why the Catholic Church had long used force against heresy was that it sometimes worked. The use of judicial terror and exemplary punishments might force dissident movements underground, where they could be more easily controlled. At the very least, their voices could be muffled. Christianity's brave talk of the blood of martyrs watering the faith has some truth to it, but the shedding of martyrs' blood can also cost the faithful dearly. If repression risked making martyrs, the alternatives were perhaps worse. By permitting a man such as Knox to go about his business in Scotland for nearly a year, and then to escape, Guise was signalling that she would not defend the Church from those who wished, not to reform it, but to overthrow it. While the Catholic reform programme flirted with evangelical ideas, the absence of any sustained effort to enforce limits to that flirtation left the Church exposed to the seductions of the new religion while undefended by the certainties of the old.

With hindsight, Hamilton's reforming project appears at best eccentric, at worst a Trojan horse for Protestantism. Within a few years of its demise, the Council of Trent's resounding declaration in favour of traditional orthodoxies had closed off the possibility of any other compromises on this scale. The perspective of the 1550s was very different. It seemed possible that the Council of Trent might reconcile Protestantism and Catholicism, or indeed that the Council might be allowed to lapse altogether. In Germany, there were not only doctrinal experiments at Cologne and elsewhere, but there was the political experiment represented by Charles V's Interim, the religious compromise he tried to impose on the Lutheran states he defeated in the late 1540s. Henry VIII had tried to impose another such compromise on England, with a degree of success while he lived, and this too explicitly informed Hamilton's programme. In France, the idea of a compromise settlement which could be imposed by a strong royal hand lasted into the 1560s and beyond. In the event, the political will needed to impose such settlements ensured that they rarely outlived their creators. Mary of Guise's unwillingness to provide any meaningful support for her bishops ensured that the Scottish compromise failed more quickly. Yet plenty of Europeans hoped for and believed in the possibility of such compromises. Their failure in Scotland should not be blamed so much on any inherent impossibility, as on the political decision not to support them. Mary of Guise was a shrewd political tactician, but she should perhaps also be credited with a hand in the destruction of Scottish Catholicism.

The firm foundations of Scottish religious life, which had been eroded by heresy and war in the 1530s and 1540s, were almost entirely dissolved by reform and politics in the 1550s. Archbishop Hamilton's reformers had explicitly abandoned some of the old orthodoxies of Catholicism. They were no longer willing to defend their Catholic inheritance without question, as Beaton had. Indeed, they were willing to pick public fights with their more old-fashioned brethren, as the squabbles in St Andrews over the Paternoster show. It was a bold attempt to create a new Catholic orthodoxy for Scotland, drawing on existing traditions and on the most innovative thinking from across Europe. Yet because they were unable to defend their new-built compromise with force, it became clear that it was built on sand. They had undermined one orthodoxy without being able convincingly to set up another in its place. Those Scottish Catholics who had vacated the old certainties – either from despair at the failings of the old Church, or because their bishops and theologians had told them to do so – now found themselves living in a house with treacherous foundations. As it collapsed under the weight of events in 1558–59, many of those who had genuinely believed in the reform programme found themselves driven towards the only religious certainty still standing: Protestantism.

NOTES

1 *CSP Scotland*, 385; Melville of Halhill, *Memoirs*, 20–1; Royall Tyler (ed.), *Calendar of Letters, Despatches and State Papers relating to the Negotiations between England and Spain*, vol. X (London, 1914), 339; Hannay, 'Some papal bulls', 32–4; Cameron, *Warrender Papers*, 31; RPC, 89–90; Sanderson, *Ayrshire*, 74.

2 Patrick, *Statutes*; Winning, 'Church councils', 334, 357.

3 Merriman, *Rough Wooings*, 19; Winning, 'Church councils', 335, 357.

4 James Kirk, *Patterns of Reform*, xii; cf. Lee, *James Stewart*, 13; Donaldson, *Scottish Reformation*, 35, 37; Cowan, *Scottish Reformation*, 87; Wormald, *Court, Kirk and Community*, 93–4; Dilworth, *Scottish Monasteries*, 33.

5 See above, ch. 1.

6 Knox, I, 291–2; AM, 1274; Lindsay of Pitscottie, *Historie*, II, 141–3.

7 Leslie, *Historie*, II, 345–6, 400. Cf. John Leslie, *De origine moribus, et rebus gestis Scotorum* (Rome, 1578), 516, 547.

8 Kenneth, 'Popular literature', 179.

9 See above, ch. 1.

10 Patrick, *Statutes*, 89–94, 110–12, 124, 163–7, 176–7, 185–6.

11 Patrick, *Statutes*, 98–103, 104–9, 126–7, 136, 147, 173–6.

12 *Registrum Episcopatus Aberdonensis*, lx–lxiv; Charles S. Romane (ed.), *Selections from the records of the regality of Melrose*, vol. 3: 1547–1706 (Scottish Text Society 2nd series 13: Edinburgh, 1917), 167–87, esp. 168–9; Cowan, *Scottish Reformation*, 87; W. Chambers, *Charters and Documents Relating to the Burgh of Peebles, with Extracts from the Records of the Burgh* (Edinburgh, 1872), 226–7, 235, 242, 253; Lindsay of Pitscottie, *Historie*, II, 142.

13 The best account of its origins remains that of Alexander Mitchell in his edition, *The Catechism set forth by Archbishop Hamilton printed at Saint Andrews* (Edinburgh, 1882), iii–xxxii.

14 Patrick, *Statutes*, 144–7.

15 Hamilton, *Catechisme*, preface fos 1r, 2r, fos 100r, 119r. Cf. Peter Marshall, 'The debate over "unwritten verities" in early Reformation England' in Bruce Gordon (ed.), *Protestant History and Identity in Sixteenth Century Europe*, 2 vols (Aldershot, 1996), I, 60–77.

16 Hamilton, *Catechisme*, fos 139r–148v; cf. fos 35r, 93v, 199r, 200r.

17 *Ibid.*, fos 83v–84r, 128v; Mitchell, *Catechism*, xxii–xxiii.

18 Hamilton, *Catechisme*, fos 7v, 22v–23v.

19 Kellar, *Scotland, England and the Reformation*, 127; Maurice Taylor, 'The conflicting doctrines of the Scottish Reformation' in McRoberts, *Essays*, 252–5; Mitchell, *Catechism*, xvi–xvii; Cowan, *Scottish Reformation*, 82–3.

20 John Durkan, 'The cultural background in sixteenth-century Scotland' in McRoberts, *Essays*, 327. Cf. Patrick, *Statutes*, 86.

21 Hamilton, *Catechisme*, fos 92v, 206r.

22 Mitchell, *Catechism*, ix–xv, xxvi–xxxii; *TA*, X, 50.

23 Patrick, *Statutes*, 90, 94, 126–7, 165, 176–7; Mitchell, *Catechism*, xv n.1. Cf. Donaldson, *Scottish Reformation*, 43–6.

24 John Hamilton, *Ane Godlie Exhortatioun sett Furth be Johane Archbischope of Sanctandrous* (RSTC 12731.2: St Andrews, 1559). On sacramental doctrine, see below, ch. 6.

25 Patrick, *Statutes*, 86; *Wodrow Misc.*, 101–3, 106, 115–6, 125, 133, 150.

26 *Wodrow Misc.*, 121, 143, 162, 164.

27 Knox, I, 291; Lindsay of Pitscottie, *Historie*, II, 141–2; see below, ch. 7. This text is unlikely to be the 'short declaration' on the Mass, as is sometimes argued: Alec Ryrie, 'Reform without frontiers in the last years of Catholic Scotland', *English Historical Review*, 119 (2004), 39–40.

28 John Bale, *Scriptorum illustrium maioris Brytanniae posterior pars* (Basel, 1559), 224; Dunbar, *Reforming the Scottish Church*, 24–5; *AM*, 1268.

29 Knox, I, 276–9, 288.

30 See below, ch. 7.

31 Knox, I, 126–7, 201.

32 Knox, I, 265–6; *AM*, 1273.

33 Row, *History*, 7–9.

34 *Wodrow Misc.*, 67.

35 Patrick, *Statutes*, 122–7, 147.

36 Hamilton, *Catechisme*, fos 18r, 88r–v, 143v.

37 *AM*, 1272.

38 *Wodrow Misc.*, 114, 125, 133, 150–1, 157–9; Knox, I, 277–8.

39 John Durkan and Anthony Ross, *Early Scottish Libraries* (Glasgow, 1961), 73, 93, 139, 148.

40 James K. Cameron, 'The Cologne Reformation and the Church of Scotland', *Journal of Ecclesiastical History*, 30 (1979), 41–2; James K. Cameron, '"Catholic Reform" in Germany and the pre-1560 Church in Scotland', *RSCHS*, 20 (1979), 105–7, 112–15.

41 Ronald G. Cant, *The University of St Andrews: a short history* (Edinburgh and London, 1970), 34–7; James K. Cameron, 'St Mary's College 1547–1574 – the second foundation: the principalship of John Douglas', in D. W. D. Shaw (ed.), *In Divers Manners: A St Mary's Miscellany* (St Andrews, 1990), 43–48; Cameron, '"Catholic Reform"', 114; Durkan, 'Cultural background', 292; James K. Cameron, 'Humanism and religious life', in John MacQueen (ed.), *Humanism in Renaissance Scotland* (Edinburgh, 1990), 165–6.

42 Annie I. Dunlop (ed.), *Acta Facultatis Artium Universitatis Sanctiandree 1413–1588* (Scottish Historical Society 3rd series 54: Edinburgh, 1964), lxiii–lxvi; see above, 20–1.

43 On this account, see Freeman, '"The reik of Maister Patrik Hammyltoun"', 55; cf. David Lindsay of the Mount, *The Works of Sir David Lindsay*, ed. J. H. Murray (Early English Text Society old series 11 *et seq.*: London, 1865–71): 'Ane Dialog betuix Experience and ane Courteour', lines 2624–31, 'Ane Satyre of the Thrie Estaitis', line 4604.

44 *AM*, 1274; Hamilton, *Catechisme*, fo. 175v.

45 Patrick, *Statutes*, 87; Burns, *True Law of Kingship*, 5–6, 32; J. H. Burns, 'The conciliarist tradition in Scotland', *SHR*, 42 (1963), 89–104; Ryrie, 'Reform without frontiers', 46.

46 Herkless and Hannay, *College of St Leonard*, 187; Durkan, 'Beginnings of humanism', 16; Knox, I, 192–3.

47 *Registrum Episcopatus Aberdonensis*, lix; Gilbert Hill, 'The sermons of John Watson, canon of Aberdeen', *IR*, 15 (1964), 4–6, 10–11; Kirk, *Patterns of Reform*, 26–7; Donaldson, *Scottish Reformation*, 34.

48 For example, Taylor, 'Conflicting doctrines', 254; Kenneth, 'Popular literature', 179; Cowan, *Scottish Reformation*, 83. For the opposing view, see Sanderson, *Ayrshire*, 75; Donaldson, *All the Queen's Men*, 26.

49 See above, ch. 2.

50 For a detailed discussion of Lindsay's views, see Edington, *Court and Culture*.

51 See, for example, Lindsay, *Works*: 'Ane Dialog betuix Experience and ane Courteour', lines 490–9, 538–684, 2613–84, 4375–400, 4639–58, 4743–973, 5690–4; 'Ane Satyre of the Thrie Estaitis', lines 1091–2, 1144–51, 2037–287, 2723–44; cf. Edington, *Court and Culture*, esp. 170, 195.

52 *ODNB*; William Lauder, *Ane Compendious and Breue Tractate, concernyng ye Office and Dewtie of Kyngis* (RSTC 15314: Edinburgh, 1556), sigs A1v, C2v, C3v–4v.

53 Lauder, *Breue tractate*, sigs B1r–B4r.

54 Wedderburn, *Complaynt*, 125, 127–30.

55 Robert vans Agnew (ed.), *Correspondence of Sir Patrick Waus of Barnbarroch* (Edinburgh, 1882), 3; Maurice Lee, 'Sir Richard Maitland of Lethington: a Christian laird in the age of Reformation' in his *The 'Inevitable' Union and Other Essays on Early Modern Scotland* (East Linton, 2003), 27–9; Craigie, *Maitland Folio Manuscript*, 33; Kirk, *Patterns of Reform*, 43.

56 Kellar, *Scotland, England and the Reformation*, 151.

57 Knox, I, 256; John Davidson, *Ane Answer to the Tractiue, set furth in 1558. be Q. Kennedy* (RSTC 6320: Edinburgh, 1563), fos 3v, 34v.

58 Lindsay of Pitscottie, *Historie*, II, 76–7; Knox, I, 437; III, 518; and see below, ch. 7.

59 As James Cameron has observed: Cameron, 'Cologne Reformation', 64.

60 *TA*, X, 50.

61 *APS*, 485, 488–9.

62 Herries, *Historical Memoirs*, 28–9; Merriman, 'James Henrisoun', 101–2; Cameron, *Scottish Correspondence*, 405.

63 Michael Yellowlees, 'The ecclesiastical establishment of the diocese of Dunkeld at the Reformation', *IR*, 36 (1985), 75–6.

64 Pollen, *Papal Negotiations*, 135, 528–30; *AM*, 1274; Cowan, *Scottish Reformation*, 87; Sanderson, *Ayrshire*, 73.

65 Pollen, *Papal Negotiations*, 7–8, 19–23.

66 *RSS*, IV, 911, 2580.

67 Knox, I, 308–9.

68 Robert Keith, *History of the Affairs of Church and State in Scotland from the beginning of the Reformation to the year 1568*, 3 vols (Edinburgh, 1844), I, 483–4; *APS*, 493; Knox, IV, 77, 83.

69 Wormald, *Court, Kirk and Community*, 96.

70 Kellar, *Scotland, England and the Reformation*, 141.

Chapter 6

1543–59: underground Reformation

'DETESTABLE HERESY RISES AND INCREASES'

In the early 1550s Scottish Catholics could be forgiven for believing that heresy had been defeated. In self-congratulatory mood, the general provincial council of 1552 declared that

> many frightful heresies have, within the last few years, run riot in many diverse parts of this realm, but have now at last been checked by the providence of All-good and Almighty God, the singular goodwill of princes, and the vigilance and zeal of prelates for the Catholic faith, and seem almost extinguished.[1]

We know, of course, that this confidence was premature, and that a few years later, the heretical infection would break out more virulently than before. Traditional, Protestant histories of the Scottish Reformation would argue that the apparent peace of the 1550s was deceptive. On this view, Protestantism was silently coalescing from simple reading-groups into formally organised 'privy kirks': a network of underground Protestant churches, waiting fully formed in the parishes and preparing for government.[2]

This movement is usually seen to have crystallised in 1555–56, when John Knox paid an extended visit to Scotland, preaching clandestinely in Angus, the Mearns, Lothian and Ayrshire. Knox arrived fresh from Calvin's Geneva, and the perfection he had seen in the church there had gone to his head.[3] He came to Scotland bearing Calvin's insistence that Protestants must separate themselves from the old Church entirely. Calvin condemned any outward conformity with Catholicism as *Nicodemism*, after Christ's disciple who had visited him by night for fear of being seen.[4] Knox insisted that to attend Catholic worship was to consent to damnable idolatry. However, the story of 'privy kirks' being seeded by Knox's preaching has always been thin on evidence. A growth in Protestant support and militancy in the 1550s has been deduced more often than it has been proved.

Was Protestantism steadily growing during the hidden years of the 1550s, so that the process was almost over by the time religious change came into the open? This is not only an impossible question to answer. For an early modern society, it is almost impossible to ask. It is misleading to apply our democratic era's interest in numbers and in rates of conversion to a hierarchical society such as that of sixteenth-century Scotland. We might wonder what level of support a notional opinion-pollster would have found for Protestantism at any given time, but the outcome of the Scottish Reformation was not decided by referendum – nor did anyone at the time believe that it should be. The questions of when, where and in what numbers Scots converted to Protestantism are clearly important. A few scraps of evidence do survive which allow us to address them. However, we must remember that these quantitative questions are less important than the qualitative ones: who were the Protestant converts, and, compared to their opponents, how deeply felt were their convictions?[5]

Assessments of the scale of Protestant support in pre-Reformation Scotland vary widely. The conservative Lord Herries detected a turning-point in the mid-1540s. 'Divisions for matter of religion and doctrine for divers years past had been but in conception; they are now at the point of birth, and ready to rise.' On his view, peace with England only redoubled these divisions. The Catholic Bishop Leslie put the crisis later: it was during the late 1550s that heresy 'flew through the people', and that most Scots moved from mocking the old faith to abandoning it.[6] However, it is less easy to find Catholics who believed at the time that the situation was desperate. It was only in 1559 that Archbishop Hamilton declared that 'Lutheranism, Calvinism, and very many other nefarious heresies are being propagated everywhere in this realm by heretics', and Henry II of France warned of 'the great number of persons who flock at all hours to . . . the said heretics'.[7] Those Catholics who before 1559 voiced generalised laments about the religious situation tended to worry about their own shortcomings, not the heretics' advances.

Likewise, Protestants were usually inclined to downplay their numbers and present themselves as a 'faithful little flock'. George Wishart lamented how few people came to hear him preach in Haddington in 1545, although this may reflect the population's fear of the Earl of Bothwell as much as any distaste for Wishart's doctrines. Ninian Cockburn, a reformer in the pay of the English, assessed the religious situation in late 1547 with gloomy relish. In his view, most Scots who claimed to favour the Gospel did so merely because that was what their English paymasters wanted to hear. He warned that the French troops who were expected to arrive in the new year would destroy the Protestants – 'but there be very few of them to destroy'. And this was in a population which, Cockburn claimed, blamed the clergy for the devastation which the war had brought to them. As so often, anticlericalism did not translate into heresy.[8]

However, not all Protestant observers were so downbeat. In particular, several compared Scottish Protestantism favourably with its English counterpart. John ab Ulmis was an associate of Heinrich Bullinger, the minister of Zurich and a tireless builder of Reformed Protestant networks. In 1551, ab Ulmis was in England, and visited Berwick-upon-Tweed. He reported to Bullinger:

> There appears to be great firmness and no little religion among the people of Scotland. . . . It is the general opinion, that greater numbers of them are rightly persuaded as to true religion than here among us in England. This seems to be a strange state of things, that among the English the ruling powers are virtuous and godly, but the people have for a long time been most contumacious; while in Scotland, on the contrary, the rulers are most ferocious, but the nation at large is virtuous and exceedingly well disposed towards our most holy religion.[9]

Ab Ulmis was a level-headed observer who did not have a particular polemical point to make. As a foreigner, able to communicate only in Latin, he was vulnerable to misinformation, but he was no fool. Nor was he alone in drawing this comparison. In 1559 the English radical Christopher Goodman made a similar point from his Scottish exile. He reproached England because 'the like thirst and zeal to his holy word and promoting of Christ's kingdom, is not amongst you . . . as is found in this people of later calling'.[10] Knox himself apparently had the same comparison in mind when he visited Scotland in 1555–56. It was his first trip to his native land in eight years, and for much of that time he had been ministering in England. He returned to Scotland with some reluctance and with low expectations. However, he was genuinely surprised by 'the fervent thirst of our brethren, night and day sobbing and groaning for the bread of life. . . . If I had not seen it with my eyes in my own country, I could not have believed it. . . . The fervency here doth far exceed all others that I have seen'.[11] Knox's hyperbole is as clear as ever, but the comparison with England is unmistakable. The point should not be overplayed, not least because England's Protestant fervour was hardly the most testing benchmark to meet. However, if three seasoned observers who knew something of both countries agreed that Protestantism was as least as strong, in numbers and in fervency, in Scotland as in England, their view is not to be dismissed lightly.

However, none of these Protestant observers was in a position to give a picture of the country as a whole. The regional variations in Protestant support were substantial, before, during and after 1559–60.[12] In 1555–56 Knox confined his itinerary to Protestant strongholds, and it was one of those strongholds,

Ayr, which provided Goodman with his refuge. There was perhaps widespread and socially significant support for Protestantism in these parts of the country, but not elsewhere. In 1559–60 an English agent claimed that Fife, Angus and the Mearns, Strathearn and Argyll were the only actively Protestant regions (the last of those no doubt reflecting its earl's influence, for there is otherwise scarcely a trace of real Protestantism in Gaelic-speaking Scotland before 1560). An anonymous early historian of the Reformation summarising the religious situation in 1558 broadly agreed: 'The greatest fervency appeared in the Mearns and Angus, and Kyle [in Ayrshire], and Fife or Lothian; but chiefly the faithful in Dundee exceeded all the rest in zeal and boldness. ... In Edinburgh their meeting was but in private houses.'[13] The priority which this author gave to Dundee and its hinterland is widely supported. In 1547, the English commander at Broughty Crag, near Dundee, gave the Duke of Somerset his opinion of the local population. Although they were reluctant to make a truce with the English,

> all the honest men and substantial men of the said town favour the word of God . . . They are much desirous here in the country of Angus and Fife to have a good preacher and Bibles and Testaments and other good English books. . . . [If] there were a bookbinder, that came hither with books, he should sell them very well.[14]

Eight years later, Knox claimed that 'the most part of the gentlemen of the Mearns' attended his clandestine preaching. Catholic fears in the region mirrored reformist optimism. After 1543 the Cistercian abbey at Cupar Angus began to insert clauses in its leases of land threatening forfeiture to any lessees convicted of heresy. One lease denounced the 'Lutheran madness'.[15]

Dundee was the probably the first burgh in the country in which a Reformed Church was publicly established – only probably, because the burgh itself did not begin formally to support the new Church until August 1559.[16] In this at least, Dundee was preceded by Ayr. Ayr's burgh council played both sides of the religious question. It began to scale down its support for the old Church in 1557. In the same year the long-standing reformist preacher Robert Achesoun came to the town and began to be styled the 'minister'. A local Protestant gave him houseroom for seven weeks, but thereafter the burgh council rented a room for him, at a cost of £4. His furnishings and living expenses continued to be provided by local reformers until well into the 1559–60 rebellion, when the burgh took over full responsibility for supporting him and reimbursed his early supporters for their expenses.[17] Ayrshire was, Knox claimed, 'a receptacle of God's servants of old', from its Lollards onwards, but it is only in the 1550s that it begins to emerge as a significant centre of reformist activity. In 1558 the Archbishop of Glasgow was worrying that 'detestable heresy rises and increases in the diocese of Glasgow', a worry which can only have been directed at Ayrshire.[18] The strength of the Earl of Argyll's Campbell affinity in the region would turn it into the Congregation's second heartland during 1559–60.

A few tentative conclusions do emerge, then, from the fragmentary evidence for the scale of Protestant allegiance before 1559. There was no rising tide. Generalised Catholic alarm is detectable only in 1559 itself. There was a significant number of reformers and reformist sympathisers in some parts of the country, principally in Fife, Angus and the Mearns, and Ayrshire. Even there, they were a minority. They may have been more noticeable than their co-religionists in conservative and conformist England, but they were still a long way from any kind of dominance. In most other regions Protestants were a rarity. It may be true that there was a wider sense of disillusionment with or detachment from the old church. Margaret Sanderson's survey of surviving pre-Reformation wills provides no positive evidence of Protestantism at all (itself a striking finding) but may suggest that some Scots were distancing themselves from traditional piety in the 1540s and 1550s.[19] If this was the case, it was certainly an opportunity for Scottish Protestantism, but it was an opportunity which had not yet been exploited. Protestant growth in the 1540s and 1550s was at best incremental, not exponential.

PSALM-SINGING AND IMAGE-BREAKING

More important than Protestantism's numerical strength was its mood, and the nature of its activities. James V's reign had bequeathed a loosely defined and open evangelicalism, informed by Lutheran theology but dominated by anticlericalism and Bible-reading. It had no organisation beyond the gathering of informal groups to read, and perhaps to break the Lenten fast together. The only other activity that we can associate with such groups is some smashing of Catholic images.[20] Reformism with this kind of profile unquestionably survived after 1543. However, a new assertiveness, and a new edge of bitterness, is visible within it. In James V's reign, Bible-reading was already moving from being an adventure for the curious to a pious act for the committed. A man burned in Stirling in 1539 tried to carry his New Testament to the stake with him, but one of the crowd snatched it from his bosom. In 1543, those who wished to burnish their evangelical credentials claimed to keep their New Testaments 'hid under my bed-feet', and to have forgone sleep to pore over the Word. Adam Wallace, executed in 1550, carried his Bible 'at his belt'; until it was taken from him in prison, it 'always . . . was with him wherever he went'.[21] In a world which Protestant doctrine was desacralising, the Bible was the only holy object left. Reformers would not be parted from it.

One symptom of this militant Biblicism was the use of the Psalms. The praying and the singing of the Psalms as a means of cementing religious identity was one of the most distinctive features of Reformed Protestantism across Europe.[22] Metrical Psalms were a form of music which was irreproachable even to the dourest Reformed theologian. They became a badge of Reformed identity, and their texts were peculiarly well suited to peoples under persecution. When Adam Wallace's Bible was finally taken from him, he spent the night before his execution 'in singing, and lauding God . . . having learned the Psalter of David without book, to his consolation'. George Buchanan, imprisoned in Portugal by the Inquisition, passed his time by composing metrical Psalms.[23] When the Edinburgh Protestant Elizabeth Adamsoun was on her deathbed, in about 1556, she asked her companions to sing Psalm 103, which she said had first taught her soul 'to taste of the mercy of my God'. More tantalising is John Knox's claim that George Wishart, shortly before his arrest in late 1545, sang Psalm 51, 'which was put in Scottish meter'.[24] The version of the Psalm which Knox put in Wishart's mouth subsequently appeared in the collection known as the *Gude and Godlie Ballatis*. The earliest surviving edition of that collection dates from 1567, but some its lyrics are clearly much older, many of them obviously predating 1559. There may have been an earlier edition of the whole collection, or some of the individual pieces may have been circulating in manuscript or printed broadsheets (although Knox's account of Wishart is hardly incontestable proof). If some form of the *Gude and Godlie Ballatis* existed in the 1540s, then Scottish reformers would have had metrical texts of up to twenty-two Psalms, as well as a wide range of other religious lyrics, many drawn from German Lutheran sources.[25] This collection may have been the hymn book of the early Scottish Reformation. It also seems likely that other, English collections of metrical Psalms were being used: Adamsoun's chosen Psalm, 103, does not appear in the *Gude and Godlie Ballatis*. And some Scottish reformers clearly did not think of their Psalms in metre at all, being more familiar with the blank verse of the English Great Bible.[26]

However, the dominant mood of Scottish Protestantism in the 1540s and 1550s was not quiet psalmody. As well as Psalms, the *Gude and Godlie Ballatis* contains a series of polemical religious ballads such as 'God send every priest a wife' and 'The Pope, that pagan full of pride'. These are the most eye-catching items in the collection for the modern reader, and early Protestants probably felt the same. The Protestant historian John Row felt that the most memorable items in the book were these ditties which changed 'old Popish Songs unto godly purposes'.[27] The regime was alarmed by this phenomenon. In June 1543 the Lords of Session denounced the spread of heretical and slanderous ballads, singling out 'the new dialogue called *Pastullus* and the ballad called *The Boar*', which had recently been printed as broadsheets.[28]

John Foxe had sight of two scurrilous verses written against the clergy which were circulating during the dispute in St Andrews in 1551–52 over the legitimacy of saying the Paternoster to saints. In the same year parliament legislated against the printing of heretical 'ballads, songs [and] blasphemous rhymes', but in 1556 the Queen Regent was still concerned about 'certain odious ballads and rhymes lately set forth be some evil inclined persons' in Edinburgh.[29] Religious lyrics, then, seem to have been at least as polemical as they were devotional. And, as in France and elsewhere, even the Psalms were used in this way. Knox claimed, rather dubiously, that when the Edinburgh authorities searched for iconoclasts in the town in September 1558, 'none could be apprehended; for the brethren assembled themselves in such sort, in companies, singing Psalms, and praising God, that the proudest of the enemies was astonished'. More plausibly, an anonymous witness described how when churches and religious houses were sacked by Protestant forces in 1559, the iconoclasts were 'praising God continually, in singing of Psalms and spiritual songs'.[30] Group singing was a seal of collective identity and a means of sanctifying violence. The piety to which it points is unnervingly aggressive.

Indeed, from 1543 onwards Scottish Protestantism unmistakably contained a militant wing. This seems to have been provoked in part by the reassertion of Catholic orthodoxy that autumn, following the end of Governor Arran's 'godly fit'. The wave of attacks on religious houses in September 1543, at the moment when the political winds changed, may have been a last-ditch attempt to force the pace of events and draw out evangelical support. However, these attacks also reflected disappointed reformist hopes. As it became clear that there was no longer any point in waiting for the regime to act, evangelicals turned to direct action.[31] In October 1543, an English spy in Edinburgh reckoned that if a papal legate came to the town he would risk being lynched[32] – although this turned out to be wishful thinking. This aggressive mood surfaced again later that autumn, in Perth, when a large group of reformers in the town was denounced. Most of them were accused of 'using and reading of the New Testament only', and escaped punishment. However, some of the group had gone beyond mere reading. They had held 'conference and assemblies in hearing and expounding the Scripture', and had washed down their doctrine with food and drink. In particular, they had eaten a goose during the Hallowe'en fast (one of their number was a butcher). It seems this core group had also wished to make a more demonstrative commitment. Three of them had stolen an image of St Francis and hanged it, 'nailing . . . ram's horns to his head, and a cow's rump to his tail'. Worse, on All Saints' Day, the morning after their goose dinner, one of them interrupted a sermon in the parish church. A friar was speaking of purgatory when Robert Lambe leapt to his feet, waved his English Bible and demanded that the friar speak only the truth, warning that the Bible would 'bear witness against you at the great day of the Lord'. He made as if to pull the friar from the pulpit by force, but the crowd prevented him. Lambe and four others were executed. This group, it seems, had begun by meeting to discuss Scripture, but some of them had felt compelled to move on to a higher level of commitment. Lambe is said to have explained his outburst by saying that 'the work of the Lord must needs be wrought openly, for it will not lurk long'.[33] The reformers' disappointments in 1543 had provoked some of them to acts of prophetic desperation. This group were known to the town as 'Christers':[34] they had acquired a distinct and separated identity, and this, perhaps, marks the point at which we can stop using the vague language of 'evangelicals' and label these people Protestants.

Such militancy was not unique to Perth. Acts of iconoclasm and sabotage were becoming common.[35] In 1544 another image of the reformers' favourite target, St Francis, was found hanged, this time in Aberdeen; the saint was no doubt victimised as a means of insulting the hated friars who bore his name. The most dramatic act of resistance, however, was the murder of Cardinal Beaton in 1546. Beaton's assassins may not have seen their deed simply as a religious act, but it was widely interpreted as such. One of the regime's first reactions to it was a general proclamation against iconoclasm.[36] Peace with England did not bring such problems to an end. In 1551, another Perth artisan, Oliver Craigie, was fined for 'molesting' the parish church and for disrupting divine service. The following year, the provincial council and a parliament agreed in denouncing those who 'make mockery' during sermons or disrupted services, 'stopping the same to be heard and seen by the devout people'.[37] Similarly, the 1552 catechism denounced the theft or vandalism of items 'ordained to the . . . ministration of the Sacraments and service of God'. This may have been aimed principally at mere burglars. The group sentenced to death in 1556 for stealing ornaments from the parish church of Forres in Moray were probably simple criminals; likewise those who looted Cambuskenneth Abbey in 1558. The Dumfries man arrested in 1552 'for striking of a priest, and taking of the sacrament out of his hands' was also as likely to have been motivated by personal malice as by any religious zeal. However, the burning of the parish church of Echt in Aberdeenshire, in 1558–59, was apparently a genuine act of religious terrorism – nor, apparently, was it the only such church-burning.[38] One Catholic claimed that the renewal of war in 1557 provoked fresh 'contemptuous tricks' and 'open insolences'. And indeed, Protestant saboteurs were dealing in anonymous intimidation as well as violence. In October 1558, a text threatening Scottish friars with expulsion from their houses began circulating. It is likely that variant copies of this Beggars' Summons surfaced in different towns, since the one which Knox saw bore the later date of 1 January 1559. In the event, remarkably enough, its threats were carried out, but it reads more like a piece of propagandist bravado than a serious statement of intent.[39]

The most notorious acts of violence were committed in Edinburgh. In 1556, images of the Trinity, of the Virgin Mary and – again – of St Francis were removed from their places and broken into pieces, provoking a furious but apparently fruitless search for the perpetrators.[40] However, the most contentious image in the town was that of St Giles, the patron of the parish. It was carried in procession each year on 1 September, the patronal festival. Sir David Lindsay (who defended the use of images of St Francis and St Dominic) denounced the St Giles's day procession as 'great idolatry / And manifest abomination', and compared the image to the Biblical idol Bel: 'A dead image, carved of one tree / As it were holy should not honoured be.'[41] In July 1558, someone decided to take him at his word. The image was 'taken out of the High Church of Edinburgh privately in the night' and, so rumour had it, dumped in the town's North Loch. The town council and Archbishop Hamilton fell to quarrelling over who would replace it. With the festival approaching, another image of the saint was borrowed from the Franciscans. Reformist agitators decided to target this image as well, and to do so on the very day of the procession. Edinburgh's small Protestant community was openly split over this plan, but a small group of Protestant saboteurs succeeded in insinuating themselves into the procession and pulling the image down. We can credit Knox's claim that this provoked uproar, if not his claim that most of the crowd supported the iconoclasts.[42]

The Protestants' explanation for these confrontational actions was that they were provoked by intensifying persecution. According to Lord Herries, the reformers' repeated accusation against the clergy during the 1550s was

> that they laboured to keep down the Reformed Religion, by fining, banishing, and execution to the death, which they termed a persecution of the saints of God. . . . Everything that fell out was a ground for the Reformed party to take hold on, to bring themselves respect, and the authority of the other party in hatred with the commons.[43]

The reaction to Walter Myln's burning in 1558 fits this picture neatly. According to Knox, Myln's death 'did so highly offend the hearts of all godly, that immediately after his death began a new fervency amongst the hole people'. Characteristically, this showed itself in anonymous protest. A cairn was built during the night at the site of Myln's burning, and rebuilt when the clergy had it dismantled. John Foxe, who was better informed about Myln's case, claimed that there was widespread disquiet at the execution, with the Archbishop's chamberlain, the Provost of St Andrews and most of the townspeople refusing to have any part in it. 'Out of [Myln's] ashes sprang thousands of his opinion and religion in Scotland.' When the iconoclastic wave struck St Andrews in 1559, a bonfire of images from the abbey was lit at the spot where Myln had been burned the previous year.[44] This is all plausible enough, but Myln's execution was an isolated event. The mass executions in Mary Tudor's England may have alarmed some Scottish Protestants, but in Scotland itself, so far from being persecuted, they enjoyed unprecedented security.[45] It is import- ant that Protestants felt that they were at risk of persecution during the 1550s, but that has to be seen as a consequence, rather than a cause, of their growing radicalisation.

Nor can we easily ascribe rising Protestant anger to anticipation of imminent victory. Indeed, while an act of iconoclasm such as the St Giles's day riot would horrify the religious establishment, it is striking that it took place in Edinburgh, which, by contrast with Perth and Dundee, was a Catholic stronghold. Terrorist acts of this kind were shocking and provocative, but ultimately more a sign of weakness than of strength. This is a militancy tinged with desperation, which rarely emerged from its hiding place except to commit acts of anonymous sabotage. In Edinburgh, as in Perth, the militants were not acting on behalf of disciplined, organised Reformed congregations, but were reckless provocateurs set apart from quietist majorities. The Prot- estant cadres were no doubt trying to force the pace of change, but it is not clear that such actions won them more than notoriety. Iconoclasm was a way for committed reformers to scratch their itchy religious activism. It was not likely to win converts.

THE RADICALISATION OF REFORM

Can Scottish Protestantism's rising mood of militancy be taken as a sign of deepening reformist commitment, separation from the old Church and forma- tion of definably Protestant congregations?[46] The evidence is inconclusive. There is one – but only one – documented example of a formally organised Protestant 'privy kirk' in the 1550s, in Edinburgh. If there were 'privy kirks' in towns such as Perth, they were, as Mary Verschuur has observed, 'very private'.[47] However, enough fragments of evidence survive for some patterns to emerge.

We have clear evidence of several organised, public Scottish Protestant congregations before 1560 – but not in Scotland. The role of exiles in the Scottish Reformation is often overlooked, perhaps because, as Knox observed regretfully, most of the first generation of exiles never returned home. Clare Kellar has recently pointed out that the Anglophone exile congregations estab- lished on the Continent in the 1550s were not simply 'English' churches. About a tenth of the exiles at Geneva and at Emden were Scots; Knox in Geneva, and John Rough and John Willock in Emden, were amongst their leaders. The

Scots were well integrated into these exile communities, persuading some of their English brethren to take Scotland's plight seriously.[48] These were not the only communities of Scottish reformist exiles, however. Less well documented, but no less important, were the Scots at the French court after the young Queen of Scots was taken to France in 1548. These were fertile years for French Protestantism, and some Scots were caught up in this. In 1551, the English ambassador Sir John Mason claimed that he had been openly using the English Prayer Book service at the French court – including the Eucharist – and that both French and Scots had joined him Sunday by Sunday.[49] Some of these Scots were perhaps predisposed to more radical views, for not all of them were in France by choice. Several of the 'castilians' captured at St Andrews in 1547 remained in French royal service. Norman Leslie, the Master of Rothes, was the leader of Cardinal Beaton's assassins, and his Protestantism is well attested. After his release, he entered French service and remained so until he was killed at the battle of Renti in 1554.[50] The French also inherited the hostages the castilians had held, in particular James Hamilton, the son of Governor Arran, who was himself known as Earl of Arran after his father's promotion to the dukedom of Châtelherault. Young Arran was converted to a passionate Protestantism during his decade in a gilded French cage, and so were some of his entourage. He was made captain of the French King's Scots guards in 1551. Soon afterwards, one of the guardsmen, Robert Norvell, was imprisoned in the Bastille for over four years 'for God's word'. Norvell had been denounced by another guardsman.[51] The Protestantism of this circle may have been less clearly established than that of Geneva, but young Arran's critical role in Scotland in 1559–60 means that France has to be recognised as one of the cradles of Scottish Protestantism.

We know of one other set of Scottish evangelical exiles: not so influential but certainly numerically stronger. During the reign of Edward VI, several self-governing 'stranger' churches were established in London and elsewhere in the south-east of England for Protestant exiles from France, the Netherlands and elsewhere.[52] There were no formally constituted Scottish exile congregations, but there were informal networks of Scottish exiles in London, and something very like a Scottish 'stranger' church did take shape in the north-east, first in Berwick-upon-Tweed and then in Newcastle-upon-Tyne. Berwick was self-consciously a Scottish town under English rule, and had indeed been firmly in English hands for less than seventy years. During the wars of the 1540s it filled with Scottish exiles, many of them Protestants. Newcastle, too, was filled with Scottish exiles. The first minister to these congregations was John Rough, followed in 1549 by his old associate John Knox, recently released from French custody. The Duke of Northumberland believed that it was Knox's reputation which had drawn so many Scots to Newcastle. Knox was beneficed in the Church of England, but he had little interest in conforming to its rites. He used the remoteness of his posting, and the effective absence of episcopal oversight in the diocese of Durham, to discard the authorised Book of Common Prayer in favour of a Eucharistic liturgy he wrote himself. This was, he boasted, 'not as man had devised, neither as the King's proceedings did allow, but as Christ Jesus did institute'. A near-contemporaneous copy of this liturgy shows it to be thoroughly Reformed in flavour, heavy with Scripture and light with almost everything else, and with communion received seated. This skeletal structure was fleshed out with long extemporary prayers. In later years, Knox fondly remembered his preaching in both towns. It had been, he recalled, vehement and politically controversial. Even in 1558–59, after Elizabeth I's restoration of Protestantism in England, Knox was keen to restart this exile ministry; it was eventually taken up by another Scottish Protestant, John McBrair.[33] The fate of these exiles during the reign of Mary Tudor is frustratingly shadowy. Some at least returned to Scotland, made significantly safer than England by Mary of Guise's non-confrontational policies towards heresy. In any case, it is clear that these are the first groups which can be called Scottish Protestant congregations.

How important these exile congregations were for their brethren at home is another matter. Exiles are eye-catching, but their influence is easy to overestimate. Young Arran's entourage did not make an impact in Scotland itself until 1559–60. The Genevans were publishing works aimed wholly or partly at a Scottish readership, as Scottish exiles had been doing since the 1530s; but the scale of production was small and the logistical challenge involved in transporting books from the Alps to Scotland considerable. There is no direct evidence of any of these books actually reaching in Scotland during the 1550s, while we know that the works of David Lindsay, for example, were widely read. The most important contribution which the exiles could make to Scottish Protestantism was in the field of preaching. Preachers could take refuge in the safety of exile; during their travels, they could draw from the wellsprings of European Protestantism, and return to share what they had learned. And if organised congregations in Scottish Protestantism were rare, there was preaching aplenty.

The brief official sponsorship of evangelical preaching during 1543 was followed by a longer period when the chaos of war and the weakness of the regime made possible some public preaching in defiance of the Church. The most spectacular such defiance was that which followed on Cardinal Beaton's assassination and the garrisoning of St Andrews castle; for a time in early 1547, Rough and Knox were able to preach in the city and beyond it.[54] The most influential preacher of the 1540s, however, was the man whom the 'castilians' claimed to be avenging, George Wishart. Wishart was a returned exile: he had spent several years in England and there is a good chance he had visited Switzerland. His ministry in Angus, Ayrshire and Lothian in 1544 and 1545 was powerful, but also unstructured. He neither preached to gathered Protestant congregations nor, apparently, encouraged them to form. As he put it, 'I taught openly, and in no corners'. Others did not remember it in quite that way, but what we know of his ministry was relentlessly public. He preached in churches, but also in the open air, when the Scottish summer made it possible. He was supported not by his hearers but by noble and lairdly protectors, who were ready (sometimes too ready) to confront his opponents on his behalf, and who took responsibility for conveying him safely from place to place.[55]

This pattern – itinerant preaching, usually under the protection of the powerful – persisted after Wishart's death. In 1547 John Rough did not restrict himself to the dubious safety of St Andrews castle, but travelled through the country, preaching as he went. His protectors eventually decided to smuggle him over the border to Carlisle.[56] Walter Myln preached not only in fields, but 'on the sea also sailing in ship', where noble protection was unnecessary. He may not have been the only reformer to take advantage of the enforced and isolated fellowship of shipboard life. David Calderwood preserved a tale of a ship's company who, when blown off course in 1546, passed the time by staging a trial of Cardinal Beaton in absentia, and burning him in effigy.[57] However, it was only noble patronage that could give such preachers the scope to be genuinely dangerous. In the early 1550s John McBrair's preaching in the diocese of Glasgow was causing alarm; he was being protected by Lord Ochiltree. In 1553 five young lairds, aided by the Sheriff of Teviotdale, brought the preacher Robert Achesoun to Kelso in the Borders for a sermon at sunrise one Friday.[58]

The clandestine nature of that meeting, however, is a sign that the times were changing. If the open-air sermon was the medium of choice in the 1540s, in the 1550s reformers addressed gathered congregations meeting behind closed doors, usually the doors of a friendly laird. This may reflect a shift towards more radical doctrines: a progress from mass appeals to the interested towards cells of committed radicals. More likely, however, it was a function of the more settled politics of the 1550s. Both ecclesiastical and secular authorities were able to exercise far more control than during the chaos of the English wars. (Intriguingly, there was a further burst of public reformist preaching in 1557, when the war with England was briefly renewed.[59]) If the authorities avoided open confrontation with Protestants during this period, the reformers returned the compliment. Preaching in private houses was normally tolerated, and on the whole it was to this that reformers confined themselves. Even so, their safety was not assured. When the old Earl of Argyll's support for his Protestant chaplain, John Douglas, became too public, Archbishop Hamilton tried to intervene.[60] Argyll was powerful enough to defend Douglas, but others were more vulnerable. William Harlow was an Edinburgh tailor who had returned from English exile in 1555. In 1558 he preached in a house in Dumfries, under the protection of a local laird, Alexander Stewart of Garlies. Word spread rapidly. Later the same day, Harlow was hauled before an official of the Dean of Nithsdale for his presumption, and his doctrine was denounced from the pulpit of the parish church.[61]

Scrapes like these make it unsurprising that for most of the 1550s, both preachers and patrons preferred to keep their activities discreet. In late 1550s Edinburgh, John Willock was protected by a group of nobles headed by Lord Seton. Knox wrote that they 'kept their conventions, and held councils with such gravity and closeness, that the enemies trembled', but such careful privacy is more obviously testament to their own fears. The Earl of Argyll claimed that 'divers houses in Scotland by us' also maintained their Protestantism 'secretly'. These included some of the most energetic supporters of Protestantism. Argyll's kinsman Robert Campbell of Kinzeancleuch, an Ayrshire laird and indefatigable Protestant factotum, hosted itinerant ministers in his household so that 'privately in his lodging, / He had both prayers and preaching'. Amongst these was Knox, who would become Campbell's life-long friend.[62] Throughout Knox's tour of Scotland in 1555–56 he was under the close protection of sympathetic lairds such as Campbell and John Erskine of Dun. At times during this visit, Knox 'taught commonly' before substantial audiences in Edinburgh and in Ayr, but even this was behind closed doors. His more normal practice, however, seems to have been to 'exhort secretly'. When he celebrated a Reformed Eucharist, that was certainly done in the utmost privacy. As Kellar has observed, there is a striking contrast between Wishart's mass preaching of 1544–45, and Knox's secrecy a decade later.[63] Privacy not only restricted the audience for preaching, but changed its nature. Knox's later hint that formal congregations were emerging in 1555–56 is belied by his own correspondence from the time. These meetings seem to have been little more than reading groups, whose literary diet included 'profane authors' alongside the Bible and evangelical theology. Adam Wallace, burned in 1550, denied that he had ever preached, but confessed to having given 'exhortation' to his fellow-reformers in 'privy places'.[64] Gathering around a laird's hearth in secretive groups eroded the distinction between preaching and discussion, and even between a minister and his flock. So far from forming into distinctive congregations, during the mid-1550s Protestantism's social shape was still fluid and informal.

Knox and his allies were keen to change this. Although he may have overemphasised his achievement in 1555–56, there is no mistaking his ambition. He insisted that Protestants should separate themselves scrupulously from the Catholic Church, and in particular that they should not tolerate the Mass.[65] He seems, however, to have been fighting an uphill battle on this point. In August 1556, after leaving Scotland, he wrote to an Edinburgh reformer, urging her to maintain what he feared was a lonely purity. Siren voices were luring her to return to the old Church for the sake of companionship, 'for avoiding danger', and for fear of tempting God through excessive scrupulosity. These voices, to Knox, were 'sweet songs of the Devil, to bring your soul asleep'. He had the same message for other Edinburgh correspondents: 'If any would persuade you that . . . we may do in external things as the blind of the world doth, believe them not.' He justified this view at length, evidently believing that his views were a long way from being an accepted orthodoxy. His specific concern that reformers should dissociate themselves from Catholic worship was matched with a general (and characteristically Calvinist) insistence that God's people should be visibly separated from the reprobate. He even advised Edinburgh's Protestant ladies on seemly clothing, fearing lest God's people appear 'more like to courtesans than to grave matrons'.[66] He may have hoped that the sheep had begun to be divided from the goats, but he had no illusions that much progress had yet been made.

Matters may have moved in Knox's direction over the next few years. We know that Knox's preaching on this trip won converts; and at least one of his associates, Robert Campbell of Kinzeancleuch, was afterwards leading his neighbours in discussing 'how orderly they might suppress / In their own bounds that idol, Mass'. By early 1559, the Dean and Chapter of Aberdeen were worried that significant numbers were deliberately absenting themselves from church, and urged that such people should be investigated for heresy. The general provincial council which met that spring heard worries that heretical gatherings were not only celebrating the Eucharist, but also conducting baptisms and solemnising marriages – cutting the last sacramental ties with the established Church. (These worries also underline the limits to Knox's personal influence, for the council named five heretical teachers behind this separatist movement, and Knox was not among them.)[67] Similar problems are implied by a lawsuit brought in 1558 by John Ross of Cragy, who owned the rights to the teinds of Perth's parish church. He claimed that 'all and sundry parishioners of the parish church of Perth' had refused to pay, despite the threat of excommunication. He was no doubt exaggerating, but this suggests something larger than a mere teind dispute – a large-scale withdrawal from the life of the old Church.[68] Withdrawal of this kind remained a minority activity even amongst committed Protestants, but some kind of separation had begun.

The clearest part of this process is theological. Scottish Protestantism began as a broadly Lutheran movement during the reign of James V, but had unmistakably become a Reformed (or 'Calvinist') one by 1560.[69] This shift is sometimes seen as a natural process of development, although there was no reason why it should have been automatic. Nor is the process entirely clear-cut. The simplest litmus test of Reformation-era theologies is the denial of

Christ's real, objective presence in the bread and wine of the Eucharist. Briefly, Catholics and Lutherans agree that Christ's body and blood are physically present, but disagree vehemently about the mode of that presence: Catholics believing that the bread and wine are entirely transformed into the substance of Christ (transubstantiation), while Lutherans see Christ's body as present together with the elements (a view sometimes, misleadingly, labelled 'consubstantiation'). Most Reformed theologies, however, argue that Christ is not physically present at all, but is present spiritually, in the believer. Confusingly for modern readers, the proponents of this radical view were known to their opponents as 'sacramentaries'.

Using this yardstick, the rise of Reformed views is unmistakable. The parliament of 1541 worried about unspecified heresies against the sacrament, but the first direct evidence of the more radical view surfaces in 1543, when the lords of the council worried that 'divers and sundry persons, our sovereign lady's lieges, are sacramentaries'.[70] During the mid-1540s, several Scottish reformers were vague – or coy – about these radical doctrines. Henry Balnaves' denunciation of the Mass in a treatise of 1548 was directed principally at the alleged abuses of votive Masses for the dead, not at the core Catholic doctrines. George Wishart may himself have visited Switzerland, and he produced a translation of the Reformed Helvetic Confession, but he avoided Eucharistic controversies in his preaching. His most controversial statement was the claim that Jews and heathens mocked Christians for worshipping 'a piece of bread baked upon the ashes' – a view which he denied holding himself. At his trial he was happy to use the term 'sacrament of the altar', loaded as it was with traditional assumptions. Yet he may have celebrated a distinctly irregular Eucharist on the morning of his execution.[71]

From the late 1540s on, however, matters are clearer. Catholic observers discerned a shift. A petition from the clergy to Governor Arran in 1547 observed that Scotland had previously been infected with the 'pestilentious heresies of Luther', but that because these had gone unpunished, 'divers of them are become sacramentaries, and specially against the blessed sacrament of the altar'. In the same year Knox preached in St Andrews that the Mass was 'abominable idolatry'. Significantly, by this point England's Protestant establishment had also shifted decisively towards Reformed views. The next Scot to face death as a heretic, Adam Wallace in 1550, affirmed at his trial that Christ's body could not be in two places at once, and admitted that he believed the sacrament to be 'but bread sown of corn'. It was, as the Bishop of Orkney said, 'a horrible heresy' – to Catholics, and also to Lutherans. It also seems, from this point on, to have become Scottish Protestantism's orthodoxy. In 1558 the Catholic controversialist Quintin Kennedy certainly saw it as such. The evangelical Scottish guardsman in France, Robert Norvell, wrote or translated a ballad in which Christ was made to say:

> This flesh ye see, ye shall not eat;
> Nor drink the blood, shed forth of me,
> My Sacrament, is drink and meat,
> That feeds, the inward man truly,
> Not for thy teeth, nor thy belly:
> I am no meat material.
> Believe, and thou hast eaten me,
> The flesh profits nothing at all.

Likewise, Walter Myln openly mocked the Mass at his trial in 1558, declaring that the sacrament was 'not to be taken carnally but spiritually'.[72]

Scottish Protestantism, then, was becoming theologically more defined and socially more distinct. Once again, however, we cannot interpret this simply as a rising tide of reformist militancy which crested in 1559–60. Such an interpretation does not do justice to the real diversity, and the real divisions, which remained within the Protestant movement.

If a process of theological consolidation and social separation was at work in Scottish Protestantism in the late 1550s, it was not unchallenged. Knox worried in 1557 that 'the winds of unstable and ill-advised opinions' were blowing on his flock. Some Protestants were as unwilling to tarry for the minister as for the magistrate. In the absence of ministers who had been 'called' in the fashion of which Reformed theologians approved, they allowed their noble protectors to preside at celebrations of the sacraments. Some apparently ministered the Eucharist to one another, without anyone acting as president.[73] There may have been divisions over questions of theology as well as of church order. John Borthwick, a Scottish reformer exiled in 1540 who was one of Knox and Foxe's heroes, tempered his undoubted Protestantism with a keen interest in astrology. In 1545 he claimed to have used his 'astrolok' to discern the future course of international affairs. Worse, in 1554 he arrived in Geneva declaring that he had received a personal revelation from God by which all Europe's Protestant churches could be united. These are not the sorts of things which good Reformed Protestants ought to have been saying. The general provincial council which met in 1549 believed that the heresies which were being preached in Scotland included such idiosyncratic beliefs as the claim that souls 'slept' from death until the Last Judgement and, even, the outright denial of immortality. Knox feared that Scotland had been infected by the heresy of the English 'Freewillers', who denied predestination in such a way as to unravel the entire Protestant doctrine of salvation.[74]

Perhaps more important than these radical and dissident currents is a strong sense of Protestant reluctance to burn their bridges with the old Church. Sanderson's survey of sixteenth-century wills detects a noticeable minority of post-1560 wills (87 from a sample of 669, or 13 per cent) which contained decisively Protestant statements of faith; none at all of the 605 wills which survive from the period 1539–58 contain such statements. This suggests that self-conscious separatist Protestant identity before 1560 was either very rare, or not yet sufficiently assertive to wish to make such statements of faith – or both.[75] We know of plenty of evangelical Scots clergy who worked to reform the old Church from within.[76] This approach was quite incompatible with Knox's radical separatism, but it remained a force within Scottish Protestantism even during 1559–60. Some at least of the congregations formed during the civil war initially used the English Prayer Book of 1549 (much more widely circulated in Scotland than its more radical successor of 1552). Knox's abhorrence even of a bowdlerised version of the 1552 book helped to split the exile congregation in Frankfurt in 1554–55; he can hardly have been reassured to find the earlier text being used in Scotland on his return there.[77] However, his purist position was not an accepted orthodoxy. During 1559 Knox's rigorist views on questions such as who should be admitted to baptism, and on what to do with the clergy of the old Church, were seen as extreme and impractical by his fellow reformers. He appealed to Calvin for support, only to find (as he had over female monarchy) that even Calvin had a streak of pragmatism which he himself lacked.[78]

In 1560 Knox ran into similar difficulties over the Book of Discipline. This was a blueprint for the structure and administration of the new Church, drawn up by a committee of six, including Knox. They were an eclectic group, but were perhaps oddly representative of Scottish Protestantism as a whole: two returned exiles, one former conformist, and three new converts. John Willock, recently returned from exile in Emden, was Knox's equal as a theologian, if not as a preacher, but his views were more those of Zurich than of Geneva. John Spottiswoode was an evangelical convert of long standing, but he had conformed outwardly, holding a benefice in the old Church until 1559 under the patronage of the reformist laird of Calder. John Winram, John Row and John Douglas were all newcomers to the Reformed faith, having made the jump only in 1559. All were also associates of Archbishop Hamilton. Winram had been a lively Catholic reformer. Row was an ecclesiastical lawyer who had spent most of the 1550s in Rome as Hamilton's agent. Douglas had been the principal of St Mary's College at St Andrews since 1547, and Rector of the university since 1552; Hamilton had, apparently, been impressed by his humanist scholarship. The sincerity of these three late converts is undoubted, but we might expect them to be less willing to anathematise the old Church than was Knox. And indeed, Spottiswoode's son, the historian and Archbishop, wrote that 'divers' of the committee wished for 'the retaining of the ancient policy [church order], and to purge it from corruptions and abuses only . . . forasmuch as they were not to make up a new Church, but only to reform it'. In other words, they wished to use the Reformation as a continuation of the Catholic reform programme by other means. Knox and Willock won through with some difficulty. Winram did, however, succeed in toning down the 'austerity' of a first draft of the Confession of Faith, later that summer.[79] Knox's vision of the Church was not the only contender within the Protestant movement before, or during, 1559–60. Its eventual (and partial) success should not be allowed to give it an air of inevitability.

More importantly, the eventual success of a radical, separatist version of Protestantism in Scotland cannot be ascribed to its radical doctrines or separatist structures. If congregations were forming in Scotland in the late 1550s, their dominant feature was not the new one of withdrawal from the old Church, but the old one of noble and lairdly patronage. Even in the burghs, any 'privy kirks' met under the protection of friendly magnates.[80] Evangelical preachers and Protestant ministers had depended on such patronage since the reign of James V, and they continued to do so. The crisis of 1559–60 was not precipitated by a mass movement which Protestant ministers built. It was made possible by reformist Catholicism and by dynastic politics; and it was driven by a curious and potent alliance between the ministers and the Protestant nobility. The Scottish Protestant underground were not the makers of the revolution of 1559–60: merely its heirs.

NOTES

1 Patrick, *Statutes*, 143.

2 On the paradigm of the 'privy kirks' and its plausibility, see Alec Ryrie, 'Clubs, congregations and the nature of early Protestantism in Scotland', *Past and Present* (forthcoming, 2006).

3 Knox wrote in December 1556 that 'the most perfect school of Christ that ever was in the earth since the days of the Apostles' could be found in Geneva; although he did not, as is often suggested, apply this description to the city as a whole. Knox, IV, 240.

4 Andrew Pettegree, 'Nicodemism and the English Reformation' in his *Marian Protestantism: Six Studies* (Aldershot, 1996).

5 Cf. Alec Ryrie, 'Counting sheep, counting shepherds: the problem of allegiance in the English Reformation' in Peter Marshall and Alec Ryrie (eds), *The Beginnings of English Protestantism* (Cambridge, 2002), 106–9.

6 Herries, *Historical Memoirs*, 14, 26; Leslie, *Historie*, II, 382–3.

7 Patrick, *Statutes*, 150; Pollen, *Papal Negotiations*, 20.

8 Knox, I, 136–8; III, 506; NA SP 50/2 fo. 77r (*CSP Scotland*, 73.1); and see above, ch. 1.

9 Robinson, *Original Letters*, 434–5.

10 NA SP 52/1 fo. 231r (*CSP Scotland*, 554).

11 Knox, IV, 217.

12 Ian B. Cowan, *Regional Aspects of the Scottish Reformation* (London, 1978).

13 *HP*, II, Appendix 39; *Wodrow Misc.*, 54. As Cowan notes, the claim that Lothian was a centre of Protestantism is dubious. Cowan, *Regional Aspects*, 20.

14 NA SP 50/2 fo. 78r (*CSP Scotland*, 74).

15 Knox, I, 250; Charles Rogers (ed.), *Rental Book of the Cistercian Abbey of Cupar-Angus*, 2 vols (London, 1879–80), II, xxiii–xxiv.

16 Knox, *Works*, I, 300; VI, 22; Flett, 'Conflict of the Reformation and democracy', 68.

17 Pryde, *Ayr Burgh Accounts*, 33, 128.

18 Knox, I, 105; Cosmo Innes (ed.), *Registrum Episcopatus Glasguensis*, 2 vols (Edinburgh, 1843), II, 583.

19 Margaret H. B. Sanderson, *A Kindly Place? Living in Sixteenth-Century Scotland* (East Linton, 2002), 155–65; see above, ch. 5.

20 See above, 65–6, 78–9.

21 Calderwood, *History*, I, 128; Knox, I, 101; *AM*, 1272–3.

22 W. Stanford Reid, 'The battle hymns of the Lord: Calvinist psalmody of the sixteenth century', *Sixteenth Century Essays and Studies*, 2 (1971), 36–54.

23 *AM*, 1273; Aitken, *Trial of George Buchanan*, xxv.

24 Knox, I, 139, 246–7.

25 Alexander F. (ed.), *A Compendious Book of Godly and Spiritual Songs, Commonly Known as 'The Gude and Godlie Ballatis'* (Scottish Text Society 39: Edinburgh, 1897), xiv–xvi, xxxii–xl, xliii–lii.

26 In 1548–49, Henry Balnaves cited the Psalms using the old Vulgate numbering, followed in the Great Bible; so did a group of Perth craftsmen in 1557, and the version of Psalm 127 (Vulgate 128) which they quoted was taken from the Great Bible. Knox, III, 439, 441; Perth Museum and Art Gallery, Original Papers of the Convener Court of Perth 1365–1717 no. 30.

27 Row, *History*, 6.

28 NAS CS7/1 fo. 368r (*ALC*, 527).

29 *AM*, 1274; *APS*, 488–9; J. D. Marwick, *Extracts from the Records of the Burgh of Edinburgh AD 1403–1589*, 4 vols (Edinburgh, 1869–82), II, 252.

30 Knox, I, 261; *Wodrow Misc.*, 58–9.

31 On which see above, p. 66.

32 *HP*, II, 65.

33 Calderwood, *History*, I, 171–5; Perth Museum and Art Gallery, Original Papers of the Convener Court of Perth 1365–1717 no. 34 fo. iv.

34 Calderwood, *History*, I, 175.

35 Kirk, 'Iconoclasm and reform', 378–9.

36 *Extracts from the Council Register of Aberdeen*, 211; *RPC*, 28–9; and see above, 18–19, 65–7.

37 Verschuur, 'Perth and the Reformation', 386; *APS*, 485; Patrick, *Statutes*, 139, 168.

38 Hamilton, *Catechisme*, fo. 58v; NAS JC1/9, sub. 7 December 1556 (Pitcairn, *Ancient Criminal Trials*, I, 393–4); *TA*, X, 111, 402–3; *Registrum Episcopatus Aberdonensis*, lxiv.

39 Knox, I, 320–1; *Wodrow Misc.*, 57–8; James Maitland, *Maitland's Narrative of the Principal Acts of the Regency During the Minority*, ed. W. S. Fitch (Ipswich, 1842), 14. Mary Verschuur's suggestion that the 'Beggars' Summons' was local to Perth is unlikely, given the second reference to it, but the discrepancy in dating may suggest that Knox was using a Perth or Dundee variant of the text. Verschuur, 'Perth and the Reformation', 452; cf. Foggie, *Renaissance Religion*, 48–9.

40 *Extracts from the Records of Edinburgh*, II, 251–2.

41 Lindsay, *Works*: 'Ane dialog betuix experience and Ane courteour', lines 2501–2, 2508, 2520–1, 2533–6.

42 *Wodrow Misc.*, 54–5; Knox, I, 256, 258–60; Leslie, *Historie*, II, 382–3; Murray, 'Excommunication of Edinburgh town council', 24–34.

43 Herries, *Historical Memoirs*, 26.

44 Knox, I, 308; AM, 1274–5; *Wodrow Misc.*, 60.

45 See above, ch. 5.

46 As argued by Kirk, *Patterns of Reform*, xi–xv, 1–15.

47 Verschuur, 'Perth and the Reformation', 400. On the Edinburgh privy kirk, see Calderwood, *History*, I, 303–4; Knox, I, 298–300; II, 151; Lynch, *Edinburgh*, 84–6; Michael Lynch, 'From privy kirk to burgh kirk: an alternative view of the process of Protestantisation' in Norman MacDougall (ed.), *Church, Politics and Society: Scotland 1408–1929* (Edinburgh, 1983), 86–7, 93.

48 Knox, I, 56; Kellar, *Scotland, England and the Reformation*, 155–83.

49 Knighton, *Calendar of State Papers Domestic . . . Edward VI*, 289.

50 RSS, III, 820; Knox, I, 225–6; APS, 467; Sanderson, *Cardinal of Scotland*, 278.

51 Robert Norvell, *The Meroure of a Chrstiane* [sic] (RSTC 18688: Edinburgh, 1561), fos 3r, 4r, 62v; John Durkan, 'James, third earl of Arran: the hidden years', *SHR*, 65 (1986), 154–66; Herries, *Historical Memoirs*, 27.

52 Andrew Pettegree, *Foreign Protestant Communities in Sixteenth-Century London* (Oxford, 1986).

53 Robinson, *Original Letters*, 434–5; Peter Lorimer, *John Knox and the Church of England* (London, 1875), 261, 290–2; Knox, III, 103, 167; V, 480, 490; VI, 20; Knighton, *Calendar of State Papers Domestic . . . Edward VI*, 747; Durkan, 'Scottish "Evangelicals"', 153; Kellar, *Scotland, England and the Reformation*, 117–18; Durkan, 'Heresy in Scotland', 328–9.

54 See above, 73, 77.

55 Knox, I, 125–9, 134–8. Lord Herries alleged that for 'some time' before the beginning of his public ministry, Wishart taught in 'private conventions'. Herries, *Historical Memoirs*, 15.

56 *CSP Scotland*, 48.

57 AM, 1275; Calderwood, *History*, I, 143.

58 *Liber Officialis Sancti Andree: Curie Metropolitane Sancti Andree in Scotia sententiarum in causis consistorialibus que extant* (Edinburgh, 1845), 167; Andrew Agnew, *The Hereditary Sheriffs of Galloway* (Edinburgh, 1893), 375; Cameron, *Scottish Correspondence*, 368.

59 Knox, I, 256; Leslie, *Historie*, II, 382–3.

60 Knox, I, 276–9, 282–9.

61 Keith, *History of the Affairs of Church and State*, I, 495–6.

62 Knox, I, 185, 237, 256, 276, 289; Charles Rogers (ed.), *Three Scottish Reformers* (London, 1874), 107.

63 Kellar, *Scotland, England and the Reformation*, 152.

64 Knox, I, 238, 245–54; IV, 135–9. On Knox's 1555–56 visit, see also Ryrie, 'Clubs, congregations'.

65 Knox, I, 247–9.

66 Knox, IV, 95, 223–4, 225–6, 230–6, 239–40.

67 Sanderson, *A Kindly Place?*, 171; Rogers, *Three Scottish Reformers*, 107; *Registrum Episcopatus Aberdonensis*, lxii–lxiii; Patrick, *Statutes*, 159–60, 186–7.

68 NAS CS 7/18 fos 165v–166r; Verschuur, 'Perth and the Reformation', 444.

69 On Scottish Lutheranism, see above, 29–36.

70 *APS*, 370; *ALC*, 528.

71 Knox, III, 519; *AM*, 1269–70; Dotterweich, 'Emergence of evangelical theology', 272–81; Lindsay of Pitscottie, *Historie*, II, 77–8.

72 *RPC*, 63; Knox, I, 194; *AM*, 1272, 1275; Kennedy, *Two Eucharistic Tracts*, 111–47; Norvell, *The Meroure*, 46r.

73 Knox, II, 253; IV, 274; Alexander Peterkin (ed.), *The Booke of the Universall Kirk of Scotland* (Edinburgh, 1839), 5; Ninian Winzet, *Certane Tractatis for Reformatioun of Doctryne and Maneris, Set Furth at the Desyre, and in ye Name of ye Afflictit Catholikis* (RSTC 25860: Edinburgh, 1562), sig. Civ. On dissident strands within early Scottish reformism, see Ryrie, 'Clubs, congregations.'

74 NA SP 1/204 fo. 81v (*LP*, XX(i), 1240); Durkan, 'Heresy in Scotland', 336; Patrick, *Statutes*, 126; Knox, IV, 637–71; Thomas Freeman, 'Dissenters from a dissenting church: the challenge of the Freewillers 1550–1558' in Peter Marshall and Alec Ryrie (eds), *The Beginnings of English Protestantism* (Cambridge, 2002), 129–56.

75 Sanderson, *A Kindly Place?*, 155–73, esp. 166.

76 For example, see Calderwood, *History*, I, 127; *Miscellany of the Spalding Club*, IV, 120–1.

77 On English liturgies in Scotland, see NA SP 52/2 no. 11 (*CSP Scotland*, 616); Knox, VI, 34; Ryrie, 'Clubs, congregations'.

78 Knox, VI, 75–7, 96–7.

79 Keith, *History of the Affairs of Church and State*, III, 15; Duncan Shaw, 'John Willock', in his *Reform and Revolution* (Edinburgh, 1967), 42–69; *ODNB*; Dunbar, *Reforming the Scottish Church*; Row, *History*, vii–x; Cameron, 'St Mary's College'; Cameron, '"Catholic Reform"', 115; NA SP 52/5 fo. 71r (*CSP Scotland*, 902).

80 Calderwood, *History*, I, 303–4.

Chapter 7

1557–59: the makings of a rebellion

As far as we know, no-one in 1550s Scotland was expecting a religious civil war. The revolt of May 1559 seemed to come from a clear sky. Before then, Scotland's few radical Protestants were angry but also impotent. The religious mood of most of the country during the preceding decade had been calm and inclined to compromise. Even in the early months of 1559, few observers of Scottish affairs showed signs of suspecting that a religious revolt was imminent. The new and shaky English regime of Elizabeth I was keen to destabilise Scotland if possible, but had no great optimism on this score. John Aylmer, the future Bishop of London, writing in the spring of 1559, hoped wistfully that the Scots might come to rue their French alliance, but he actually expected them to invade England rather than turn against France. 'The piddling Scots ... are always French for their lives', he wrote shrewishly, showing no signs of believing that the Scots might ever be anything other than 'pricks and thorns in our sides'.[1] Others close to the regime in London were hoping to kindle faction and religious division in Scotland, but with little hope that such divisions already existed. In January 1559, Sir Henry Percy met the Duke of Châtelherault on the Border. He sounded out this most malleable of Scottish lords on the possibility of an English alliance. Châtelherault agreed that many Scots favoured the Gospel, and claimed that he personally would prefer an English to a French alliance, but insisted that nothing could be done. All he could promise was that, in the event of renewed Anglo-French war, some Scots would drag their feet and give intelligence to the English. England had heard promises like this before.[2] If Châtelherault did not anticipate the rebellion, neither did John Knox. Judging from his correspondence, as late as April 1559, his primary concern was with English affairs. While he believed that Scotland 'now beginneth to thirst for Christ's truth', his main priority was to visit England, and in particular his 'poor and dispersed flock' in Northumberland.[3] He returned to Scotland when he did, not because he intended to lead a revolution, but because he was not welcome at his preferred destination, England.

Even when the rebellion had started, observers and participants were slow to recognise the magnitude of the events. John Jewel, soon to be Bishop of Salisbury, wrote in May 1559 that there had been 'some disturbances, I know not of what kind, respecting matters of religion'. He was interested, but did not expect riot to become revolution.[4] The English lieutenants along the Border took a closer interest, but they, too, only slowly realised what was happening. Sir James Croft expected the stirs to be settled within a few days, and the Earl of Northumberland was for a time convinced that an agreement had been reached. Sir Henry Percy, a Borderer of old, was uneasy even at the end of June, when he heard that the Congregation were planning to march on Edinburgh. He still found it natural to treat a Scottish army that close to the Border as hostile, although he admitted that in this case it seemed unlikely.[5] If the English were disorientated, so too were the Scots. Mary of Guise herself seems to have been wholly surprised by the violence and determination of the Congregation's resistance, nor were the Congregation themselves following any kind of predetermined plan. The storm blew up from clouds no bigger than a man's hand, and took a course which none of the participants could have predicted.

When it eventually came, the rebellion was a rising both against the Catholic establishment and against perceived French oppression. If a religious revolt was unexpected, perhaps anti-French feeling was more apparent. It has often been suggested that the 1559–60 war was as much about nationalism as religion.[6] This argument has recently come under trenchant attack from Pamela Ritchie, whose account of Scottish politics in the 1550s emphasises the popularity of the French in general and of Mary of Guise in particular.[7] The point deserves further examination. The Franco-Scottish 'Auld Alliance' had deep roots, as did the Anglo-Scottish enmity from which the Scots had suffered so grievously in the 1540s. Was there real hostility between France and Scotland by 1559? If so, how had it come about, and how did it feed into the rebellion?

Anglophile Scots and English imperialists had long argued that the French alliance was a one-sided relationship in which the stronger ally exploited the weaker. In the 1540s the English polemicist Nicholas Bodrugan deplored the alliance as a 'bloody league' which led to Scotland's being laid waste and the Scots slaughtered as cannon fodder for the French. His colleague William Patten warned the Scots against 'the feigned friendship of France . . . that for a few crowns do but stay you still in store for their own purpose'. Some Scots agreed. John Eldar hoped to see France plucked from Scotland's heart. James

Harryson described the French as 'indeed our ancient enemies': 'For what other thing do we but serve them for their money, to our own utter destruction, to the spilling of our own blood, to the burning of our towns, and to the waste and spoil of our whole native country? And at this, do the Frenchmen laugh; they take pleasure, sitting at home in security.' He described the French alliance as an 'iron hook, that hath caught and killed afore now, the most part of our ancestors . . . while the French lose not a man, but a few golden crowns'. Eldar and Harryson, of course, were simply earning their 'golden crowns' from another foreign source, but their argument had real force. Some English writers struck particularly close to the mark. Edward Seymour's 1548 *Epistle* foresaw that Scotland risked becoming 'the camp and plain, betwixt [England and France] to fight on'. He also warned that if foreign help was sought against an invader, the cure could be worse than the disease: when the Hungarians had called on Turkish military help against the Habsburgs, they had effectively mortgaged their kingdom to their saviours. This was an uncomfortably precise description of France's role in Scotland after 1548.[8]

The Franco-Scottish alliance had survived for two and a half centuries despite its inequality. Scotland's role in tipping the balance of the Hundred Years' War in France's favour, and the physical distance between the two kingdoms, had ensured that Scotland had usually been a genuine ally, not a client state. The Scottish view of the alliance in 1543 was that 'France requireth nothing of them but friendship, and would they should continue and maintain the honour and liberty of their realm'.[9] Until then this had almost been true. In the 1540s, however, the nature of the alliance changed fundamentally, for three reasons. The ambition and power of Valois France made the alliance more unequal than ever; the extremity of Scotland's need during the 'Rough Wooings' left the Scots exposed to exactly the danger of which Somerset had warned. Most importantly, the succession of a woman to the Scottish throne was as tempting a prospect to France as to England. After 1548, with the child Queen in France and pledged to the Dauphin, Scotland was virtually turned into a French protectorate. Henry II regarded himself as the effective sovereign of Scotland, and took a close interest in its government.[10] How did the alliance respond to this unprecedented change in its shape?

Many Scots were genuinely grateful to the ally who had, again, rescued them. The poet Richard Maitland of Lethington exulted at Henry II's recovery of Calais in 1558, urging all Scots to praise 'your most tender friend that noble king'. He also celebrated the Queen's marriage to the Dauphin in 1558 by writing not only of the nation's 'great blitheness and joy inestimable' but also of the 'true fraternity' between Scots and French. This joy at least was widely shared. When the royal marriage finally went ahead, it was another sign of the attention which France was lavishing on its ally, attention which was noticed and appreciated. In 1550 the privy council formally thanked Henry

II for his labours on their behalf. He had, they said, 'preferred the rest and ease of this realm to his own particular profit', and they were 'indebted to his highness more than they are able presently to acquit'. The debts they spoke of were not simply moral. The French cemented the alliance with cash as well as gratitude. As Mary of Guise had been advised in 1548, Scottish loyalty was not so great that money would not make it more secure, and indeed, French largesse was considerable. 'There was never a Scotsman in Scotland', Sir George Douglas believed, 'but he was better French than English, forasmuch as they were pampered with money, pensions, and lands'. In 1560, the Congregation still feared that the lure of French money could cost them support.[11]

Gratitude for French help was real enough, but this did not mean genuine affection. As Jenny Wormald has commented, 'throughout its history, the Auld Alliance had worked best when the French and Scots did not try to live together, and particularly when the French kept out of Scotland'.[12] The presence of significant numbers of French troops in Scotland after 1548 was a continuous source of friction. Soldiers billeted on a civilian population are rarely popular. Even in the midst of the war, in October 1548, a fist fight between a Scot and a French soldier in Edinburgh quickly boiled over into a full-scale riot which the French tried to quell by firing indiscriminately into the crowd. The following year, a group of Breton sailors ravaged the isle of Cumbrae. In 1550, French soldiers were being put on trial for 'sundry attempts upon our Sovereign Lady's lieges'.[13] The return of peace eased these problems but did not end them. In the same year, Edinburgh's entire town council was imprisoned for refusing to provide horses for the French. There were persistent problems relating to victualling the soldiers. In 1552, several French soldiers were accused of scrumping vegetables from a Dundee garden, and a small riot broke out. When soldiers did pay for goods, there was a widespread reluctance to accept French coins in payment. The regime's menacing endorsement of the foreign coin could not still the fear that it was debased. The cost of provisions was inflated by the extra mouths which needed feeding, fuelling resentment amongst the soldiers and their hosts alike. According to a Spanish envoy, such resentments only spurred the French to bring in more soldiers. In 1555, Mary of Guise had to issue a proclamation requiring her people to sell food to the troops. In the same year, a parliamentary act worried about the 'murmurs and slanders' raised against the French soldiers, whose effect was 'to stir the hearts of the subjects to hatred' against the French.[14]

Such hatred came the more easily because it was often reciprocated. Even French officialdom could be impatient with the Scots. The Seigneur d'Oisel, France's ambassador in Scotland, was openly annoyed by the Scots' unjust treatment (as he saw it) of the Frenchmen in their midst. In France itself, it was the cost of the Scottish war which was unpopular. Brittany, that other territory which had recently been absorbed by French dynasticism, was particularly loath to pay for imperial schemes in Scotland. The duchy's receiver-general, lamenting the endless expense of defending Scotland, wished 'that Scotland were in a fish-pool'. In 1548, the English envoy Nicholas Wotton was told that the Bretons cursed the Scots for their high taxes. In 1559–60, the Normans, too, were said to be adamantly opposed to fighting for the Scots, and suspicious of the self-aggrandisement of *les Guise*. The Scots may have been the darlings of the French court in 1550, but within weeks of the outbreak of hostilities in 1559 they were being treated as pariahs, and the Scots guards were coming to blows with French soldiers.[15]

Even when the French lauded their ally, they never doubted their own innate superiority. Scotland was commonly seen in France as a land of savages. The French cleric Estienne Perlin, who visited Scotland in 1551–52, was effortlessly superior towards his hosts. 'This little country is useful and necessary to us, as much so as the richest.' Although he was dismayed by how much he was charged for his lodging, he insisted the Scots were bold and courageous allies. Yet he had no doubt of Scotland's place in the order of things: 'How happy oughtest thou to esteem thyself, O kingdom of Scotland, to be favoured, fed, and maintained, like an infant, on the breast of the most puissant and magnanimous King of France, the greatest lord in the whole world.'

Not all visitors to Scotland were so positive. For French soldiers, Scotland was a hardship posting. The country was poor, the diet unpalatable ('the beggarliness of the land', John Aylmer noted sourly, was not able 'to feed the fine-mouthed French men') and the climate harsh. In February 1560, the English ambassador in Scotland wrote: 'The winter hath been so unkind that the French long after the summer. Their misery is so great . . . that I wonder what hope they have to escape with their lives.' Their sufferings, however, do not match those of the first French troops sent to Scotland during the Rough Wooings, in 1545. Knox remembered with bitter enjoyment that 'they learned to eat (yea, to beg) cakes which at their entry they scorned. Without jesting, they were so miserably treated, that few returned to France again with their lives'. The English received a trickle of French deserters complaining of poor pay and worse food. Seymour claimed in October 1545 that 'the Frenchmen do find such misery and scarcity in the country, that both they be weary of the same, and likewise the Scots be weary of them'. Those Frenchmen who did return home had bloodcurdling tales to tell. One contingent of French soldiers returning from Scotland in 1546 allegedly 'swore they would never return there again while they lived . . . because of the bad climate and the brutishness of the people'. They claimed that their comrades had been killed by the Scots as food both for livestock and for people. We do not need to believe the accusation of cannibalism to accept that they had not come away with a positive impression of their ally.[16]

Scotland's political classes, however, had a different view. As a group, they had no animus against France – quite the opposite. However, they were jealous of any infringements of their own rights. Even in the most stirring declarations of Scottish loyalty to France, there are robust statements of the value which the Scottish magnates placed on 'the old liberty and freedom'.[17] By the end of the 1550s, some Scottish magnates clearly felt that these liberties were being curtailed. This was not a general resentment of the French, but an opposition to French policy for Scotland in three linked areas: war, domestic policy and patronage.

Since the disaster of Flodden, and even before it, the Scottish political establishment had become wary of aggression towards England. Defence against invasion was one thing, but carrying the battle to the enemy was another, especially if unprovoked. In 1543, the French ambassador in Scotland was told categorically that the Scots would not invade England.[18] France's foreign policy was more ambitious. When the French alliance brought Scotland into a war with England in 1557, these differing approaches came to the fore. As Ritchie has pointed out, there was no Scottish opposition to the war as such. The Scots were willing both to mount cross-border raids and to defend their own side of the Border. However, Mary of Guise's proposal for a full-scale invasion of England was another matter. The attempt to raise forces for the invasion ran into opposition: the Scots feared that they would be defeated, and that France, already at full stretch, would be unable to rescue them. When the army reached the Border, on 17 October 1557, the principal Scots noblemen called a halt to the invasion. The mutiny was led by the Duke of Châtelherault and the Earls of Morton and Argyll. Châtelherault later claimed that this was because they did not wish to fight someone else's war, but it was probably not so straightforward. At the time, rumour attributed their decision to bad weather, desertion amongst their own soldiers and fear of stout English opposition. Bishop Leslie later thought that they were reluctant to risk a battle from which Scotland potentially had more to lose than to gain. What is clear is that Guise was incensed at being crossed in this way. She 'raged and reproved them of their promises . . . arguments grew great between them'. She 'sorrowed and wept openly', and swiftly 'dispersed her camp in great choler'.[19]

This was not an ideological disagreement, merely a dispute over tactics. After all, Guise no more wished to see a Scottish army defeated than did Châtelherault. The incident matters partly because of Guise's furious reaction. Her trust in her nobles was severely dented. Perhaps remembering how James III had been faced with a *coup d'état* when similarly stopped on the way to war in 1482, she set about importing a substantial French bodyguard for herself. More importantly, the mutineers clearly felt that they were being excluded from policy-making. One leading nobleman, the Earl of Huntly, initially backed the invasion. Revealingly, however, he gave in when the others asked him, pointedly, 'whether he would be a Scotsman or a Frenchman'. It was an accusation to which Scots were becoming sensitive. In June of the same year, the Earls of Westmorland and Cassillis had been negotiating on behalf of their rival Queens, and the Englishman had casually referred to the Scots as 'French'. Cassillis bridled, insisting, 'I am no more French than ye are a Spaniard'. Westmorland stoutly admitted that he did see himself as a Spaniard, since his King, Philip, was Spanish. By the same logic, he expected a Scot, whose Queen was betrothed to a Frenchman, to see himself as French. But Cassillis would have none of it. Back in the 1540s, he told Westmorland, the Scots had resolved 'that we would die, every mother's son of us, rather than be subjects unto England. Even the like shall ye find us to keep with France'. The Scots nobility were willing to fight for their allies (especially against England), but they would not be used by them. Yet the alliance of equals which they wanted was no longer possible.[20]

The 1557 mutiny also reflected longer-established concerns about Scotland's domestic administration. The attempt to levy hefty taxes in 1556 to pay for defences had of course been unpopular – taxes always are – but resentment had been concentrated on Guise's attempt to make a comprehensive inventory of all lands and goods. To her, this was simply sound administration, but many Scots feared it was a prelude to a general seizure of property, or at least to that foreign innovation, a perpetual tax.[21] Guise abandoned the plan with some exasperation. She was becoming used to her policy innovations being treated with disproportionate suspicion. Scots who respected the French and shared their religion still deprecated 'their precise dealing alike with all sorts of people, not distinguishing the qualities of persons'. To Guise, however, the Scots' dogged insistence on their traditional dignities was an annoyance. Early in 1557, she wrote to her brother, the Cardinal of Lorraine: 'This people, especially the great lords, are so little desirous of justice, that . . . one cannot talk of [or] demand this justice without their instantly saying that one wants to change their laws. . . . They will not endure it, and say that these are laws of the French, and that their old laws are good.' Guise was not describing opponents of the French alliance, but those who wished to preserve the alliance as it had once been. The fear that this was not happening seems to have been widespread. It was rumoured (falsely) that the young Queen was not going to be married to the Dauphin at all, but rather palmed off on some lesser French nobleman – a symbol of Scottish subjection. The death of four Scottish emissaries to France in 1558 was widely, although certainly falsely, blamed on poisoning. Rumour held that Lorraine would seize the dead men's benefices. The presence of French soldiers in Scotland could also be read in such terms. Guise herself had little sympathy for such worries, writing to Lorraine: 'They are more difficult to manage than ever. God knows, brother mine, what a life I lead. It is no small thing to bring a young nation to a state of perfection.' Her subjects, however, did not feel that they needed to be perfected.[22]

For those Scots who suspected that the French alliance was eroding their liberties, the most sensitive subject of all was that of patronage. The involvement of Frenchmen in the administration of Scotland edged Scottish nobles out of one of their traditional roles. Guise was aware of this sensitivity and did what she could to ease it, but she was readier to cede incomes and dignities than power. Her council was broad and inclusive, but it had little real authority. The Earl of Huntly retained the title of Chancellor of Scotland, but the power was held by Yves du Rubay, the Frenchman whom Guise appointed as Vice-Chancellor. Rubay was the most visible and the most resented of a clique of Frenchmen through whom the Queen Regent conducted much of her business. This resentment was not, it is important to stress, born from anti-French feeling as such, but from exclusion from power and patronage. Guise's most powerful minister was the Seigneur d'Oisel, France's ambassador and, in effect, Scotland's foreign minister throughout the 1550s. He was widely trusted by the Scots, not least because none of them wanted his job. The most instructive example, though, is Mary of Guise herself. When she travelled to France in 1550, she probably hoped to remain there with her daughter, but was persuaded to return to Scotland in 1551 because no-one else had the authority to hold the alliance together. She was unique: French, yet known and trusted by the Scots. However, her personal qualities could only partially conceal the reality that Scotland's government was now under French control. When she was gravely ill in early 1559, the rumour was that she would be succeeded by a council of three: du Rubay, d'Oisel and the Duke of Châtelherault. Scots would be left with a minority voice in the administration of their own realm.[23]

Catholic and Protestant chroniclers of this period agree that Guise's exclusion of Scots from her patronage was a source of profound resentment. Bishop Leslie wrote of the 'ire and anger' which Guise's French clique provoked, although he was careful to blame this on the machinations of du Rubay and his associates rather than on Guise herself. In October 1559, the Congregation produced a detailed history of France's alleged attempt to conquer Scotland by stealth. The monopolisation of offices was at the heart of their complaints. The French office-holders, it was alleged, not only held a stranglehold over the business of government; they had also seized the most lucrative posts. The Congregation described this as a violation of the promise made by France in 1548 to preserve Scotland's laws, customs and nobility.[24] These views were informed by the bitterness of civil war, but there had been earlier protests to the same effect. In 1556, a group of lairds – three hundred of them, we are told – assembled in Edinburgh to lodge a protest with Guise. Their spokesmen, the Lairds of Calder and of Wemyss, demanded both that she withdraw the planned tax assessment (which she did), and that she cease sidelining the nobility. It was in the nobles, they insisted, that the strength of the kingdom resided, not in the wealth of the Crown. Excluding the nobility from power would reduce Scotland to 'bare earth or . . . a thing spiritless'.[25]

Scotland was not yearning for a chance to throw off the yoke of French subjection; much less to embrace an alternative, English allegiance. The long-standing Scottish view 'that they would never strike a Scot if an Englishman stood by' still obtained. A few Scots can be found being positive towards England in early 1559; but these were either weathercocks such as Châtelherault, or politicians such as William Maitland of Lethington, keen to keep their options open.[26] Few Scots believed that the French alliance had turned into conquest. Many of them were, however, wary of the possibility that it might do so. French policy, French placemen and French soldiers were generally viewed not with hostility, but with suspicion. There was no inevitable nationalist clash coming. However, the wariness which had crept into Scottish views of France meant that Mary of Guise's political room for manoeuvre was limited. If a crisis should arise, in which she was accused of tyranny, many of her subjects would be inclined to believe it.

COMPROMISE AND ITS ENEMIES

That crisis duly came in May 1559, but our knowledge of the events leading up to it is unsatisfactory. There are few relevant documents from the late 1550s. We are mostly reliant on later histories, many of them very late, and all of them soaked with hindsight. An anonymous manuscript entitled *A Historie of the Estate of Scotland* provides some very useful detail, although its Protestant bias is heavy.[27] Our most important source is John Knox's history, but Knox's account of this period is exceptionally problematic. He had access to many essential documents, some of which would otherwise be lost, but he himself was in exile until May 1559. His personal knowledge of events was therefore limited and (of course) self-centred. As a result, his account is not only biased but also seriously confused in its chronology. It is, nevertheless, where we have to begin.

Knox had fled Scotland before a heresy accusation in 1556, but in March 1557, four of the most powerful Protestant nobles invited Knox to return: the Earl of Glencairn; Lord Erskine; Lord Lorne, who would soon inherit his father's earldom of Argyll; and Lord James Stewart, an illegitimate son of James V. They judged that the danger was past: 'we have no experience of any more cruelty to be used than was before'. There is no great mystery as to why. War with England threatened, and we know that one immediate consequence of this was that the religious environment became still more permissive. In Scotland's decentralised military system, the leading nobles became nearly autonomous during wartime. During the war that followed, there was public Protestant preaching in Edinburgh and elsewhere for the first time since the height of the Rough Wooings. Guise was, as we have seen, under considerable political pressure. Repressing religious dissidence was simply not a priority. Knox was being invited to join a Protestant resurgence which was already under way.[28]

Knox set out from Geneva with some reluctance, reaching Dieppe in late October. There he found letters warning him that matters had changed. Those who six months before had sworn that they were 'ready to jeopard lives and goods' for the Gospel were now instructing Knox to stay put. One Protestant (who disagreed with this decision) told Knox that the reformist nobles were regretting ever having invited him to return. Knox was understandably annoyed, and wrote several sharp letters in reply, upbraiding the Protestant nobles for neglecting the spiritual duties which, in his view, their elevated station carried. Knox claimed that these letters provoked five Protestant lords to sign the pledge known to historians as the First Band of the Lords of the Congregation, on 3 December 1557.[29]

What are we to make of this sequence of events? Why would these lords first summon Knox, then rescind their invitation, and then band together in the name of religion? It is clear even from Knox's account that his fiercely separatist agenda was not shared by his noble backers. Alarmingly radical political ideas were emerging in the Anglo-Scottish church in Geneva. Knox and his friend Christopher Goodman were arguing that Protestants in Mary Tudor's England should resist their apostate and tyrannical government with force. Knox transferred some, but not all of this radicalism to the Scottish situation. He told his noble fair-weather friends in October 1557 that their people were being oppressed, and that 'you ought to hazard your own lives (be it against kings or emperors) for their deliverance'. They had a duty to reform 'public enormities'. In December, however, he warned them against open rebellion and urged that they obey established authority in all things lawful. Only if they were not granted toleration might they 'attempt the extremity', and by this he merely meant that they might unilaterally establish Reformed worship in defiance of the regime. The following year, he wrote that they might resist the tyranny of the clergy, but not that of the Queen Regent.[30] This softer line has attracted a good deal of comment. Jane Dawson has ascribed it to Knox's theology of covenant, in which more was expected of the English because more had been given to them. Scott Dolff has recently argued that Knox's view was also informed by a 'divine pragmatism', in which God did not expect the Scots to rise in rebellion because there was no prospect of victory.[31] However, Knox's concern seems to have been less the fear of unsuccessful rebellion and more the hope that rebellion would be unnecessary. He still hoped that the Queen Regent might co-operate. She had, after all, protected him in 1556. In the same year, he urged her in an open letter to 'study how that the true worshipping of God may be promoted, and the tyranny of ungodly men repressed'. In December 1557, he was still pressing the Protestant nobles to 'seek the favours of the authority'. The following April, Knox admitted that he had been worried that excessive zeal might discredit the Gospel by provoking unnecessary tumults and uproars.[32]

If even Knox had not yet given up on Mary of Guise as a supporter of reform, the Protestant nobles had high hopes of her. Their stated reason for revoking their invitation to Knox was 'that new consultation was appointed for final conclusion of the matter': that is, they were negotiating with the Queen Regent, and they did not want one of the most tactless men in Christendom crashing around in the midst of delicate diplomacy.[33] It is in this context that the band of December 1557 should be seen. The band has been seen as 'a decisive step' towards Protestant separatism,[34] but its text is studiedly vague. It simply committed the signatories to promote the Gospel and to protect its ministers and one another. Even this, however, was too controversial for some. Five noblemen signed it: three of the four who had invited Knox, plus the old Earl of Argyll (who had less than a year to live) and the Earl of Morton (who, despite this, refused to commit himself openly to the Congregation until April 1560). Scotland's most prominent Protestant, Lord James Stewart, was conspicuously absent. He, and any others whom the signatories may have hoped to attract, apparently felt that such a move was too confrontational.[35] Yet the actual demands which the five signatories made were modest enough. They wished to be permitted to hear Protestant preaching behind closed doors, 'without great conventions of the people thereto' – that is, they wished to formalise what some of them were already doing. Secondly, 'the Common Prayers' and extracts from the Bible were to be read in parish churches, using 'the order of the Book of Common Prayers'. This clearly meant the English Prayer Books of Edward VI, but perhaps the conservative book of 1549 rather than its more radical 1552 replacement: certainly, the wording does not imply a precise attachment to any one text.[36]

Formalising *de facto* toleration, and a vernacular liturgy for the daily offices of matins and evensong (not for the sacraments): these were not unrealistic demands. The vernacular Bible was already legal. The vernacular catechism which was supposedly read from the pulpit every week included the Paternoster and the Ave Maria in Scots.[37] The next year, the same demands resurfaced in a different form. In July 1558, 'certain brethren of Dundee' were summoned for religious offences. Knox claimed that it was at this point that Dundee 'began to erect the face of a public church Reformed', under the leadership of the minister Paul Methven. The summons, however, suggests that matters had not quite reached that point. The named offenders, George

Luvell and David Ferguson, were certainly radicals: Luvell had been suspected of iconoclasm back in the 1530s, and Ferguson would later become a firebreathing Reformed minister. In 1558, however, they were merely accused of 'using and wresting' Scripture, 'disputing upon erroneous opinions', and breaking the Lenten fast. Methven was certainly working in the area, but it seems that his ministry, like that of the other Protestant preachers, was still anchored in gentry households.[38] An open breach with the old Church had not yet been made.

Indeed, this shot across the reformers' bows did not provoke resistance, but a further attempt at negotiation. A delegation of reformist lairds petitioned Guise, led by Sir James Sandilands of Calder, who had pressed Guise to review her plans for taxation in 1556; perhaps he was chosen for this task because of this previous success. The terms of this petition are very similar to the demands drawn up by the Protestant lords six months before. The petitioners asked for clerical discipline – an uncontroversial platitude. They asked for 'Common Prayers, in our vulgar tongue' for all who wished to participate. They justified this request by referring to the legalisation of the English Bible, and carefully emphasised that at such gatherings they would pray for the Queen and the realm. They asked for informal preaching to be permitted at these gatherings, promising to guard against any disorder which this might cause. More radically, they asked for the sacraments to be administered in the vernacular, and for the laity to receive both bread and wine in the Eucharist. Neither request was unthinkable for a Catholic, and there were encouraging German precedents, but no-one in Archbishop Hamilton's circle had yet gone this far. Even so, this was again a measured and realistic set of proposals. The later Protestant writer who claimed that the petitioners had asked for a full-scale Reformed sacramental ministry was seriously distorting their purposes. The response to these reasonable requests was itself reasonable. The Dundonian heretics were bailed. Some amongst the clergy even offered a public debate – a remarkable concession, granting a platform to heretics – but, predictably, disagreement over the ground rules scuppered this idea. The clergy then put forward counter-proposals of their own. They would concede vernacular prayer and even baptism, behind closed doors, if the reformers would admit their adherence to the essentials of Catholic theology. This, of course, they would not do, but Guise herself refused to take sides. She promised a parliament to consider the Protestants' petition, and assured them that in the meantime she would continue to tolerate their activities.[39]

In 1557–58, then, it seemed plausible to both moderate Protestants and reformist Catholics that a viable religious compromise might be reached: a workable ceasefire, if not a final settlement. The outlines of such a compromise were already clear. Protestant preaching would be permitted in private.

A vernacular liturgy would be used in some or all parish churches: for matins and evensong, and perhaps also for the sacrament of baptism. The hierarchy would undertake not to treat such activities as heresy, and the reformers would refrain from any more provocative direct action. The Queen Regent would act as guarantor. This was not terribly different from what was already happening in some parts of the country. However, in 1558 it was already obvious that the difficulty would lie in policing the boundaries of such a compromise. A compromise could only work if the Church or the regime retained the right to prosecute those Protestants who violated it. It may have been for this reason that the bishops decided to renew their prosecution of heresy. The otherwise peculiar decision to burn Walter Myln in April 1558 – the first burning for eight years – should probably be interpreted as a public warning. If so, however, it was fatally undermined by Mary of Guise's refusal to support it. The bloodshed no doubt frightened some, as it was meant to, but it seems to have alienated many more.[40]

Most reformers continued to look for a compromise, but as we have seen, an angry and activist minority had no interest in politics. It was Protestants of this kind who, in defiance of their co-religionists, committed a public outrage on 1 September 1558, by attacking the St Giles's day procession in Edinburgh. This was an extremely effective act of terrorism. It created ripples across Europe. By the time the story reached Zurich, it had grown in the telling to become a popular uprising which established a Reformed Church and forced the Queen and nobles to flee. Similar rumours seem to have reached John Foxe in Basle.[41] The reality was less dramatic, but it did drive a wedge between the religious parties and place any possible compromise under considerable stress. The bishops could not allow such a provocative act to pass in silence. The culprits were untraceable, and no fresh summonses for heresy were yet issued; Guise probably persuaded Hamilton to wait until the parliament was over. But relations had soured. Further burnings were in the air.

In November 1558, therefore, the promised parliament assembled amidst renewed religious tensions. Its principal business was, literally, the crowning act of the Franco–Scottish alliance: Queen Mary's new husband, Dauphin Francis, was granted the crown matrimonial of Scotland.[42] The Protestant lords, however, took the occasion to submit another petition to Mary of Guise, and to lay a protestation before the parliament as a whole. Again, they asked merely to be allowed to read and expound Scripture in assemblies, 'to invoke the name of God in public prayers' and to minister the sacraments. Yet their language was now fiercer, and more precise in its theology. This perhaps reflected the influence of the newly returned exile John Willock. Moreover, both petitions now focused on a newly pressing problem: the heresy laws. Strikingly, they did not reject the laws altogether, but asked that they be taken out of the Church's control. The existing procedures, it was argued, violated natural justice, because the churchmen were being judges in their own cause. However, the petitioners protested their loyalty to Guise, whom they clearly still trusted. And indeed, Guise continued to seek their trust, accepting the petitions and promising to deal fairly with them.[43]

With hindsight, Protestants saw Guise's openness as a bitter deception. The chronology, they thought, spoke for itself. As long as Guise needed political support in order to grant Francis the crown matrimonial, she strung the Protestants along with empty promises; but once the parliament was over she turned on them. And indeed, in December 1558, she permitted the bishops to summon Willock, Methven and three other leading preachers on charges of heresy. Although this summons was rescinded, it was renewed in April 1559, sparking the outbreak of rebellion in May. Guise certainly moved from being the reformers' great hope to being their most dangerous enemy within a few months. It is not easy, however, to paint her as a dissembling Catholic fanatic. As we shall see, even during the rebellion she was open to religious compromises. On her deathbed, remarkably, she asked to see Willock, spending some time in private conversation with him.[44] She never seems to have had fierce or partisan religious convictions. If she had, she might have proved better able to deal with those who did. Why, then, did her policy change so abruptly between November 1558 and May 1559? Two reasons are immediately apparent: the shifting international political situation, and the gradual collapse of the attempts at religious compromise.

Mary Stewart's marriage to Dauphin Francis in April 1558, and the grant of the crown matrimonial to Francis at the end of the year, were political triumphs for Mary of Guise, which cemented her and her family's commanding position within Franco-Scottish politics. However, there was no obvious reason why these achievements should change her religious policy. Two other momentous international events did. One was the death of the English queen, Mary Tudor, on 17 November 1558. This not only weakened the Anglo-Spanish alliance which had been cemented by Mary Tudor's marriage to Philip II of Spain, but also left a disputed succession. Elizabeth Tudor quickly occupied the English throne, but some Catholics argued that her birth and therefore her claim was illegitimate, and that the rightful queen of England was therefore Mary Stewart, Queen of Scots, Princess of France and daughter of Mary of Guise. This changed the diplomatic logic of Scotland's religious policy entirely. The English succession dispute turned on whether Elizabeth was the legitimate daughter of Henry VIII, and thus on whether Henry's repudiation of Rome had been justified. This was, in other words, a contest between a Protestant, Tudor claim and a Catholic, Stewart–Guise–Valois claim. As Francis and Mary quickly claimed the titles of King and Queen of England, and denounced Elizabeth as a heretical usurper, it would have been hard for Mary of Guise to avoid adopting a more overtly Catholic religious policy. Moreover, her Protestant subjects, who had once been harmless, were now potentially an English fifth column.

The impact of the English succession crisis on Guise is, however, easier to deduce than to demonstrate. The same is not true of the other great international event of these months: the treaty of Câteau-Cambrésis, concluded in April 1559 after some months of negotiation. This was a peace between Philip II of Spain and Henry II of France, ending a lifetime of Habsburg–Valois warfare. Scotland and England were both comprehended in the treaty. The return of peace immediately lessened Guise's political dependence on her magnates. However, Câteau-Cambrésis also signalled a shift in French religious policy. Henry II had agreed a peace which cost France painful concessions partly because of his conviction that France's heresy problem was becoming urgent. Peace was a precondition for a serious crackdown on religious dissidence, and in 1559 France embarked on just that. The policy extended to France's Scottish province. As the treaty was being concluded, the Cardinal of Lorraine sent the Sieur de Béthencourt to Scotland with instructions for his sister Mary of Guise. Sir James Melville of Halhill, a Scot in French service, testified that Béthencourt was instructed to rebuke Mary of Guise for her 'gentle bearing' towards heresy. According to Melville, Guise was most reluctant to change her policy, both because of her personal respect for the Protestant nobles and also because she feared a confrontation. However, she did as she was told. It was this, Melville wrote, which lay behind Guise's proclamation on Maundy Thursday, 23 March 1559, that failure to conform to Catholic rites on the approaching Easter Sunday would be treated as heresy. This proclamation led directly to the final summons of the preachers who violated it, and so to the outbreak of the rebellion.[45] Scotland was going to be drawn into France's religious struggles, whether its Queen Regent approved or not.

If she complied with Béthencourt's instructions, however, it may be because there were few other options open to her. The possibility of a workable compromise was evaporating, partly because of the Protestant militants. In the autumn of 1558, the document known as the 'Beggars' Summons' first appeared, demanding that the friars vacate their hospitals in favour of the poor. In November, the Protestant lords' long-delayed invitation to John Knox was at last renewed.[46] We cannot be sure why the battle-lines were hardening in this way, but the St Giles's day riot in Edinburgh seems to have been one catalyst. Those reformers who did not themselves approve of the iconoclasm nevertheless feared a Catholic backlash. One of the petitions laid before parliament that autumn demanded that 'if any tumult or uproar shall arise amongst the members of this realm for the diversity of religion, and if it shall chance that abuses be violently reformed, that the crime thereof be not imputed to us'. The blame lay rather with those clergy who had had the chance to reform abuses and had not done so. The iconoclasm was forcing moderates to choose sides.[47]

It was against this backdrop that Guise's summons to the preachers was issued in December 1558. Like her summons of the Dundee reformers six months before, this drew forth a protest from the Protestant lairds, but now their mood was less accommodating. According to Knox, they came to her not with proposals for negotiation, but with an ultimatum. Once they had done so, 'every man put on his steel bonnet'. If this is true, it was the first overt threat of armed resistance. Guise, however, continued to make conciliatory noises. She discharged the summons of the preachers, and made what would turn out to be a final attempt at compromise.[48] She arranged for a convention of the nobility and a general provincial council of the Church to meet, in parallel, in March 1559. Knox believed the purpose of the council was to 'give some show to the people that they minded reformation', but Guise evidently hoped there would be substance behind the show. She sent a list of requests to the council from the 'temporal Lords and Barons' who had met with her in convention. We know that there was 'contention . . . for matters of religion' at this convention, but the statement which Guise wrung out of it was a detailed blueprint for religious compromise. It called for learned preaching in every parish in the country at least once per month, and asked that 'the Common Prayers with Litanies in our vulgar tongue be said in every parish church upon Sundays ánd other holy days'. It did not ask for the sacraments themselves to be said in the vernacular, but called for 'a godly and fruitful declaration . . . in English tongue' to be read aloud when they were celebrated, explaining their meaning: this was an intelligent and imaginative compromise. At the same time, it demanded that action be taken against iconoclasm and against those who 'pretend to use the sacraments' without proper authorisation. Hearing of this, the English commanders on the Border concluded that 'the matter is pacified'.[49]

However, real compromise was slipping from reach. Neither the Protestants nor the hierarchy now entirely trusted the Queen Regent to guarantee a deal. She had even had to strong-arm the convention into adopting her ideas, with little support other than from her French inner circle. And while the provincial council adopted most of the suggestions made to it, including the declarations on the sacraments, it rejected vernacular prayers, which were the keystone of the proposed settlement. They represented too sharp a departure even for Scotland's reformist Catholics. Perhaps the Protestants too would now have refused to accept such a settlement, which would have involved such a degree of conformity to the old Church. Under the cover of the peace negotiations with England, Protestants such as Maitland of Lethington and Kirkcaldy of Grange were already exploring whether Elizabeth's new regime might assist them. These is no evidence that they were contemplating rebellion, but they

did want to strengthen their negotiating hand. It was under these circumstances that Guise, urged on by Béthencourt and her brothers, issued the proclamation demanding Easter conformity. She had already, in February, issued
a proclamation in Dundee and other east coast towns against iconoclasm and
Lent-breaking, threatening the death penalty for violators. After her appeal
for Easter conformity had been rejected, it was clear that the possibility of
compromise had passed. Guise was going to have to do as her brothers wished,
and use her new-found political independence to crack down on heresy. The
preachers were again summoned for heresy, this time being required to
come to Stirling on 10 May.[50]

The febrile, mercurial state of religious politics during the interval that
followed can be gauged from a remarkable set of events in Ayrshire. Two of
the leading religious controversialists clashed there after Easter: Quintin
Kennedy, the Catholic–reformist Abbot of Crossraguell, and John Willock,
whom (until Knox returned to snatch the title) Protestants were calling
'Primate of their religion in this realm'. Their confrontation provides a
snapshot of the state of the religious parties. Before Easter, Willock had
preached in Ayr that the Mass was idolatry, and claimed that several ancient
theologians – notably Irenaeus and Chrysostom – supported this view.
Kennedy, who arrived in the town on Easter Sunday, was incensed, and
proposed a formal disputation with Willock. He aimed to prove that the
ancient Fathers of the church supported his own interpretation of Scripture, not Willock's. He suggested to Willock that they each name twelve
judges, and that they should collectively submit to the judgement of these
twenty-four men, even to the point that the loser should confess himself
guilty of heresy. It was a bold proposal. This most articulate of Catholic
reformers clearly believed that there was still time for talking, and that he
could win over some of his opponents. He claimed that Willock's appeal to
the Fathers had persuaded a great many of his hearers, and believed that if
this could be debunked, the tide could be turned.[51]

Willock and his supporters had a different view. Although he swiftly
accepted Kennedy's proposal, he also changed its terms. Although he had
cited the Fathers, he was not willing to allow them to be arbiters of the matter, and wished to restrict the disputation to Scripture alone. He also named
his arbiters: a daunting list of local lords and lairds, headed by the Earl of
Glencairn. Kennedy realised that a trap was being laid for him. The negotiations for the disputation continued with all the trust of spiders preparing to
mate. (Happily for us, the two men refused to meet, so the entire exchange
took place on paper.) Kennedy insisted that a simple argument over Scripture,
as Willock suggested, would be a waste of time, for they would simply disagree; it was the same theme on which he had written the year before.
He suspected that 'it is but difference that you desire, and not to have the

matter at a perfect trial'. He also feared that Willock would bring a substantial crowd of supporters with him. In the end, since Willock refused to accept his demands, Kennedy stayed away from the disputation. Willock did appear, backed, Kennedy claimed, by Glencairn and more than four hundred armed men. The Protestants were no longer interested in real discussion, or in playing the Catholic reformers' games. And their resolve could only be strengthened by incidents such as this, in which the Catholics undeniably lost face.[52]

In the face of Guise's ultimatum, however, their response was less certain. This was partly a matter of geography. There were two distinct and geographically separate centres of Protestant strength, the east coast towns and the southwest. There were contacts aplenty between the two regions, but there was not yet a single 'Congregation'. It was only on 31 May, after the rebellion had begun, that the two groups formally banded together, and then they referred to themselves as distinct 'Congregations'. Both groups, independently, sent delegations to Guise to protest; Glencairn led the westerners, while the eastern Protestants were represented by a more lowly gathering of lairds, of whom the most prominent was John Erskine of Dun.[53] However, the most exalted of the Protestant nobles – Lord James Stewart and the Earl of Argyll – were not involved in either protest. Guise rebuffed both sets of petitioners. We do not know how the westerners responded to this, but the eastern lairds assembled first at Dundee, the burgh most sympathetic to their cause. There they decided to accompany the preachers to Stirling. Presumably they hoped that, as before, a show of force would persuade the Queen Regent to talk.

It was at this stage that the easterners were joined by John Knox. Having finally established that his views on female monarchy had made him unwelcome in England, he answered the call to return to Scotland, apparently with some reluctance. If his timing in denouncing the 'monstrous regiment of women' had been unlucky, his timing in returning to Scotland was exquisite. He landed in Edinburgh on 2 May. Learning what was afoot, he quickly made his way to Dundee, probably arriving there on the 5th. The Protestants quickly received him into the heart of their counsels. This, at least, is the impression given by a letter addressed to Guise from the eastern lairds on 6 May. It survives only in a later copy in Erskine of Dun's archive, but it gives every impression of being written by Knox. Its rolling, melodramatic preacher's cadences; its lengthy citation of dreadful warnings from the Old Testament; and its insistence that in the Church Guise was 'a servant and no Queen' are all vintage Knox. He had apparently already adopted the role he was to fill for the next eight months, as the Congregation's secretary. Yet the substance of the letter showed that the reformers had not yet stepped over the brink. It reminded Guise of 'our old hope toward you'; they had not forgotten her toleration. There was no threat of violence, simply an earnest request for the summons to be rescinded.[54]

The crisis was broken, and the stand-off turned to rebellion, by another terrorist act. By Thursday 11 May, the reformist lairds, with Knox among them, had reached Perth. Perth had recently 'received the Order of Common Prayers'. Whatever this meant, it clearly had not affected the lives of the monasteries and other traditional ecclesiastical institutions in the town; but it did mean that Knox was able to preach there. The date was significant. Guise's deadline had expired, and the preachers had been outlawed as a consequence. It was another sign that, this time, she meant what she said. Moreover, the next day, the 12th, was 'Flitting Friday': the Friday before Whitsun, the customary day for evictions to take place. The 'Beggars' Summons' of the previous winter had threatened the friars with just such an eviction. The threat must have seemed empty when it was made, but the coincidence of dates had made it painfully apt. Exactly what happened on 11 May is unclear. Knox, our only eyewitness, wrote a detailed account several years later, in which he admitted that he had preached a sermon 'vehement against idolatry'. After, or during, this sermon, a priest passed by on his way to Mass. Knox claimed that a boy in the crowd threw a stone at the priest and missed, striking instead the tabernacle on the altar of the church. 'Immediately the whole multitude that were about cast stones, and put hands to the said tabernacle, and to all other monuments of idolatry, which they dispatched.' It is a frighteningly plausible account: a explosion sparked off by accident, after one of the most inflammatory preachers in Christendom had spent an hour or more liberally lacing the situation with petrol. But Knox probably also lit the match. In a letter written shortly after the event he described the iconoclasm as a deliberate response to the outlawing of the preachers. Other witnesses agree that it was premeditated, and the destruction certainly seems to have been controlled and thorough.[55] The later image of furious mobs suited the reformers well, as it allowed them to distance themselves from disorder.

Whether premeditated or not, however, the iconoclasm was not an accident. It was a culpable act of political violence; an attempt to force the pace of change and to precipitate a conflict which most people on all sides wished to avoid. It forced Guise into a military response, and forced the Protestant lairds to choose sides. As so often in politics, violence worked.

NOTES

1 John Aylmer, *An Harborowe for Faithfull and Trewe Subiectes, Agaynst the Late Blowne Blaste* (RSTC 1005: London, 1559), sigs P4r, Q2v.

2 *CSP Foreign 1558–59*, 59, 262.

3 Knox, VI, 11–20.

4 Hastings Robinson (ed.), *The Zurich Letters*, 2 vols (Cambridge, 1842, 1845), I, 24.

5 *CSP Scotland*, 455, 457, 460, 463, 469, 474.

6 For example, Cowan, *Scottish Reformation*, 115; Donaldson, *All the Queen's Men*, 28, 31–2.

7 Ritchie, *Mary of Guise*.

8 Bodrugan, *An epitome*, sig. D3v; Patten, *Expedicion into Scotlande*, sig. b7v; BL Royal MS 18.A.xxxviii fo. 14v; Harryson, *Exhortacion*, sigs F7r–G2v; Seymour, *Epistle*, sigs B5v–6v.

9 Merriman, *Rough Wooings*, 104–5; *HP*, II, 79.

10 Ritchie, *Mary of Guise*, 28–31.

11 Wedderburn, *Complaynt*, 2; Craigie, *Maitland Folio Manuscript*, 27–32; Pollen, *Papal Negotiations*, 429; *RPC*, 86–7; Cameron, *Scottish Correspondence*, 242; *HP*, II, 126; NA SP 52/4 fos 162r–164v (*CSP Foreign 1560–61*, 315).

12 Jenny Wormald, *Mary Queen of Scots: A Study in Failure* (London, 1988), 83.

13 Leslie, *Historie*, II, 315–16; Cameron, *Scottish Correspondence*, 315; *RPC*, 105.

14 *RPC*, 100–1, 106, 108–9; Flett, 'Conflict of the Reformation and democracy', 48; *CSP Foreign 1559–60*, 42; Tyler, *Calendar of Letters relating to Spain*, X, 339; *TA*, X, 281; *APS*, 499–500.

15 Tyler, *Calendar of Letters relating to Spain*, X, 341; *CSP Foreign 1547–53*, 77, 264; NA SP 68/7 fo. 13r (*CSP Foreign 1547–53*, 341); *CSP Foreign 1559–60*, 408, 853; *CSP Foreign 1558–59*, 868, 888; Melville of Halhill, *Memoirs*, 85.

16 *LP*, VI, 975; XX(ii), 308; Carpenter, 'David Lindsay and James V', 144; Hume Brown, *Early Travellers*, 73–9; Aylmer, *Harborowe*, sig. Q3r; NA SP 52/2 no. 38 (*CSP Scotland*, 642); Knox, I, 123; NA SP 49/8 fo. 209r (*LP*, XX(ii), 524); M. Bryn Davies, 'Boulogne and Calais from 1545 to 1550', *Bulletin of the Faculty of Arts, Fouad I University, Cairo*, 12 (1950), 44.

17 *RPC*, 87; *APS*, 481, 507.

18 Dickinson, *Two Missions*, 43, 45.

19 Ritchie, *Mary of Guise*, 180–8; Cameron, *Scottish Correspondence*, 409; LPL MS 3195 fos 177r–v, 248r, 253r; *CSP Foreign 1558–59*, 262; Leslie, *Historie*, II, 372.

20 LPL MS 3195 fos 253r, 265r; NA SP 51/1 fo. 35r (*CSP Scotland*, 416).

21 *CSP Scotland*, 411; Herries, *Historical Memoirs*, 29–30; Knox, I, 402; Pollen, *Papal Negotiations*, 429.

22 Pollen, *Papal Negotiations*, 428–30; Leslie, *Historie*, II, 385; *CSP Foreign 1559–60*, 45; *CSP Foreign 1547–53*, 305; Knox, I, 263–4, 404–7; Maitland, *Maitland's Narrative*, 5, 12.

23 Ritchie 61–95, 126–8; *CSP Foreign 1547–53*, 255; NA SP 59/1 fo. 147r (*CSP Foreign 1558–59*, 522).

24 Leslie, *Historie*, II, 354, 442; *CSP Foreign 1559–60*, 42, 45; Knox, I, 292.

25 Leslie, *Historie*, II, 362; Herries, *Historical Memoirs*, 29–30.

26 *HP*, II, 126; *CSP Foreign 1558–59*, 262, 269.

27 *Wodrow Misc.*, 51–85.

28 Knox, I, 267–8; on preaching during 1557, see above, 129.

29 Knox, I, 268–74.

30 Knox, I, 272; IV, 284–5, 461–520.

31 Jane Dawson, 'The two John Knoxes: England, Scotland and the 1558 tracts', *Journal of Ecclesiastical History*, 42 (1991), 123–40; Scott Dolff, 'The two John Knoxes and the justification of non-revolution: a response to Dawson's argument from covenant', *Journal of Ecclesiastical History* 55 (2004), 58–74.

32 Knox, IV, 83, 251–2, 285.

33 Knox, I, 269.

34 Wormald, *Court, Kirk and Community*, 114; Kirk, *Patterns of Reform*, 12.

35 Knox, I, 273–4; *CSP Scotland*, 698, 722, 751; *HP*, II, Appendix 39; Burns, *True Law of Kingship*, 141; Lee, *James Stewart*, 27–35. As Jane Dawson has recently pointed out, it was John, Lord Erskine who signed the band, not, as usually stated, John Erskine of Dun. Dawson, *Politics of Religion*, 24 n. 52.

36 Knox, I, 275–6; Gordon Donaldson, *The Making of the Scottish Prayer Book of 1637* (Edinburgh, 1954), 5–7.

37 Hamilton, *Catechisme*, fos 175r–193r.

38 *TA*, X, 369–70; *Wodrow Misc.*, 53; Knox, I, 300–1. On Luvell and Ferguson, see *TA*, VI, 307; Yellowlees, 'Dunkeld and the Reformation', 45; Lindsay of Pitscottie, *Historie*, II, 137.

39 Knox, I, 300–7; *Wodrow Misc.*, 53–4; Herries, *Historical Memoirs*, 34–5; Buchanan, *History*, II, 399.

40 See above, 111, 125–6.

41 *CSP Foreign 1558–59*, 212; John S. Wade, Thanksgiving from Germany in 1559: an analysis of the content, sources and style of John Foxe's *Germaniae ad Angliam Gratulatio'* in David Loades (ed.), *John Foxe at Home and Abroad* (Aldershot, 2004), 215. On the St Giles's day incident, see above, p. 125.

42 *APS*, 506–7.

43 Knox, I, 309–15.

44 *CSP Scotland*, 812.

45 Melville of Halhill, *Memoirs*, 76–8; *Wodrow Misc.*, 56; Wormald, *Court, Kirk and Community*, 115–6; Kellar, *Scotland, England and the Reformation*, 186.

46 Knox, I, 274. On the Beggars' Summons, see above, 31, 124–5.

47 Knox, I, 314.

48 *Wodrow Misc.*, 55; Knox, I, 257–8.

49 Patrick, *Statutes*, 149–52, 156–60; Knox, I, 291; Wodrow Misc., 55–6; NA SP 59/1 fo. 147r (*CSP Foreign 1558–59*, 522); Leslie, *Historie*, II, 397–9.

50 NA SP 59/1 fo. 147r (*CSP Foreign 1558–59*, 522); *TA*, X, 416; Knox, I, 317; Lindsay of Pitscottie, *Historie*, II, 142.

51 *Wodrow Misc.*, 265–8.

52 *Ibid.*, 265–76.

53 Knox, I, 344; Herries, *Historical Memoirs*, 36; Maitland, *Maitland's Narrative*, 23–4.

54 Knox, VI, 21–2; *Miscellany of the Spalding Club*, IV, 88–92.

55 Knox, I, 321–2; VI, 22, 23; *Wodrow Misc.*, 57; Gordon Donaldson, '"Flitting Friday": the Beggars' Summons and Knox's sermon at Perth', *SHR*, 39 (1960), 175–6; Lindsay of Pitscottie, *Historie*, II, 145.

Chapter 8

1559–60: from rebellion to revolution

FROM PERTH TO LEITH: THE COURSE OF THE REBELLION

In the course of a few days in May 1559, Scottish Protestantism went from being an underground movement in an outwardly Catholic country to an armed revolt against established authority which was implementing dramatic changes in the territory it controlled. The revolt quickly escalated into civil war, as the rebels amassed an impressively wide body of support from within the country. Scotland's neighbours hastened to intervene. The first foreign troops arrived in August 1559, and by the early months of 1560 the war had turned into a brutal slogging match between English and French expeditionary forces. The English victory of that summer cemented what the Protestant rebels had achieved, and allowed them give those achievements a degree of legal backing. The result was a violent social, political, diplomatic and religious rupture, and the creation of a new, Protestant, pro-English Scotland.

This extraordinary series of events presents its own set of historical problems. Having spent most of this book piecing together scattered shards of evidence, we now find ourselves deluged with evidence, as all of Western Europe focused its attention on Scottish Protestantism. What happened during 1559–60 is therefore tolerably clear. But the sheer oddity of those events makes the questions all the more pressing. How did this local rebellion become an international war? What drove the different groups of rebels, and what breadth of support were they able to command? How was it possible for them to turn for assistance to the auld enemy without being damned as English stooges? How were the English, who had lost an internationalised war in Scotland in the 1540s, able to win one ten years later? And how did the war affect the religious life of Scottish parishes?

The rebellion itself may be thought of as a drama in three acts.[1] In Perth, on 11 May 1559, following a sermon by John Knox, there was an iconoclastic riot. The town's churches and monasteries were stripped of the paraphernalia of Catholic worship and taken over for Reformed usage. Mary of Guise, the Queen Regent, decided to suppress this open defiance by force. A loosely organised band of Protestant lords, lairds, townspeople and preachers prepared to defend the town. A truce was negotiated, allowing Guise's forces entered Perth. However, the Protestants, styling themselves 'the Congregation', did not disband their forces. Indeed, when Guise was seen to have violated the terms of the truce by her actions in Perth, two of Scotland's most powerful nobles went over to the rebels – the Earl of Argyll, and Lord James Stewart, James V's illegitimate son. The Congregation now proceeded through Fife, ransacking Catholic churches as they went, and in mid-June they 'reformed' St Andrews itself. Significant parts of the country – Angus, the Mearns, Fife and substantial areas of the south-west – were under the Congregation's effective control. The rebels also began to put out feelers to Elizabeth I's England, in search of support. Meanwhile, their armies turned towards Edinburgh, and after a brief stand-off in Fife, Guise's forces fell back without a fight. At the end of June the Congregation occupied the capital. It felt like victory.

The second act of the drama showed that Guise was not to be written off so easily. From her refuge in Dunbar, she fought back on several fronts. Her propaganda impugned the Congregation's motives, insinuating that Lord James was plotting to seize his father's throne. It was probably not true, but it was both plausible and effective. At the same time, she negotiated with the rebels, deliberately dragging out the talks. Time was on her side. The Congregation's forces were feudal levies, liable to serve only for short periods, while Guise's own French troops were expecting reinforcements. By the end of July, the stalemate was turning against the Congregation. They agreed a truce, and withdrew from Edinburgh to their bases in Fife and in the west. The truce permitted some Reformed worship, but its terms were unclear and the Congregation were probably right to doubt whether Guise would keep her word. They regrouped, and began to look in earnest to England. Elizabeth I's Protestant regime was sympathetic, but wary of giving open assistance. Eventually, however, some English money made its way to the Congregation, with promises of more to follow.

Meanwhile, Guise used her French reinforcements to fortify Leith, the port which has since been swallowed by Edinburgh but which was then a separate town. This provoked genuine alarm, and brought some significant newcomers to the Congregation's ranks: in particular James, Duke of Châtelherault, the heir to the throne. Châtelherault's commitment to the religious cause was always lukewarm, but that of his son, the young Earl of Arran, newly escaped from gilded captivity in France, was passionate. Buoyed by these new supporters and by English money, the Congregation re-occupied Edinburgh on 16 October. They demanded that the fortification of Leith cease and the French soldiers leave the country, and when Guise rebuffed them, they ceremoniously declared that she was deposed. They hoped to take Leith by assault. However, their enthusiastic, ill-equipped and disorganised forces were no match for professional French troops. The first few skirmishes proved humiliating for the rebels. At the same time, Guise succeeded in choking off their financial lifeline by intercepting £1000 sterling which the English had sent to keep their soldiers in the field. The Congregation's support melted away with embarrassing speed, and on 6 November they left Edinburgh for the second time, in something close to a rout. Guise had successfully called their bluff.

The third act opened with a last, desperate plea being sent from the retreating Congregation for English help. As they waited, the enemy brought the battle to them. In December and into January, French forces rode a series of brutal, punitive raids into the Congregation's heartlands, and in particular into Fife. Guise received further reinforcements from France, although fewer than she hoped: more than a thousand men were drowned in December shipwrecks en route to Scotland. Finally, Elizabeth was persuaded to act. In January 1560, an English navy arrived off the east coast of Scotland, blockading any French traffic. The French troops in Fife were left exposed, and hastened back to Edinburgh. French raids continued in the west, but in April a substantial English army arrived. The Congregation's forces rallied, and many previously undecided Scots now joined them. They entered Edinburgh for the third and last time. Guise's army was now bottled up in Leith, and a grim little siege began. Guise herself, her health deteriorating fast, withdrew to the neutral ground of Edinburgh castle. The siege was tense, bloody and anticlimactic. A major English assault on 7 May was botched. The English feared that Guise's forces would be reinforced by French or, worse, by Spanish troops, but no reinforcements came. Instead, as Leith was battered and its food and ammunition became scarce, a French delegation arrived to negotiate a surrender.

France's growing internal turmoil made prosecuting a war on the other side of the North Sea an impossibility. Moreover, Guise herself was now mortally ill; she died on 11 June. Within a week, a ceasefire was agreed, and a treaty followed on 6 July. The French – more than 4,000 of them, including women and children – were evacuated. The English forces also withdrew. Scotland continued formally to acknowledge its French King and Queen, but its government was now, in effect, committed to the Congregation. In August, a parliament sealed the victory by reaffirming the new English alliance, and by passing a series of acts which established Reformed Protestantism as the official religion of Scotland.

GATHERING THE CONGREGATION

It is plain enough that, by May 1559, attempts at religious compromise in Scotland had failed. It is less clear why that failure provoked open rebellion. It was a shift which the regime clearly did not expect. If the iconoclasm of May 1559 forced the lairds in Perth to choose sides, why did they choose rebellion, rather than the safer cause of law and order? And when they had done so, how did they prove able to recruit steadily more Scots to their cause – nobles, lairds and commoners?

The obvious answer is religious zeal. Yet such answers often make historians uneasy. We are well aware that religion was commonly used as a hypocritical cloak for all kinds of uglier motives. A historical figure who claims religious motivation, or claims a higher moral purpose, invites scepticism. In such a case, we are inclined to search for ulterior motives, and if we find them, to assume that they discredit any more idealistic pretensions. However, excessive cynicism in this area can be as misleading as excessive credulity. Even the finest religious and moral convictions are rarely uncontaminated by baser concerns. Yet merely because someone may benefit from professing a belief does not mean that that profession is false. Indeed, many people find it easier sincerely to embrace beliefs if they stand to gain from them. The danger of underestimating the power of religious motivation is real.

And indeed, the religious issue was at the centre of the Congregation's programme not only when the revolt first broke out, but throughout the war. Their earliest negotiations with Guise focused exclusively on their demand for religious freedom. In May 1559, even when they appealed to Scotland's Catholic nobles for support, they had no other issue to raise but religion, stressing the injustices they had endured and the clergy's corruption. Religious freedom was the focus of the band which united the eastern and western forces on 31 May 1559. Another band, drawn up in Edinburgh in mid-July, committed the signatories to 'maintaining of the true religion of Christ, and down-putting of all superstition and idolatry', without mention of political or nationalistic questions. The truce or 'Appointment' agreed with Guise at the end of July likewise focused on the religious issue. In mid-June the English agent Sir James Croft was clear about the Congregation's priorities: they were 'fully bent to set forth God's word'.[2]

One of the rebellion's most striking features is the respect which the lords accorded to their preachers. John Knox was an unlikely diplomat, but from May 1559 to January 1560 he was the Congregation's principal secretary. His responsibilities included delicate negotiations with an English regime which he had gravely insulted by his ill-timed fulmination against female monarchy. In May, he and his more level-headed colleague John Willock were responsible for securing the Earl of Argyll and Lord James Stewart's agreement to guarantee the truce at Perth. The peak of the ministers' influence, however, came in the autumn. Knox took the lead in cajoling potential sympathisers into providing real military support in the run-up to the second occupation of Edinburgh; and he was more than a go-between. An English journal of the second occupation emphasises that almost every day, the lords convened to hear a sermon from Knox, Willock or Knox's friend Christopher Goodman. Before taking important policy decisions they regularly heard sermons, in which the preachers expounded the godly view of the question before them. During that occupation the Congregation also named a council governing religious policy, consisting of Knox, Willock, Goodman and the evangelical Bishop of Galloway, Alexander Gordon. Knox was also asked to oversee a proposed scheme to turn some of the old Church's incomes to military use. These plans came to nothing as the Congregation were forced into a rapid retreat, but when they rallied at Stirling on 8 November, Knox preached what he clearly felt was the sermon of his life to the lords. Lord Herries believed that Knox's preaching on that occasion was responsible for reviving the Congregation's courage and determination.[3] The ministers were not window-dressing for this rebellion; they were at the heart of its counsels. Nor would the lords have subjected themselves to such a punishing regime of preaching if their religion had been merely for show.

Their commitment showed itself in more than sitting through sermons. The Congregation's three main leaders were unmistakably sincere in their Protestantism. Lord James Stewart, the Earl of Argyll and the young Earl of Arran had all shown their commitment to the new faith during the 1550s, when they had nothing to gain from doing so. All would continue to do so after the rebellion, despite the vicissitudes of politics and (in Arran's case) the onset of madness. In 1559–60, these three idealistic young men – all in their mid-twenties – impressed all around them with their zeal and sincerity. The gushing English emissary Thomas Randolph marvelled at their 'singular wisdom and godliness'.[4] Nor were religious motives confined to this core group of leaders. In December 1559, Maitland of Lethington claimed that religious opinion was the decisive factor in determining support for the Congregation. Those who were animated merely by dislike of the French he saw as effectively neutral. Even in the midst of the siege, Guise's negotiations with the Congregation's leaders centred on the religious question. Maitland and Lord James were insistent on the issue, as was the Master of Maxwell, father of the (Catholic) historian Lord Herries. Their colleague Lord Ruthven was 'more unyielding than any of the others'.[5] If the Congregation's leaders were not personally committed to the new religion, most of them found it politic to pretend to be so.

There is also evidence of wider support for the reformers during 1559–60: not a majority of the country by any means, but a significant movement in some areas. William Kirkcaldy of Grange claimed that in the Congregation's heartlands, in Fife, Angus and the south-west, 'by the forth-setting of religion and hatred of the Frenchmen we get the hearts of the whole commonalties'. Lord Herries agreed that in those regions the reformers 'had the affections of the people'. In St Andrews, the band of July 1559 in support of the Protestant cause was signed by 304 men: perhaps a third of the entire adult male population of Scotland's ecclesiastical capital, including the provost of the town and at least some of the bailies. In other towns, the reformers did more than sign bands. If we are to believe Knox, the sack of Bishop Hepburn's palace and of nearby Scone Abbey in May 1559 was the work of Dundee rioters who blamed Hepburn for Walter Myln's death. In the same way, the friaries in Edinburgh were looted shortly before the Congregation's first occupation of the town; local reformers were taking advantage of a temporary power vacuum to finish the business they had started when they had attacked the St Giles's day procession the year before. By midsummer, Protestant support within Edinburgh was considerable, although well short of a majority. Bishop Leslie remembered bitterly that 'the people' of Edinburgh were 'allured with hope . . . of liberty, and a new kind of life'. The real test of Edinburgh's allegiance came when the Congregation withdrew in July 1559. The 'Appointment' made with Guise permitted Edinburgh freedom of religion, but what this meant was unclear. Was the town to make a collective decision, or were its citizens each to be free to pursue his or her chosen faith? Guise proposed a public meeting at which a vote would be taken, but the reformers vigorously protested at the idea that 'our religion now established . . . shall be subject to voting of men'. In other words, both sides assumed that the Catholics would win any such vote. Yet the reformers were still numerous. When they 'answered with one voice that [they] would not leave their profession', Guise was forced to abandon her scheme. They were permitted to retain St Giles's church until the second expulsion of the Congregation in November. Guise's forces taunted them but did not attack them.[6]

This episode is revealing both of the weakness and the strength of Scottish Protestantism at this point. Numerically, it was not particularly strong. Yet the determination of its adherents was unnerving. When the Congregation evacuated the town for a second time in November, a significant number of Edinburgh Protestants left with them, preferring to abandon their homes than to conform in their religion and appeal to Guise's mercy.[7] Guise's supporters and the neutrals lacked all conviction; the reformers were full of passionate intensity. This gave the committed Protestants a power out of all proportion to their numbers.

Belatedly, as Mary of Guise recognised the determination of the coalition which was forming against her, she set about trying to break it apart and to isolate its leaders. This was not an obviously hopeless task, but in the event she was almost wholly unsuccessful. If the committed core of Protestant nobles was small, Guise could have counted her faithful lords on her fingers. She was staunchly supported by Lord Seton and by several of the bishops, including Archbishop Hamilton. The Earls of Bothwell, Eglinton and Cassillis remained more or less loyal. Most of the rest of Scotland's magnates were fair-weather friends at best.[8] The reasons for Guise's failure to mobilise any wider support are important, because they shed light on the initial motives of the Congregation; on how the rebels eventually succeeded in building such a broad coalition; and on the underlying weaknesses of Guise's regime. Her central allegation was that the Congregation were guilty of sedition or outright treason, and while at some points this rang uncomfortably true, she was never able decisively to discredit them.

The most obvious accusation to which the Congregation's leaders were open was that they were usurpers. The Duke of Châtelherault and his son, young Arran, had been heirs presumptive to the Scottish throne since the death of James V, but were painfully aware that the prospect of Queen Mary's having children endangered this position. Lord James Stewart was James V's son, and his illegitimacy did not necessarily render an attempt on the crown impossible. In October 1559 Guise was telling anyone who would listen that the Congregation's religious motives had been hijacked by dynastic ambition. English observers, familiar with a more rough-and-ready approach to dynastic legitimacy, seem to have assumed that one or both of these claims lay behind the Congregation's actions. In August 1559, England's perennial ambassador to Scotland, Ralph Sadler, was even instructed to urge Châtelherault and Lord James to see the revolt in these terms. Some in the French court, too, feared that religion was a cloak for an attempt by Lord James to seize the throne.[9]

These charges were dangerous, but, it seems, illfounded. Lord James and the Hamiltons must have entertained the possibility of usurping the crown, but they made no real moves in that direction, either in 1559–60 or at any other time. If we are looking for evidence that Lord James coveted the throne, the closest we can come is the comment of Elizabeth I's Chief Minister, William Cecil, when he first met Lord James in June 1560. According to the Victorian edition of the Scottish correspondence, Cecil told his Queen that Lord James was 'not unlike either in person or qualities to be a king soon'. However, this is a mistranscription. The original letter plainly says, not that Lord James would be 'a king soon', but that he was 'a king's son'.– which was of course a simple statement of fact. The previous year Lord James had even offered to accept voluntary exile if his religious petitions were granted (admittedly a bluff which was most unlikely to have been called). The ambitions of the Congregation's leaders were real – Lord James presumably wished to be Regent, and young Arran wished both to maintain his family's rights to the succession and also to marry the English Queen – but those ambitions were both limited and passably honourable.[10]

Guise's accusations of sedition worried the Congregation's leaders. Aware that such accusations were damaging them, they insisted that their cause was simply one of religion. This in itself is an intriguing fact: initially, the Protestants clearly felt that they could recruit more support by appealing to religion than by opposing tyranny. Justifying their tactics to the English in August 1559, they lamented 'how difficult it is to persuade a multitude to the revolt of an authority established'.[11] It was not only the multitude that needed persuading. There were several prominent Protestants who refused to join the revolt, either from loyalty to the established authority or from distaste for working with the auld enemy. Lord Erskine had heard Knox preach in the mid-1550s and had been one of the five signatories of the band of 1557, but in 1559, despite the expectation that he would declare for the rebels, he remained studiously neutral. Edinburgh castle was under his command, and he refused to yield it either to the Congregation or to Guise. He used the bargaining power which control of Scotland's most powerful stronghold gave him to press both sides towards negotiations, and in 1560 he allowed Guise to retire there to die. Nevertheless he was an enthusiastic supporter of the parliamentary Reformation in August 1560.[12] Another signatory of the first band, the Earl of Morton, was equally dilatory during the war and equally committed after it, although in his case personal rivalry with the Hamiltons may have been as significant as loyalty to the regime. Robert Lockhart was a long-standing Protestant whose sincerity even Knox affirmed, but in the autumn of 1559 he was persuaded to act as a mediator between Guise and the Congregation.[13]

The Earl Marischal's case is more striking still. His Protestantism is unmistakable. He was pardoned for using heretical books in 1544. He attended George Wishart's sermons in 1544–45 and John Knox's in 1556, and recommended Knox's preaching to the Queen Regent. He stoutly supported the Protestant Confession of Faith in the August 1560 parliament. He was also an early advocate of the English alliance: he was one of the ambassadors who negotiated it in 1543, and in 1545 bound himself afresh to the English cause. Yet in 1559–60 he gave no open support to the Congregation during the rebellion, and firmly opposed the English alliance he had once advocated. The English ambassador described Marischal as one of the leading opponents of the new order in general and of the rapprochement with England in particular. Perhaps he no longer trusted England; or perhaps he would not break faith with the Queen Regent, whose deathbed he attended in 1560.[14] It is commonly implied that the rebels of 1559–60 had to turn to political grievances in order to muster support, because their religious agenda was only a minority interest.[15] The reminder that some powerful magnates were sympathetic to the Congregation's religious agenda but balked at open rebellion suggests a different view. The Congregation's recruitment problem was not only a matter of persuading those uninterested in Protestantism to join their cause. Equally significantly, they needed to persuade those sympathetic to the Protestant cause that rebellion was both a just and a necessary means to advance it.

In the rebels' recruitment generally, necessity was probably more important than justice. The Congregation succeeded in persuading large numbers of Scots to support them not so much because their arguments were irrefutable as because they were seen to be winning. Likewise, for some crucial figures, the decision was dominated by questions of personal rather than of national interest. In the battle which was fought during the summer of 1559 to secure the allegiance of the Duke of Châtelherault, Scotland's most eminent and least decisive nobleman, the critical question was the fate of the Duke's son, the young Earl of Arran. One of the earliest and most vital favours which the English performed for the Congregation was to assist in smuggling Arran out of France and back to Scotland. The Congregation knew that securing Arran's escape was an absolute precondition if Châtelherault were to join them.[16]

Châtelherault did at least remain firmly committed to the Congregation thereafter (his son's zeal perhaps left him little choice). Many other waverers came and went according to the perceived fortunes of war. Indeed, much of the Scottish political nation was never actively committed to either side. A large minority supported the Congregation; a much smaller number were staunchly loyal to Guise; the majority watched from the sidelines. Most of them wished, as Richard Maitland put it, to 'lie lurk and do no more / To see which side shall have the victory'. When the reformers had the wind at their backs, as in October 1559, their following increased, and it was said that if they could guarantee English support, 'the whole country would follow'. Inevitably, however, friends who had been won so easily disappeared when the rebels' fortunes turned. As the second occupation of Edinburgh unravelled in November 1559, magnates who had been promising support fell dumb and soldiers began to desert. As the Congregation withdrew from the town, 'the spiteful tongues of the wicked railed upon us, calling us traitors and heretics: every one provoked other to cast stones at us. One cried . . . "Fie, give advertisement to the Frenchmen that they may come, and we shall help them now to cut the throats of these heretics" '.

The arrival of English forces in 1560 swung the pendulum the other way. Guise's Scottish forces suddenly scattered; even those loyal to her, such as Lord Home, began quietly to negotiate with the English. The arrival of the English army in April produced another flood of Protestant recruits, but many of these – including the Earl of Morton – quickly withdrew as the possibility of a negotiated settlement resurfaced. As the siege closed around

Leith, the neutrals returned. After a fire in the besieged town seemed to herald a French defeat, the Duke of Norfolk wrote that 'the Scots do marvellously come in'. If Leith fell, he wrote, 'there will be left but few Scots in Scotland, but that they will be open enemies to the French'.[17] Conservative burghs such as Aberdeen and Peebles began to hedge their bets, providing token assistance to the Congregation. Some magnates did the same, often trying to negotiate favourable religious or political terms for themselves. The Earl of Huntly played a complex double game for most of the spring and summer of 1560, allowing his illegitimate brother Alexander Gordon to support the reformers, while he himself gave them little but warm words. His price for greater support was to be allowed 'supreme authority in the north' and to be rewarded with lands seized from die-hard supporters of Guise. But although he was not given any such assurances, he eventually, and reluctantly, signed the reformers' third band anyway. By then, it was prudent to back the unmistakable winners.[18]

Both sides put a great deal of effort into wooing these neutral lords, but it is not clear whether it was worth it. The neutrals' military contribution to the civil war was marginal. In January 1560, the Master of Maxwell recruited a group of Dumfriesshire lairds to the Congregation, but he had little faith in 'so great a number of inconstant and broken men'.[19] Such indecision was common in 1559–60, but the indecisive had little effect on the outcome. A seventeenth-century Earl of Leven began his history of this period with the following observation: 'Rational men may be said most ordinarily to be acted in all their undertakings either by a religious or civil principle, as they are swayed either by conscience or interest. It is obvious to the observation of all that such as are led by the former are more tenacious than those who are ruled by the latter.'[20] The rebellion was led, and its outcome determined, not by the majority of waverers who pursued self-interest, but by the tenacious minority who were ruled by their consciences.

THE END OF THE AULD ALLIANCE

It is a commonplace that, as the 1559–60 war progressed, the Congregation's avowed purposes shifted from being narrowly religious to become more nationalistic. Protestantism became less important than anti-French sentiment, and the Congregation also led the political nation in embracing the English alliance which had been so firmly rejected a decade before. Yet if religion was as central to the rebellion as I have argued, how did the religious and nationalistic issues come to be so intertwined? And how was it possible for so many Scots to turn with such alacrity to the auld enemy?

From the beginning of the revolt, one of the Congregation's demands was that Guise's French troops should have no part in Scottish affairs. The truce at Perth in May 1559 required that French soldiers be barred from the town. By early July, during the first occupation of Edinburgh, this had grown to a demand that all French troops should leave the country. Indeed, the Congregation's most controversial action during that occupation was probably an attempt to undermine the French presence: they seized the coining-irons used to mint money. Their justification was that Guise had been debasing the coinage, which was true; but the debasement had been carried out largely so that the French troops could be paid, and the Congregation were clearly interested in putting a stop to this. Seizing the coining-irons – a symbol of sovereignty – was a tactical error, since it allowed Guise to paint the Congregation as rebels and robbers. By the time Edinburgh was abandoned in late July, there was no more talk of expelling all the French, but the 'Appointment' drawn up with Guise did specify that Edinburgh itself should be demilitarised.[21] The arrival of fresh French forces during August, and the fortification of Leith, turned this into the Congregation's dominant theme. From then on, their principal and unwavering demand was for a complete withdrawal of French forces. The Protestant crusade had become an anti-French purge.

There was an obvious logic to this. Guise's French army was the principal obstacle to a Protestant settlement. Its removal was a necessary prerequisite for a Protestant establishment. As Clare Kellar puts it, 'the forces of their foreign oppressors were the legions of Antichrist, and their fight for freedom and for the true faith was one and the same struggle'.[22] The Congregation's willingness to call on English help can also be seen as merely instrumental: a necessary means to an end. However, this will not quite do. Many of those who joined the Congregation during the course of the rebellion were clearly much more anti-French than pro-Protestant. Moreover, the Congregation's leadership themselves became increasingly committed to the anti-French cause. It was a cause which, by the autumn of 1559, had acquired a life of its own.

As Lord Herries later put it, hatred of the French 'was the occasion that many of [the] Queen Regent's best friends in Scotland joined with the Congregation, although they differed from them in religion'. This does not, of course, mean that anti-French sentiment was stronger than Protestantism, merely that it was more widespread. Nevertheless, it is clear that while the Scottish elites were divided over religion, by the early autumn of 1559 they were becoming united by their opposition to France. When the Earl of Argyll was raising support from the McConnells and other Highlanders in September 1559, his only message was that France was conquering Scotland by stealth. In early October, young Arran was trying to win over the Catholic Lord Sempill. He acknowledged that Sempill was 'not resolute in your conscience towards the religion' – a polite evasion – but he emphasised French oppression and appealed to Sempill to protect 'the commonwealth and liberty of this your native country'. Sempill himself was not persuaded, but Archbishop Hamilton feared that Arran's wider efforts to win support in this way were bearing fruit. The reformers believed that although many Scottish lords might be neutral in religion, there was none 'so blind that he sees not the manifest ruin of our commonwealth ... intended by the French, so imprudent that he considers not his own peril'. According to the Duke of Norfolk, the Borderers who joined the Congregation in January 1560 supported the rebels 'so far forth as concerneth the expulsion of the French authority and rule out of Scotland', but were not persuaded of the religious cause. The Congregation's final appeal to the neutral lords, in March 1560, made no mention of religion, but appealed to them as 'true native Scotsmen' to resist French tyranny – and also referred unproblematically to the impending arrival of English forces, as if it were natural for 'true native Scotsmen' to look for help from that quarter.[23]

The universal testimony of Scottish and foreign observers is that, by the end of 1559, the French were widely loathed as tyrants and oppressors. The Duke of Norfolk initially feared that this was an elaborate charade intended to lull English suspicions of the Scots before a fresh Franco-Scottish invasion, but when he arrived in the north he was persuaded otherwise. 'The enmity and daily hostility between the French and the Protestants is so manifest ... as I cannot judge that they would make any such train to trap us.' However, it is also clear that this common hatred was grounded in several distinct grievances. William Cecil emphasised in June 1560 that there were many factors which had fired anti-French feeling, and commented that 'all this nobility of Scotland hate the French, and be devoted to England, yet some be for one respect and some for another'.[24]

As we have seen, until 1559 the latent suspicion towards France and French motives in 1550s Scotland remained merely latent.[25] It became inflamed partly because the Congregation deliberately exacerbated it. When Argyll was trying to persuade the McConnells to join the cause in September 1559, his argument was that 'the French are coming in and setting down in this realm to occupy it and to put forth the inhabitants thereof, and suchlike to occupy all other men's rooms piece and piece, and to put away the blood of the nobility'. As a warning, he cited the example of Brittany, another independent realm which had been joined to France by a marriage alliance, only to be absorbed into the French state. Argyll was not alone in this approach. At the height of the propaganda war, in October 1559, the Congregation were busily picking at old wounds, real or imagined, which could be blamed on France. Two formal manifestos drawn up early that month claimed that the French had been secretly plotting a takeover of Scotland ever since 1548. They cited the steady exclusion of Scots from positions of authority; the billeting of a rapacious and underpaid French army on Scotland; and the debasement of the coinage. They also made much of the young Earl of Arran's imprison-ment. All this was held up against the promise made in 1548 that Scotland's laws and privileges would be respected. The lords' formal declaration that Guise was deposed harped on these same injuries, lamenting how an 'army of strangers . . . was laid by her Grace upon the necks of the poor community of our native country'.[26] The Congregation's ulterior motive for attempting to irritate their countrymen against France is plain enough, but they did have some genuine grievances on which to work.

In truth, however, these long-standing complaints were merely pretexts. Until 1559 Guise herself had been trusted and the protection of France accepted as, if nothing more, the lesser of two evils. It was only immediately before and during the rebellion that these views changed. They did so almost entirely in response to actions taken by Guise and by the forces under her command.

The pattern was set during the very first confrontation of the rebellion, at Perth in May 1559. As Pamela Ritchie has recently argued, this situation was badly mishandled by the Queen Regent. In order to defuse the immediate crisis, Guise agreed a truce whose terms she would not or could not keep: demilitarisation of the town, an amnesty for the iconoclasts and a promise to consider the religious issue at a forthcoming parliament. She may have hoped to bend, rather than break this agreement. Her decision to occupy the town with Scots soldiers, rather than Frenchmen, indicates such an approach. However, the assertive manner of her entry and the trigger-happy behaviour of her troops (who shot dead a boy during the reoccupation of the town) suggests that re-establishing her authority mattered more to her than meti-culously observing the terms of the truce. Guise was, as Ritchie has argued, convinced from the beginning that the rebels' religious agenda was a cloak for more sinister motives. Her suspicions were seemingly confirmed by the Protestants' sacking of the Charterhouse, where King James I was buried. She was, simply, unwilling to negotiate with traitors. Yet the most powerful Protestant nobles, Argyll and Lord James Stewart, took a different view of the Perth affair. Urged on by their rebellious friends, they used the occasion to test Guise's good intentions by acting as personal guarantors of the terms of the truce. If she had observed those terms, it would have demonstrated her good faith, and the Protestant advocates of confrontation would have been isolated. But if, as turned out to be the case, she broke her word, she could be openly opposed as a tyrant.[27] It was an important step in persuading instinct-ive loyalists that Guise could not be trusted.

Her reputation, and that of France, suffered worse damage after the second truce of the rebellion, the July 'Appointment'. Guise had successfully faced the Congregation down and forced them to withdraw from Edinburgh. Their seizure of the coining-irons had seemed to demonstrate that their motives were indeed more political than religious. Her accusations of rebellion, Knox admitted, 'made us odious in the ears of the people'. Some parts of the country, notably the Borders, were beginning to mobilise for the Queen Regent. It may be, of course, that the Appointment was inherently unstable. The promise of a parliament to tackle the religious question had done no more than postpone the conflict, and the Congregation, too, were endangering the peace, by seeking English military support. However, it was Guise who more blatantly signalled an end to negotiation. The arrival of more than a thousand fresh French troops in late August 1559, and the subsequent fortification of Leith, did more than anything else to reverse the Congregation's fortunes. The English had been warning that the Guise faction now in control of France intended to extend its newly militant anti-Protestant policy to Scotland, and the arrival of the troops seemed to confirm this. It was widely read as a violation of the Appointment, providing a pretext for Scotland's most senior nobleman, Châtelherault, to join the rebels. Châtelherault had guaranteed the truce at Edinburgh in much the same way as Argyll and Lord James had at Perth, and with much the same effect. Moreover, it was this violation which galvanised the Congregation to reoccupy Edinburgh in October; and it was Guise's refusal to vacate Leith which was at the heart of their case for deposing her.[28]

The fortification of Leith provoked genuine outrage. It gave credence to the claim that the French intended conquest, and were establishing a permanent and unassailable base of operations. By the end of September the Congregation were assuring the English that 'our defection from France is great', and that the fortification of Leith was the main reason for this. When young Arran appealed to Lord Sempill to defend his country, the fortification of Leith was his best evidence of French malice. Like others, he thought it particularly ominous that the French soldiers were accompanied by their wives and children. This looked less like a temporary expeditionary force than a conquering army. Rumour claimed that the French troops were jokingly awarding the rebels' titles to themselves. 'One was styled Monsieur de Argyll; another, Monsieur le Prior; the third, Monsieur de Ruthven.' True or not, such rumours could only reinforce the impression that Guise intended a plain conquest. Nor did Guise or her troops do anything to dispel this impression. After the Congregation's second retreat from Edinburgh, the Protestant worship which had been tolerated there during the autumn was suppressed, and French troops were garrisoned in the capital itself: a normally terse chronicler observed with displeasure that foreign soldiers had never been lodged in Edinburgh before. In September, the level-headed Protestant Henry Balnaves thought that 'the enterprise of Leith hath inflamed the hearts of our people to a wonderful hatred and despite of France, wherethrough I think there shall follow a plain defection from France for ever'.[29]

Worse was to come during the winter of 1559–60, the darkest phase of the war for the Congregation. Their attempt on Leith in early November having failed, their military weakness was painfully exposed. The French now launched a series of merciless counterattacks which confirmed all the Scots' worst fears. 'The oppression and violence used by the French', Lord Herries remembered, was 'the greatest cause' which alienated the Scots from them. Even during the skirmishes of November 1559, the French were reckless of civilian casualties in Edinburgh. Thereafter, they behaved like an army of occupation – or, as Knox put it, 'four thousand of the most desperate throat-cutters that were to be found in Europe'. Two expeditions became particularly notorious. In January 1560, a French raiding party marched deep into Fife, systematically destroying crops and households. 'Wherever they passed', one witness wrote, 'there was great harm done to the poor by the men of war'. Local landowners were ordered to destroy their own fields and mills, so as to deny provisions to the Congregation's forces. The Congregation's resistance to this raiding party was limited to guerrilla action and piracy, but there seems to have been some spontaneous resistance from the local population. It did not help that the French were indiscriminate in their destruction, with Guise's supporters suffering alongside the Congregation.[30] A second major raid, by 2,000 men to Glasgow in March, showed the same face. This time there was a pitched battle, against a much smaller Protestant force under the command of the Earl of Glencairn's son, which was cut to pieces after a fierce resistance. Most of the Protestant captives were hanged on the spot. However, the French forces were unable to devastate the country as they had before. Thomas Randolph, the English agent in Glasgow, reported that their behaviour was 'so intolerable that they engendered unto themselves much hatred of many that otherwise favoured them well. The country gathered so fast upon them that they departed both sooner then they determined, and in better order then they came, for fear to have been fought with'. Nevertheless, they inflicted considerable damage on the way home. Soon after this, when the French withdrew into their fortress at Leith in the face of the English advance, they did their best to lay waste the surrounding countryside, and 'left no thing which the very enemies could have devised'. It was indeed as national enemies that they were now being seen.[31]

Sixteenth-century warfare was not a gentle business, and the brutal tactics of the French made some military sense. However, there is no doubt that they profoundly alienated most Scots and gravely undermined the legitimacy of their cause, even amongst Guise's supporters. In December 1559, it was reported that French soldiers' cruelties had driven Lord Seton, Guise's most faithful noble backer, to withdraw to his own estates. The Earl of Bothwell allegedly sheltered a fugitive from the French, and the Earl of Huntly was distancing himself from the Queen Regent. Other loyalists suffered directly from the French raids. In February 1560, even Archbishop Hamilton was backing away from Guise. 'Their case is pitiful', crowed Randolph, 'when their clergy beginneth to fail them'. One episode from the January raid could stand as a symbol of the whole enterprise. During the French retreat, the Congregation's light forces under Kirkcaldy of Grange tried to cut them off at Tullibody by destroying the bridge there. However, the French escaped by demolishing the parish church and using its roof timbers to build a makeshift bridge. This was a resourceful and professional army, but the ruthlessness of its methods was trampling the Catholic cause in Scotland underfoot.[32]

We have already seen how the callous brutality and imperial pretensions of English policy towards Scotland in the 1540s alienated any Scottish support England might have had.[33] In 1559–60, France fell into the same trap. By the spring of 1560, the Scots were still divided over the religious question, but no-one dared avow support for the French alliance as it then stood. In April 1560, Randolph wrote: 'I see all men here so affectioned to the utter expelling of the French from hence, that whosoever has any thought to the contrary is esteemed no less the enemy to the cause than if [he] had cut five hundred throats.' When the French garrison in Edinburgh withdrew that month, their departure was followed by mob violence directed at those Frenchmen who had been foolhardy enough to remain in the town. In July, after the treaty, when English ships were evacuating the French survivors, William Cecil wrote with dark irony: 'Here is goodwill of all parts: the French to be gone, we to carry them, and the Scots to curse them hence.'[34] The 'Auld Alliance' ended bitterly.

By mid-1560, that bitterness was matched with a remarkable degree of trust between the Scots and their 'auld enemies of England'. It was a trust which came late in the day. Knox's idiosyncratic Anglophilia apart, the Congregation's early appeals to England had some wariness about them, and understandably so. They were treacherously negotiating with a foreign power, and knew that if they succeeded they might find themselves riding a tiger. It was necessity rather than affection which drove the reformers into the arms of the English. This wariness continued into the autumn of 1559. In September the English Borderers were still carrying out raids in the west, from which some of the Protestant lords suffered. Yet English help was keenly looked for and warmly received when it began to arrive. The care with which English agents smuggled the young Earl of Arran from his refuge in Geneva to England and thence to Scotland was rewarded with considerable gratitude, not only from his father Châtelherault but apparently from a great many Scots. Young Arran was second in line to the throne; the French had imprisoned him but the English had set him free. It was a sign that times were changing. While the Congregation were still insisting that England agree to respect

Scotland's 'liberties, laws, and privileges', they were now also suggesting that England occupy fortresses such as Eyemouth and Broughty Crag, which England had held under unhappier circumstances in the 1540s. By November 1559, the Congregation's appeals to England had become much more full-hearted, with only the briefest of reference to Scotland's status as a realm subject to the new King and Queen of France. This reflected the reformers' desperation at that point of the war, but it also reflected the real trust that had begun to be built between the old enemies.[35]

That trust bore fruit when English forces arrived in Scotland. The enthusiasm with which the Scots greeted their new-found English friends surprised everyone, not least the English. A Scottish witness remembered that in January 1560, Admiral Winter's ships 'were thankfully received and well entreated, with such quietness and gentle entertainment betwixt our nation and them, as no man would have thought that ever there had been any variance'. Randolph agreed that the arrival of the English ships sparked celebrations. 'I never saw people make greater joy of any felicity that ever befell unto them than these do.' And he added: 'There hath been an old prophesy that there should be two winters in one year, which, now they say, now is fulfilled by reason of Winter the admiral's arrival upon the seas; in which year many wonders should chance in Scotland.' An English herald travelling overland to Edinburgh in February met an equally warm reception. Scots he met en route were pressing him to know when the English were coming 'to deliver them out of their misery and captivity of the French'. When the army finally arrived in April, Scots and Englishmen 'with great humanity embraced each other as if there had never been hatred or enmity'. The English were surprised by how easily the allies worked together: the Scots 'have not broken their promises, but rather amplified them'. Even the soldiers of the two armies avoided any confrontations. In June, Randolph claimed that 'since our camp arrived here there was never quarrel or disorder between the English and Scottish that ever blow was given or sword drawn' – it was, he said, 'a miracle'.[36]

A more tangible sign of this miracle was the unexpected ease with which the English forces in Scotland secured supplies locally. Victuallers flocked to them. One soldier noted, with surprise, that provisions were considerably cheaper in Edinburgh than they had been in Berwick. Even in rural areas, despite the damage done by French raids and unfamiliarity with English coins, the army was able to secure sufficient rations at a reasonable price. Knox explained that 'the people of Scotland so much abhorred the tyranny of the French, that they would have given the substance that they had, to have been rid of that chargeable burden'.[37]

Yet while enmity with France was a necessary condition for Anglo-Scottish reconciliation, it was not sufficient. If the French fell into the English trap of the 1540s, the English, critically, avoided it. Partly by good judgement, and partly by good luck, the English managed to convince most Scots that their ambitions in Scotland in 1559–60 were limited and honourable. There was no fear that the English intervention would be, as so often before, a prelude to attempted conquest. This was partly because England went out of its way to demonstrate its friendly intentions. William Cecil and others in the new English regime had served under Protector Somerset and had seen his mistakes at first hand. They were determined not to repeat them. A key memorandum on English policy towards Scotland in August 1559 took as a truism that Scotland could be governed only by a Scot. This was given substance by England's assisting one likely governor, the young Earl of Arran, to return home. Cecil was well aware of the goodwill which this generated and worked to exploit it. Even when the Congregation pleaded for English intervention in December 1559, Cecil was still scrupulous about respecting Scottish sensibilities. He rejected the possibility of English forces' garrisoning an entire Scottish town as a guarantee of the Congregation's fidelity, claiming that England 'would rather maintain all the towns in the Scots' hands than have them out of theirs'. The English army's model behaviour was not due to mere soldierly goodwill. The Duke of Norfolk insisted that 'foraging, robbing, and wasting of the country where they be is not now to be suffered, except we would make enemies of friends' – as the French had done. When some Scottish merchandise which had been seized at sea by the French fell into English hands, it was carefully returned to its owners. During the Anglo–French negotiations which ended the siege, Cecil repeatedly insisted that the Scots not be excluded; rather, the commissioners were to 'deal plainly with them in the whole matter'. In particular, he refused to countenance any deal which compromised Scottish religious liberty.[38] The English did their best to behave towards Scotland as good neighbours.

This attitude was not entirely false. Plenty of English Protestants had an internationalist outlook after their years of exile, and saw assisting Scottish Protestantism as a matter of conscience. John Aylmer's view in 1559 was that 'he is one of our brethren, if he be a faithful Christian; it is manners, faith and behaviour, and not nations, that make men strangers one to another'. Even Cecil prayed, no doubt sincerely, that 'this terrestrial kingdom of Christ may be dilated through this noble Isle'.[39] Yet Cecil's concerns, and those of most other English observers, were dominated by other matters. Aylmer's religious internationalism was matched by a pungent nationalism which drew him into the unguarded, notorious and much misunderstood claim that 'God is English'. And although the regime itself took care not to talk about imperial union or English suzerainty to the Scots' faces, those ideas had not disappeared. As Stephen Alford has shown, the claim of English suzerainty was one of the ways in which Cecil persuaded his suspicious Queen that she had a right to intervene in Scotland.[40]

However, the English regime's thinking was dominated neither by religious idealism nor by imperialist aspirations, but by brutally practical concerns. One anonymous note from 1559 lists the advantages to be had from 'amity and friendship' with Scotland, including access to Scottish fishing and (more dubiously) to Scotland's gold mines. For this author and for every observer, however, the main fear was that French domination of Scotland was a prelude to a conquest of England. The English helped the Congregation because doing so offered a chance to disrupt the Franco-Scottish alliance and so to secure England's northern border. It was a chance which observers of Scottish affairs feared might not return. Cecil's most substantial discussion document on Scottish policy, drawn up in August 1559, offered many reasons why England should not intervene, but only one why it should: self-defence.[41]

Paradoxically, this bluntly self-interested approach did more to foster Scottish trust of England than any amount of diplomatic soft soap. In 1559, the weakness of England's international position was painfully obvious. A queen whose succession was disputed had inherited a divided country which had just suffered a humiliating military defeat at French hands. England was in no position to embark on any foreign adventures. Its parsimonious and conservative queen was already showing the scepticism to grandiose plans and imperial glories which would colour English diplomacy for decades. The British rhetoric of the 'Edwardian moment' had no interest whatsoever for Elizabeth.[42] Compared to Henry VIII's alarming enthusiasm for intervention in Scotland in 1543, her manifest reluctance either to risk her resources on a Scottish expedition, or to risk open confrontation with France, was positively reassuring to Scots. English caution about any kind of intervention in Scotland throughout 1559 was intensely frustrating to the Congregation, but it certainly made it clear that England had no imperial ambitions. Indeed, it was the Scots who were pleading for English troops. They even compared Elizabeth unfavourably to Henry VIII, complaining that he had been far more willing to commit resources to Scotland than she was. But the English dragged their feet. They were much readier to offer the Scots encouragement than substantial support. Cecil even asked the Scots for advice on how to solve their dilemma: how could they help the Congregation without provoking the French? Although Cecil himself was quickly convinced that intervention was worth the risk, the Queen was far more sceptical. In November, when £1,000 sterling sent from England to support the Congregation was stolen en route by the Earl of Bothwell, Cecil was so afraid that Elizabeth might wash her hands of the whole enterprise that he did not even dare tell her about the theft for more than a week. Throughout 1560, the Queen worried about the Scottish campaign's prospects, begrudged its cost and doubted its value.[43] No-one could doubt her determination to withdraw her forces from Scotland as soon as possible. During 1559–60, for the first if not the last time, Elizabeth demonstrated the political power of playing hard to get: a policy which was all the more effective because the reluctance was genuine.

One final piece of good luck helped to ensure that Scotland saw England as more trustworthy than France in 1559–60. Since James V's death, the presence of a female sovereign had destabilised Scotland's international position. During the 1540s, the competition between England and France was not for a Scottish alliance, but for a Scottish marriage which would allow the victor to swallow the kingdom entirely. In 1559, however, Mary Stewart was married and England had an unmarried Queen Regnant of its own. There was now no danger that England would absorb its neighbour by marriage. Indeed, many Scots and some Englishmen hoped that the situation had been reversed. Elizabeth was being pressed to marry Arran, who was second in line to the Scottish Crown; a dynastic union might conceivably have emerged, but this time with the smaller country providing the husband.[44] In fact, Elizabeth herself appears never seriously to have considered the marriage, and by 1561 Arran's growing mental instability had made it impossible. During the critical months of the rebellion, however, this helped to persuade the Scots that an honourable friendship with England was a real alternative to a suffocating French embrace. The diplomatic revolution was complete.

WINNING THE WAR

The propaganda war, then, was decisively won by the Congregation and the English. This, however, need not have been decisive. Realms are not conquered by books, but rather by blood. The Congregation's helplessness in the face of the French onslaught, and England's obvious international weakness, helped to cement the Protestant alliance, but hardly made that alliance terrifying. How, in the end, was the war won?

The Congregation's weakness was clear enough. While the lords could sometimes field a substantial army, they could neither equip it to the most modern standards nor maintain it in the field for any length of time. This, more than anything else, accounts for the war's peculiar ebb and flow. Cecil understood the Scots' weaknesses: 'the way to overcome them', he wrote in August 1559, 'is to prolong time, and not to fight with them, but stand at defence'. This was exactly what the French did. They fortified an almost impregnable base at Leith, which could both receive supplies by sea, and serve as a base for punitive raiding. These tactics may not have won the Scots' love, but they were brutally effective. The French could outlast, outspend and outmanoeuvre the Congregation's makeshift forces. The Congregation's first withdrawal from Edinburgh, in July 1559, was a result of thinning forces and dwindling food supplies. By mid-August the Congregation had only 500 men under arms. The attempt to re-mobilise in the autumn was delayed by bad weather, which slowed the harvest and meant that men could not be spared. The second occupation of Edinburgh was a fiasco. An assault on Leith was planned – ladders ordered, artillery brought into position, and wood prepared for firing the ditches. Yet even before the first skirmishes in early November, the rebels were running out of money. The theft of £1,000 sterling sent from England cut off their only financial hope, and their army dissolved. Their untried and inexperienced forces had also, as young Arran admitted, been outclassed in battle. By mid-November their position was desperate. Knox was pursuing a half-baked scheme to raise funds from individual Protestant sympathisers in England. When the French offensive was renewed in January, the Congregation had difficulty even maintaining guerrilla forces. When the Congregation did engage the French, they did so in a dangerously disorganised way. The Earl of Argyll and Lord James Stewart were close to bankruptcy. The eastern and western Protestant centres were quarrelling, and were in danger of being cut off.[45]

As the Congregation weakened, the French forces were gathering strength. From August onwards, Guise received a steady trickle of reinforcements. By the end of the year she had some 4,000 men under arms. France was also pressing for the Pope to send an inquisitor to Scotland to enforce Catholic orthodoxy. Guise's own leadership was also a considerable asset, her charisma and fighting spirit respected on all sides. However, the French had problems of their own. Guise was seriously ill from October 1559 onwards, and preparations were made to recall her to France. In November it was rumoured that she was dead, but she was tougher than her enemies hoped. She was very sick, but, Randolph said, 'some say the devil cannot kill her'. In April, however, her sickness returned with renewed force, and she died in June. Throughout this period, then, her effectiveness as a leader was much reduced.[46]

Moreover, the war was straining France itself. King Henry II had died on 10 July, following a gruesome jousting accident. Francis and Mary, King and Queen of Scots, now became King and Queen of France, and real control passed to Mary of Guise's brothers, the Duke of Guise and the Cardinal of Lorraine. *Les Guise* quickly ran into difficulties, however. Over the winter, the supply of troops to Scotland faltered. The sheer technical difficulty of transport across the North Sea in winter was a part of the problem. Two separate shipwrecks off the Dutch coast cost the lives of well over a thousand French soldiers, and prompted rumours that the whole enterprise had provoked God's wrath. More importantly, raising the necessary money and men within France was proving unexpectedly difficult and controversial. The huge expenses and disruption associated with the Scottish war, let alone a possible English war, provoked talk of a compromise. France had only just concluded a ruinously expensive European war and was gravely in debt. It was trying to hire German mercenaries rather than raising French troops, but these too would have had to be paid. Worse, religious disaffection in France itself was slipping out of control. There were rumours of religious unrest, and the Cardinal of Lorraine apparently feared that, like his counterpart at St Andrews, he might be assassinated. In March 1560, a scheme by French Protestants to seize the young King at Amboise was unmasked, thoroughly alarming the already unsettled regime. As these domestic threats mushroomed, the possibility of sending further reinforcements to Scotland receded. Promises of more troops continued through the spring and summer, but the date on which they could be expected to arrive kept slipping back. By April, France was reduced to asking Protestant Denmark to send troops to Scotland, unpaid: a request which was rejected with polite contempt. Bishop Leslie's judgement was clear: the French were unable to intervene decisively in Scotland because they were 'wholly engaged in repressing the seditions' in their own country.[47]

Guise's last realistic chance for reinforcements came from an unexpected quarter: Spain. The mere fact that Spaniards, as well as Germans and Danes, were paying attention to this crisis demonstrates how, by the spring of 1560, the struggle over Scotland had become western Europe's main flashpoint. Spanish interest, particularly, was a sign that religion was becoming the fault-line of European politics, for it was remarkable that the King of Spain should even consider helping his old enemies, France, against his old allies, England. Philip II had been watching Scottish events closely since the autumn, but had forbidden his subjects to assist either side. After the conspiracy at Amboise, however, rumours began to circulate in France that Spain would take up the Catholic cause in Scotland. In April 1560 England was suddenly gripped with fear of Spanish intervention. Nicholas Wotton, one of England's most experienced diplomats, was convinced that a Spanish expeditionary force was coming, and that England should rapidly make whatever peace it could to avoid the nightmare of simultaneous war with both France and Spain. The English army in Scotland even asked for instructions on how to respond to Spanish forces if they landed. Philip denied having any such plans, but rumour in the Spanish Netherlands contradicted him. In mid-April preparations for a sizeable sea-borne military expedition were being made in Antwerp, said to be destined for Scotland. Intriguingly, the Netherlandish political establishment was vehemently opposed to this. The English agent in Antwerp was taken aback by the strength of pro-English feeling, which blamed the supposed war on 'the practice of the Spaniards and priests'. In fact, however, this planned expedition appears to have been mere bluff. The ships and troops remained in the Netherlands. While Philip wished to deter the English if he could, he was not willing to intervene directly. Nor would an intervention have been risk-free for Spain, given the constant Turkish threat in the Mediterranean. At best he was willing to lease ships to France – a safe offer to make, given France's near-bankruptcy. The possibility faded, and Guise and her troops were left alone.[48]

This isolation was the fundamental reason for Guise's defeat. Victory depended on the regular supply of fresh men and materiel. In 1560 that supply dried up, principally because Scotland was not the only country then afflicted by religious discord. France was beginning its own long descent into religious civil war. As William Ferguson has observed, French rule over Scotland was the first casualty of the French Wars of Religion.[49] However, this was more than bad luck. The French and Scottish Reformations were connected. Scots such as the young Earl of Arran had been converted in France, and Scottish and French Protestant nobles were in regular contact.[50] Even in the Netherlands, the rumours of a Spanish invasion of Scotland were inflaming religious discord. The same religious contagion that had burst out in Scotland was incubating in France and elsewhere, and contact with the Scottish outbreak served only to exacerbate the condition. Just as revolutionary religion had been decisive in the beginning of the Scottish rebellion, so it was decisive in determining that rebellion's outcome.

The result of the Congregation's military weakness, and of France's fail- ure to resupply Guise, was that the war in Scotland in 1560 was on a rather small scale. This meant that even in its weakened state, a second-rank power such as England could tip the balance. Nevertheless, the victory was not easily won. Leith was, one English witness recorded, 'marvellously fortified, trenched, and replenished with a sufficient number of valiant soldiers'. The best hope always lay in starving it out, and from the first despatch of naval forces this was the principal English objective. The naval blockade set up from January certainly alarmed the French. From the first arrival of the English, French cargo ships were being seized or run aground. Yet the blockade was not impenetrable. The first English target was the small French base on the island of Inchkeith, in the Firth of Forth, which they apparently hoped could be quickly starved into surrender. However, in February Lord Seton twice successfully resupplied the French garrison there by night, and in March three French munitions ships reached the island. In June, the Inchkeith garrison even managed to seize an English supply ship. Another small French garrison, at Dunbar, had done likewise in May.[51]

When English land forces arrived in April, their situation was precarious. Fearing the arrival of French or Spanish reinforcements, the English did not expect to have the leisure to starve Leith into surrender. Their Scots allies were keen to assault the fortress, but the more experienced English soldiers were daunted by Leith's fortifications. When Lord Grey of Wilton, the commander of the English force, first saw Leith, he doubted that it could be assaulted, and pressed for a negotiated solution – much to the dismay of the Congregation. However, he also threw a noose around the town, and began to tighten it. The siege proper began on 6 April, when a French sortie from Leith was forced to retreat. From 12 April onwards there were daily bombardments of the town. By the following day the English were digging trenches. 14 April was Easter Sunday, and high Mass was celebrated in the besieged town by one of Archbishop Hamilton's chaplains; during the service an English cannonball smashed through the window of the church. (No-one was hurt, which the French understandably saw as miraculous.) The following day, a major French raid on the English positions destroyed four cannon and inflicted heavy casualties. After this the English became both more cautious and more merciless. During the night on Easter Wednesday, the town was subjected to a general bombardment. One soldier recalled that the English 'shot very terribly, from eleven o'clock till it was two in the morning. . . . The stones in the street, the tiles, and slates of the houses flew so about the street, that the women and children made such piteous noise and cry that it was heard in our camp'. There were daily skirmishes. On 22 April English cannon brought down the spire of Leith's church. The English earthworks were creeping closer to Leith, under constant fire – and also constant rain; heavy storms reduced the entire battlefield to a quagmire. The ground was 'marshy and rotten' at the best of times, but the rain made it 'so deep and foul' that heavy guns could not easily be placed. Nevertheless, the English commanders' hopes of a successful assault were rising. On 30 April, a fire broke out in Leith, much to the excitement of the besiegers. Grey's report of it, written that night, bears the excited postscript: 'Yet it burns, yet yet.' It was a hopeful sign.[52]

The assault came on 7 May, and was a disaster. The English artillery failed to breach Leith's fortifications, and, catastrophically, the ladders which had been prepared to scale the walls turned out to be too short. Apparently, no-one had anticipated that ladders set on a field of mud and weighed down with soldiers would sink some way into the ground. The result of this miscalculation was a slaughter. The assailants suffered at least a thousand men dead and injured; the survivors' morale was badly shaken. The Congregation's forces, which had participated ineffectually in the assault, melted away, and the English, too, suffered from considerable desertion. The English commanders blamed one another. The Duke of Norfolk, who had previously been an enthusiast for the assault, now thought that another 15,000 men would be needed. Indeed, the English briefly felt besieged themselves, with munitions running low and the people of Edinburgh suddenly less keen to welcome such incompetent liberators. Mary of Guise, it was said, roused herself from her sickbed to watch the assault from the ramparts of Edinburgh castle, and once the outcome was clear went to Mass to give thanks for victory.[53]

However, the assault was a side-show and the victory an illusion. The war would be won not by tactics but by logistics. English reinforcements continued to arrive, while supplies ran dangerously low in Leith. As early as April, the French had been reduced to eating their own horses. On 12 May a French party stole out of Leith to gather cockles and periwinkles on the seashore, only to be set upon by English cavalry and to suffer dozens of casualties. A month later they tried to gather shellfish again and suffered the same fate. An English wag composed a poem taunting them: 'As oft as for cockles you run to the sands / God send your brave soldiers to fall into our hands.' (He thoughtfully translated this into French and had copies thrown into the besieged town.) One English diplomat recommended that deserters not be allowed to leave Leith, in order to prevent the French from eking out their supplies. Yet deserters did begin make their way out; by June they were spreading tales of a garrison on the brink of famine, reduced to eating unmilled seedcorn and whatever fish they could catch. These stories were probably exaggerated. There does not seem to have been actual starvation in Leith, although by the end of May the men had been put on reduced rations of ten ounces of bread a day. But while they could hope to catch fish, they had no way of replenishing their exhausted gunpowder. Mary of Guise's death in the early hours of 11 June only reinforced the hopelessness of their position. France sent, not reinforcements, but ambassadors to negotiate a surrender. The terms included the provision that all those in Leith should be safely returned to France. Cecil, who came north to negotiate the peace, was relieved at this outcome. There were over 3,600 fighting men left in Leith, and he noted that they 'are for all their scarcity of victual very well looking, all very well armed. . . . If they had stood to, it should have been the occasion of the shedding of a great deal of blood'.[54]

REFORMATION IN WARTIME

The 1559–60 war was, latterly, grim; but it was also localised. Most of Scotland saw little or no fighting, but fell quickly under the control either of the Congregation or of neutral lords who were keen to maintain good relations with the reformers. This control meant that religious reform was not merely a future aspiration. Although a comprehensive settlement of the religious question was not possible until the parliament of August 1560 (if then), reformers on the ground had no need to tarry for the magistrate. They could begin to build the new Jerusalem in the parishes.

Their first priority was destruction. The iconoclastic 'cleansing' of Catholic churches was a vital first step both for theological and political reasons. Theologically, Reformed Protestants were clear that idolatry was intolerable; and politically, iconoclasm was an unmistakable and irrevocable statement of

allegiance. It was an act of defiance which brought clarity to a confused political situation, by forcibly dividing a population into supporters and opponents
of what had happened. It was also the means by which a community was
physically changed from Catholic to Protestant; and because the destruction
was far easier than any possible rebuilding, it aimed to make that change
irreversible. The vigour of this process in Scotland impressed observers. In
August 1559, John Jewel, in London, summarised the Scottish news for Peter
Martyr in Zurich:

> Every thing is in a ferment in Scotland. Knox, surrounded by a thousand
> followers, is holding assemblies throughout the whole kingdom. . . . All the
> monasteries are everywhere levelled with the ground: the theatrical dresses, the
> sacrilegious chalices, the idols, the altars, are consigned to the flames; not a
> vestige of the ancient superstition and idolatry is left.

In a slightly double-edged reference to the legendary excess of northern
barbarians, Jewel added: 'You have heard of *drinking like a Scythian*; but this
is *churching it like a Scythian*.'[55] For Englishmen disappointed by their Queen's
sober caution, the Scots' achievement seemed heady indeed.

The pattern of iconoclasm which was begun in Perth spread across the
country. As the reformers dispersed across Fife in June 1559, 'as they passed,
where they found in their way any churches or chapels, immediately they
purged them, breaking down the altars and idols in all places where they
came. And so praising God continually, in singing of Psalms and spiritual
songs, they rejoiced that the Lord wrought thus happily with them'. Their
cleansing mission took them to St Andrews. It was the site of Knox's first
sermon, twelve years earlier. Now he preached again, on Christ's cleansing of
the temple, triggering another wave of destruction. 'Before the sun was down,
there was never inch standing but bare walls' – this chronicler was exaggerating, but not wildly. Some images were symbolically burned for heresy on
the spot where Walter Myln had been executed. The nearby town of Crail
was also 'ransacked and spoiled'. In Edinburgh, the initial purge took place
even before the Congregation's forces arrived, allegedly provoked by the friars' attempts to sell off their goods – for the preachers' scruples about
not looting church property were not universally shared. Whether there
was personal violence is less clear. The pro-Catholic historians Bishop Leslie
and Lord Herries both claimed – very plausibly – that there was; however,
there is no contemporaneous evidence to support them. In any case, by the
autumn the abbeys of Scone, Melrose, Jedburgh, Kelso, Paisley, Dunfermline
and Kilwinning had been purged. In December, the Reformation even reached
conservative Aberdeen, when bands of reformers from Angus and the Mearns
arrived 'to destroy and cast down the churches and religious places' of the
burgh. There, as in Edinburgh, the iconoclasts' job was partly done for them

by the burgh council, which removed valuables from the churches in order to prevent them from being looted. The motives were different but the effect was the same.[56]

This destruction was itself a notable achievement for the reformers. Restoring Catholic worship in the wake of the iconoclasm would have been very difficult, and this was certainly one of the Protestants' aims. According to Herries, Knox cried in his 11 May sermon at Perth, 'Pull down the nests, that the crows might not build again!' It was done. When Guise reoccupied the town and Catholic worship was (briefly) restored there, the priests were forced, Knox noted with satisfaction, to say Mass using a 'dicing-table', because 'all the altars were profaned'. Altars could be reconsecrated, but more costly damage was also done. At St Andrews, and presumably elsewhere, Mass books were burned, cutting off the church's liturgical memory.[57] Catholic practice could not be stamped out as easily as Catholic buildings could be ransacked, but an earnest attempt was made at this too. One chronicler claimed, regretfully, that once the rebellion had begun 'none durst say Mass; no sacraments [were] used in the old fashion'. In fact, Mass did continue to be said in some areas. It was ostentatiously restored in Edinburgh when Guise's forces retook the town, and some other clergy celebrated it – or tried to do so. A few religious communities withdrew to less visible settings where they presumably maintained some of their liturgical life. In Aberdeen, a kind of Catholic 'privy kirk' survived for much of the 1560s. Yet the speed and scale of the suppression is still surprising. By August 1560, although the Reformation parliament was worried about priests who 'stubbornly persevere in their wicked idolatry', it believed that this was only done 'in quiet and secret places'. When the Jesuit Nicholas de Gouda visited Scotland in 1562, he was categorical: 'No religious rite is celebrated in any part of the kingdom.'[58] The suppression of Catholic worship was a remarkable success story.

Catholic structures and property, too, were under threat. In November the Congregation threatened to deprive priests who defied Reformed ministers. In December they took steps to close down the old ecclesiastical courts, some of which were still functioning. The Congregation also began to look to the old Church's property to pay for their own war effort. A proclamation in late October offered substantial pensions for those injured in the war, or for the widows of those killed, 'and this to be gathered of the papists' goods'. More systematic attempts to pay for garrisons in this way were also made. These seizures of church property were irregular and, as it turned out, often temporary, but their impact was real enough. In mid-1560, Archbishop Hamilton complained that a large number of clerics' houses, including those of bishops, had been 'spoiled from them violently since this insurrection'.[59]

The suppression was not, however, principally a matter of violence. If there was violence threatened against the Catholic clergy, it was veiled. We know of a priest in Peebles who felt coerced into conforming, and who eased his conscience by drawing up a deed claiming that he had acted 'for fear of his life . . . not from any hatred of his old religion'.[60] However, there were to be no Catholic martyrs made in the Scottish Reformation until the 1570s. Catholic clerics and previously loyal lay people conformed to the new Church in large numbers and with remarkable speed. Looking back with disgust on the collapse of Scottish Catholicism, the polemicist Ninian Winzet asked:

> How that might be, that Christian men professing, teaching, and preaching Christ and his word so many years, in one month's space or thereby, should be changed so proudly in so many high matters into the plain contrary men. At Easter and certain Sundays after, they taught with great appearing zeal, and ministered the sacraments to us in the Catholic manner: and by Whitsunday they changed their standards.

A marginal note dates this transformation: 'A sudden change to be in the faithful, 1559.' Winzet's explanation was not that these clergy were compelled, but that they were 'hypocrites, and temporisers with the time'. If so, however, hypocrisy was remarkably thick on the ground, and thickest at the nation's spiritual capital, St Andrews. Knox testified as early as June 1559 that 'divers canons of St Andrews have given notable confessions, and have declared themselves manifest enemies to the Pope, to the Mass, and to all superstition'. The most notable of these was their subprior, John Winram, who may have had covert reformist sympathies for some time.[61]

By early the following year, some tougher nuts had started to crack. Thirty-eight Catholic priests formally repented of their idolatry and proclaimed their conformity to the new religion in St Andrews during February and March 1560. Admiral Winter was personally present at one such recantation, but there is no other indication that they were extorted by force. The last of these recantations was the most dramatic. John Grierson was the provincial of the Dominican friars in Scotland, one of the best-disciplined orders. He himself was an exceptionally experienced heresy-hunter. He had been one of Patrick Hamilton's judges, and one of Walter Myln's; he had petitioned James V to act against Lutherans in 1534; and in 1559, he was appointed to enforce clerical celibacy across the country. On 17 March 1560, he formally renounced his allegiance to Rome and his faith in the Mass – although he retained his office of provincial until his death in 1564. Nor were the high-profile recantations confined to St Andrews. In February 1560, the provost of the collegiate church of Lincluden declared his intention to marry. There was a string of public confessions in Edinburgh in June 1560. It was even rumoured that Lady Stonehouse, Archbishop Hamilton's mistress, would join the rush to repent.[62] No doubt some penitents were purely cynical, but these reports have the tang of religious revival about them. The acknowledged corruption of the old

Church; the muddying of its doctrines by reform efforts; the destruction of the physical fabric which was so important to it; the fervour and apparent moral purity of reformers who were widely perceived as 'clean fingered';[63] their sense of momentum; and the unmistakable verdict which God was giving through the Congregation's victory, would all combine to make genuine conversions during this crisis very possible.

If these personal conversions were to be made national, however, a new, Reformed Church would have to be erected in the place of the old one. Here, predictably enough, progress was more piecemeal. Reformation in the parishes could never have been the work of a moment. Yet with all recognition of the importance of continuity, the changes wrought in 1559–60 still seem dramatic enough. In September 1559, Knox claimed that the ministry was established and the sacraments 'rightly ministered' in Edinburgh, St Andrews, Dundee, Perth, Brechin, Montrose, Stirling and Ayr. The reformers were expelled from Edinburgh in November 1559 but swiftly re-established themselves the following April. Ayr, which had had a resident minister since 1557, sent to Edinburgh in 1559 to secure another one. During the war, Ayr's burgh council even paid for Christopher Goodman to go on a missionary trip to the Isle of Man. Moreover, if full-scale Reformed ministry was initially established only in the burghs, preaching was considerably more widespread. There were Protestant sermons on the east Borders in late August, and even Aberdeen thought it politic to invite preachers to the town in December 1559. The ripples of reform were spreading outwards. One witness claimed that after the Congregation's second retreat from Edinburgh, the preachers redoubled their efforts, 'so that, by means of the trouble, the Religion was in all places better reformed and established'. We know that by the end of the year even small towns such as Dalmellington in Ayrshire and Crail in Fife were establishing the ministry.[64] A Protestant establishment was beginning to appear.

The nature of that establishment was not yet decided. Was this to be full-blown Reformed Protestantism in the style of Geneva, Zurich or Emden, or the more traditionally structured English version? Some favoured the latter. There was much talk of 'Common Prayer' being used. In January 1560, Randolph wrote that 'the common prayers' used in Scotland 'are the very same, or differ very little, from those of England', although they were shorn of some of the ceremonies which hotter Protestants found most obnoxious. In July 1559, Kirkcaldy of Grange claimed that when the Mass had been suppressed, 'the Book set forth by godly King Edward is read in the same churches'. No doubt he expected his English correspondent to be impressed by this. In fact, however, the English made no discernible attempts to impose their brand of Protestantism on their Scottish allies – not yet.[65] This remarkable restraint, coupled with the uncompromising vision of the leading Scottish ministers, meant that even before the Book of Discipline and the Confession of Faith were drawn up in 1560, the wind was blowing strongly in favour of a fully Reformed settlement.

The clearest sign of this was the imposition of discipline, to regulate public morals and control access to the sacraments. This was a particular priority for Reformed Protestants, and eventually the Scots even outdid Calvin by insisting that discipline was a necessary mark of a true church. The first regular, recorded system of discipline was erected in St Andrews. where there was a functioning disciplinary court, or 'kirk session', by October 1559. On 27 October Robert Roger, a shipwright, did public penance for adultery and so acquired the distinction of being Protestant Scotland's first recorded moral offender. Further cases followed in November, when Knox himself took up residence in St Andrews. He was to remain there until Edinburgh was re-taken in the Spring. Another Reformed practice – the structured theological discussions known as 'exercises' – was well established in St Andrews by 1562, and may also have been in place very early. But St Andrews was not alone. Randolph wrote in June 1560 that 'it is almost miraculous to see how the word of God taketh place in this country. They are better willing to receive discipline here than in any country that ever I was in'. Where kirk sessions had not yet become established, the secular authorities sometimes took it on themselves to impose a similar discipline in the meantime. Edinburgh's Protestant town council issued a decree against 'idolaters, whoremasters and harlots' in June 1560, requiring all such people to testify publicly to their repentance. Six months later Stirling's burgh council was helping to enforce the church's strictures against blasphemy in the same way. The willingness of various burgh councils to pay for the new Church, from Bibles through communion bread to clothes for the minister, speaks to the same active support for the emerging structures.[66] It was perhaps inevitable that the collapse of the old Church's systems of enforcement would draw the secular authorities into fulfilling the resulting social vacuum. It was not inevitable that they would do so in the way which the Reformed ministers had hoped, nor that they would subsequently cede their new-found powers to the Church.

By the summer of 1560, Scots were being pressed to conform not only to long-established moral standards, but to new doctrinal ones. In Peebles, the rector was publicly denounced in August for failure to act according to what his accuser called 'the custom and practice of the realm' – that is, to preach and minister the 'Common Prayers'. In godlier burghs, those who refused to conform found themselves the targets of discrimination, or worse. In Stirling, a cleric attempting to claim a benefice in July 1560 was opposed on the grounds that 'he has not as yet recanted his old traditions'. Again, St Andrews led the way. In May 1560 six people were hauled before the kirk session for making abusive remarks about the new establishment or, in some cases, about Knox personally. More followed later in the year. The new Reformed

Eucharist was evidently a particularly contentious point in a new Church's life. When one deacon had been issuing tokens for admission to the sacrament, a Walter Adie had said to him, 'Will ye give me a ticket to be served the Devil's dirt? I shall buy a pint of wine and a loaf, and I shall have as good a sacrament as the best of them all shall have'. He was made publicly to repent for this. The new establishment was beginning to enforce itself: less fiercely than the old one, yet more thoroughly.[67]

The success which the reformers had in beginning to build this new establishment, even while the war was continuing, inevitably raises the question: what would have happened if they had lost that war? If the French had succeeded in securing reinforcements, if the English had withdrawn, and if Guise or her successors had succeeded in reasserting French dominance over Scotland, what would have become of Scottish Protestantism?

The Reformed ministers feared that a French victory would mean full-scale religious tyranny. The rebel lords were not so excitable, but they, too, had clearly lost all trust in France's goodwill and expected deprivation or worse. These fears matched the hopes of some of their opponents. In the early stages of the war, when France's mood was shocked but bullish, there was talk in the French court of making examples of Argyll, Lord James Stewart and Erskine of Dun. However, this instinctive reaction was quickly overtaken by realism. From late 1559 onwards, a series of peace proposals were put by the French. The common theme of these was the concession that the Scots might govern their own internal affairs, including religion, as long as they maintained the French alliance and obedience. It was a distasteful concession for the French, in particular for the young King, Francis; in May 1560 he personally insisted that his Scottish subjects 'shall live in the old religion, neither having churches according to their fashion, nor the Interim as they demand, in order to live according to their opinion'. Yet this document may have been a forgery designed to lure the Spanish into the war by convincing them of the purity of France's motives; and even if it was genuine, it was quite unrealistic. As early as September 1559, some in France were muttering that it was better to accept a Protestant Scotland as an ally than to compel it to be an enemy. In March 1560, before the English army arrived, the French proposed a peace deal in which they would withdraw their troops and allow religious liberty, in exchange for a reaffirmation of Francis and Mary's just title to Scotland. The old Church would be protected, but a Reformed Church would be permitted to establish itself as well. Similar offers were renewed in April. They were rejected, largely because the English doubted and the Scots scorned France's good intentions.[68] Yet it is hard to see these offers as anything but the acknowledgement of a political reality. Scotland was a decentralised kingdom which could not be governed effectively without the co-operation of its magnates. By 1560, too much of that political establishment had become alienated from the old Church for Catholicism effectively to be re-imposed. A French reconquest of Scotland was entirely possible but, as Mary Stewart recognised on her return in 1561, the new religion had to be permitted some legal space if that reconquest was to be turned into tolerably stable government.

The Reformed Church established itself in 1559–60 with remarkable speed, but also with remarkable firmness. This was not a matter of pre-existing 'privy kirks' stepping in to take over Scotland's religious life. Rather, it was a sudden yet profound change which took place during the war itself, as political events forced Scots rapidly to reassess their allegiances, and to abandon their various attempts at compromise. The collapse of Catholic reform, and the widespread perception of sudden and brutal French tyranny, quickly closed off political options that had been part of the mainstream. Trust in the auld allies could probably have been recovered, but it would have to have been bought back in the currency of religious freedom. French Scotland could have returned after 1559–60. Catholic Scotland could not.

NOTES

1 There are several contemporary or near-contemporary narratives of these events, notably those in Knox, I and II; *Wodrow Misc.*, 51–85; Leslie, *Historie*, II; Dickinson, *Two Missions*, 57–179. For one of the better modern narratives, see Lee, *James Stewart*.

2 Knox, I, 326–31, 337–8, 344–5; *CSP Scotland*, 503; David Hay Fleming (ed.), *Register of the Minister, Elder and Deacons of the Christian Congregation of St Andrews . . . 1559–1582* (Scottish History Society 4: Edinburgh, 1889), 7; NA SP 52/1 fo. 68r (*CSP Scotland*, 465).

3 Knox, I, 343, 465–73; VI, 99; CCCC MS 105, 299, 301–3, 310, 317; *CSP Scotland*, 550.1, 559; Herries, *Historical Memoirs*, 46.

4 NA SP 52/3 fo. 68v (*CSP Scotland*, 734); *CSP Foreign 1559–60*, 176; Dawson, *Politics of Religion*; Lee, *James Stewart*; Durkan, 'James, third earl of Arran'.

5 BL Harleian MS 289 fos 68v–69r (*CSP Foreign 1559–60*, no. 392); Dickinson, *Two Missions*, 151–5.

6 NA SP 52/1 fos 143v, 153r (*CSP Scotland*, 505.1, 510); Herries, *Historical Memoirs*, 47; Hay Fleming, *Register*, 8–10; Knox, I, 360–3, 388–92; VI, 26; Dunbar, *Reforming the Scottish Church*, 35–6; Leslie, *Historie*, II, 405; Marwick, *Extracts from the Records of Edinburgh*, III, 47–9.

7 *CSP Scotland*, 566.

8 *Ibid.*, 566, 659, 661. The third Earl of Cassillis had been a Protestant, but the fourth Earl, who succeeded in November 1558, was a staunch Catholic.

9 *CSP Scotland*, 521, 549, 599; CCCC MS 105, 299.

10 NA SP 52/4 fo. 29v (*CSP Scotland*, 821); Melville of Halhill, *Memoirs*, 78–80, 82.

11 Knox, VI, 62.

12 Knox, I, 249, 273–4, 375–6, 459; *CSP Foreign 1558–59*, 908; *CSP Scotland*, 591, 879; *HP*, II, Appendix 39.

13 Knox, I, 247, 273–4, 433–4; *CSP Foreign 1558–59*, 908; *CSP Scotland*, 698, 722, 751, 879; NA SP 52/1 fo. 153r (*CSP Scotland*, 510); *HP*, II, Appendix 39.

14 *Sadler SP*, I, 93–4, 99; *LP*, XVIII(ii), 76; XIX(i), 350, 709.2; XX(ii), 144; *RSS*, III, 820; Knox, I, 126, 251–2; *CSP Foreign 1558–59*, 908; *HP*, II, Appendix 39; *CSP Scotland*, 812, 879, 881, 886, 891.

15 Donaldson, *All the Queen's Men*, 31–2; Donaldson, *Scotland: James V to James VII*, 86–7; Ritchie, *Mary of Guise*, 229–31.

16 *CSP Scotland*, 487, 499.

17 Craigie, *Maitland Folio Manuscript*, 33; *Sadler SP*, I, 515; Knox, I, 459–60, 465; *CSP Scotland*, 628, 629, 641, 698, 713, 722, 728; NA SP 52/2 no. 38, SP 52/3 fo. 151r, SP 59/2 fo. 214r (*CSP Scotland*, 642; *CSP Foreign 1560–61*, 2, 23).

18 NA SP 52/2 nos 25, 43, SP 52/3 fo. 94r (*CSP Scotland*, 647, 744.5; *CSP Foreign 1559–60*, 650); *CSP Scotland*, 682, 744.3–6, 751, 756, 812; *Extracts from the Council Register of Aberdeen*, 322; Chambers, *Charters and Documents Relating to Peebles*, 260.

19 NA SP 59/2 fo. 180r (*CSP Foreign 1559–60*, 562, where wrongly transcribed).

20 Edinburgh University Library, Laing MS III.308, pt. II, fo. 1r. This is a fragmentary and unpublished history of the reign of Mary Stewart.

21 Knox, I, 342, 367, 371–2; *CSP Scotland*, 485, 503; NA SP 52/1 fo. 143r–v (*CSP Scotland*, 505.1).

22 Kellar, *Scotland, England and the Reformation*, 192.

23 Herries, *Historical Memoirs*, 50; Cameron, *Scottish Correspondence*, 426, 427, 429; BL Harleian MS 289 fo. 69r (*CSP Foreign 1559–60*, no. 392); NA SP 52/2 nos 25, 96.1 (*CSP Foreign 1559–60*, 650; *CSP Scotland*, 699.1).

24 NA SP 52/2 no. 21, SP 52/4 fo. 29r (*CSP Scotland*, 626, 821); *CSP Foreign 1560–61*, 152 n.

25 See above, ch. 7.

26 Cameron, *Scottish Correspondence*, 427; *CSP Foreign 1559–60*, 42, 45; Knox, I, 444–9.

27 Knox, I, 324, 341–7; Ritchie, *Mary of Guise*, 214–17; Pollen, *Papal Negotiations*, 18.

28 Knox, I, 380, 413–17; VI, 23, 81; *CSP Scotland*, 501, 535, 552; *Wodrow Misc.*, 67–8; *CSP Foreign 1558–59*, 732, 823, 888.

29 NA SP 52/1 fos 216r, 258r (*CSP Scotland*, 545, 577); Cameron, *Scottish Correspondence*, 429; Knox, I, 397, 406; III, 421; *Diurnal of Occurents*, 272.

30 Herries, *Historical Memoirs*, 50; *Wodrow Misc.*, 74–6; Knox, II, 3–14, 61; *CSP Scotland*, 566, 607, 639; NA SP 52/2 nos 39, 43 (*CSP Scotland*, 642, 647).

31 Dickinson, *Two Missions*, 83–7; NA SP 52/2 no. 94 (*CSP Scotland*, 697); *Wodrow Misc.*, 80–1; Knox, II, 57.

32 *CSP Scotland*, 596.4; NA SP 52/2 no. 43 (*CSP Scotland*, 647); Knox, II, 13–14; *Diurnal of Occurents*, 55.

33 See above, ch. 4.

34 NA SP 52/3 fo. 68r, SP 52/4 fo. 180v (*CSP Scotland*, 734; *CSP Foreign 1560–61*, no. 335); Dickinson, *Two Missions*, 91.

35 Knox, VI, 31; NA SP 52/1 fos 76r–v, 158r (*CSP Scotland*, 471, 511.1); *CSP Scotland*, 522, 540; *CSP Foreign 1558–59*, 998, 1221, 1274; BL Additional MS 23108 fos 111–12v (*CSP Scotland*, 589).

36 *Wodrow Misc.*, 78, 82–3; NA SP 52/2 nos 38, 58.1, SP 52/3 fo. 83r, SP 52/4 fo. 40r (*CSP Scotland*, 642, 662.2, 743, 826).

37 *CSP Scotland*, 649, 703, 709.1; CCCC MS 105, 305; Knox, II, 64–5.

38 *CSP Scotland*, 537; *CSP Foreign 1558–59*, 1240; NA SP 52/1 fo. 298r, SP 52/3 fo. 245r, SP 59/2 fo. 195r (*CSP Foreign 1559–60*, 400, 933; *CSP Foreign 1560–61*, 133); *Wodrow Misc.*, 79; *CSP Foreign 1560–61*, 134.

39 Aylmer, *Harborowe*, sig. L4v; Robinson, *Zurich Letters*, I, 40, 67; Knox, VI, 52.

40 Aylmer, *Harborowe*, sig. P4v; Alford, *Early Elizabethan Polity*, 59–60; *CSP Scotland*, 440; *Sadler SP*, I, 378–9.

41 CCCC MS 105, 283; NA SP 52/1 fo. 76r–v (*CSP Scotland*, 471); *CSP Scotland*, 486; *Sadler SP*, I, 378.

42 Jane Dawson, 'Anglo-Scottish Protestant culture and integration in sixteenth-century Britain' in Steven G. Ellis and Sarah Barber (eds), *Conquest and Union: Fashioning a British State, 1485–1725* (New York, 1995), 109.

43 Knox, VI, 37–8, 69; *CSP Scotland*, 507; *CSP Foreign 1558–59*, 1239; *CSP Foreign 1559–60*, 165, 243; *CSP Foreign 1560–61*, 32.

44 *CSP Scotland*, 537; NA SP 52/1 fos 68r–v, 76r–v (*CSP Scotland*, 465, 471); ASP, 605–6.

45 *Sadler SP*, I, 381; *CSP Scotland*, 504, 511, 549, 566, 580.1, 613; Knox, I, 452–3; II, 6–7, 40–3, VI, 68, 100–1, 103; NA SP 52/1 fo. 258r (*CSP Scotland* 577); CCCC MS 105, 308, 314; *CSP Foreign 1559–60*, 198; Jane Dawson, 'Clan, kin and kirk: the Campbells and the Scottish Reformation' in N. Scott Amos, Andrew Pettegree and Henk van Nierop (eds), *The Education of a Christian Society* (Aldershot, 1999), 220–1.

46 Pollen, *Papal Negotiations*, 19–23, 35–6; CCCC MS 105, 309; *CSP Scotland*, 549, 585, 590, 591; *Sadler SP*, I, 499.

47 Knox, II, 4; *CSP Foreign 1559–60*, 155, 290, 418, 427, 549, 552, 580, 658, 685, 837, 962, 971; *CSP Scotland*, 685; *CSP Foreign 1560–61*, 16; Dickinson, *Two Missions*, 131, 147; Leslie, *Historie*, II, 444.

48 *CSP Scotland*, 741–2, 760; *CSP Foreign 1559–60*, 220, 904, 905, 919, 1025, 1046, 1052, 1082, 1102; 6*CSP Foreign 1560–61*, 26, 51, 109, 116, 187, 268; NA SP 70/13 fo. 129r (*CSP Foreign 1559–60*, 1036). For a detailed, colourful and not wholly reliable narrative of this episode, see Michael Burn, *The Debatable Land: A Study of the Motives of Spies in Two Ages* (London, 1970), 107–21.

49 William Ferguson, *Scotland's Relations with England: A Survey to 1707* (Edinburgh, 1994), 72.

50 Leslie, *Historie*, II, 419; and see above, ch. 6.

51 CCCC MS 105 pp. 217; *CSP Foreign 1559–60*, 441, 467n; Dickinson, *Two Missions*, 59, 71–81, 167, 177.

52 *CSP Scotland*, 724.1, 736, 749, 759, 765.1; Dickinson, *Two Missions*, 97–119, 135; Leslie, *Historie*, II, 436–7; CCCC MS 105, 305; *CSP Foreign 1560–61*, 3; NA SP 52/3 fos 153r, 163r (*CSP Scotland*, 766.1, 769).

53 *CSP Scotland*, 777, 778, 780, 790; Dickinson, *Two Missions*, 145; Knox, II, 66–8.

54 *CSP Scotland*, 792.1, 797; Leslie, *Historie*, II, 438; Dickinson, *Two Missions*, 149, 157–9, 167; CCCC MS 105, 218; *CSP Foreign 1560–61*, 116, 166, 182, 388; NA SP 52/4 fo. 162r (*CSP Foreign 1560–61*, 315).

55 Robinson, *Zurich Letters*, I, 40.

56 *Wodrow Misc.*, 58–61; *CSP Foreign 1558–59*, 1399; Knox, I, 347–50, 359–60; VI, 78; Herries, *Historical Memoirs*, 37–41; Leslie, *Historie*, II, 405, 443; *Extracts from the Council Register of Aberdeen*, 315–17, 323–6; Marwick, *Extracts from the Records of Edinburgh*, III, 42. On St Andrews, see Jane Dawson, ' "The face of ane perfyt reformed kyrk": St Andrews and the early Scottish Reformation' in James Kirk (ed.), *Humanism and Reform: The Church in Europe, England and Scotland, 1400–1643* (Studies in Church History Subsidia 8: Oxford, 1991), 413–35, some of whose conclusions are questioned by Foggie, *Renaissance Religion*, 52; on Aberdeen, see White, 'Impact of the Reformation'.

57 Herries, *Historical Memoirs*, 38; Knox, I, 345; VI, 24; *CSP Foreign 1558–59*, 862.

58 Innes, *Black Book of Taymouth*, 129; Knox, I, 391–2; Leslie, *Historie*, II, 420–2; Keith, *History of the Affairs of Church and State*, III, 3; *CSP Scotland*, 872; Verschuur, 'Perth and the Reformation', 296–7; White, 'Impact of the Reformation', 94–5; *APS*, 535; Pollen, *Papal Negotiations*, 135.

59 *CSP Foreign 1559–60*, 348, 421; Knox, VI, 53; CCCC MS 105, 307; *CSP Scotland*, 559; Leslie, *Historie*, II, 443; Keith, *History of the Affairs of Church and State*, III, 2.

60 Chambers, *Charters and Documents Relating to Peebles*, 259.

61 Ninian Winzet, *The Buke of Fourscoir-thre Questions* (RSTC 25859: Antwerp, 1563), sig. A5v; Knox, VI, 26; Dunbar, *Reforming the Scottish Church*, 35–6.

62 Hay Fleming, *Register*, 10–18; Foggie, *Renaissance Religion*, 37–8, 279; *ALC*, 422; Patrick, *Statutes*, 163; Donaldson, *Scottish Reformation*, 51; NA SP 52/4 fo. 39v (*CSP Scotland*, 826).

63 *Wodrow Misc.*, 119.

64 Knox, I, 390–1, 465–73; VI, 78; Marwick, *Extracts from the Records of Edinburgh*, III, 63–5; *Wodrow Misc.*, 73, 83; Pryde, *Ayr Burgh Accounts*, 30–1, 33; *CSP Foreign 1559–60*, 485; Kirk, *Patterns of Reform*, 14.

65 *Wodrow Misc.*, 67; Marwick, *Extracts from the Records of Edinburgh*, III, 48; Knox, VI, 22, 34; NA SP 52/2 no. 11 (*CSP Scotland*, 616); Alford, *Early Elizabethan Polity*, 60.

66 Hay Fleming, *Register*, 5–6; Dawson, ' "The face of ane perfyt reformed kyrk" ', 424; NA SP 52/4 fo. 39v (*CSP Scotland*, 826); Marwick, *Extracts from the Records of Edinburgh*, III, 65; R. Renwick (ed.), *Extracts from the Records of the Burgh of Stirling, AD 1519–1666* (Glasgow, 1887), 77; Pryde, *Ayr Burgh Accounts*, 31, 132.

67 Gunn, *Book of Peebles Church*, 167; Renwick, *Extracts from the Records of Stirling*, 63; Hay Fleming, *Register*, 33–6, 44.

68 *CSP Foreign 1558–59*, 823, 902, 930, 1331; *CSP Foreign 1559–60*, 809; *CSP Foreign 1560–61*, 124, 131; *CSP Scotland*, 731, 741.

Conclusion:
the Scottish Revolution?

The Scottish Reformation was a long time coming, but when it came it came dramatically. In early 1559 Protestants were an outlawed minority in a Catholic and pro-French state. In less than eighteen months, they won a civil war, created a new Protestant and pro-English establishment, and outlawed the practice of Catholicism in turn. The speed and decisiveness of these events were bewildering to those who lived through them, and they are scarcely less so for historians.

Traditional histories of this period – especially Protestant histories – liked to see this upheaval as inevitable: an irresistible Protestant tide breaching Catholicism's decayed defences. This book has suggested a different narrative. Scottish Catholicism had its weaknesses in the early sixteenth century, but it also had considerable vitality, and its lively spirit of self-criticism testifies to its ability to renew itself. Its financial difficulties were perhaps less damaging than its clumsy systems of discipline, which weakened its response to the arrival of Lutheran heresy. More serious, however, was the limited space which James V's regime gave to the heretics and their fellow-travellers. After the King's death, these Protestant sympathisers found a heady moment of opportunity in the foreign-policy crisis of 1543. For a short time Scottish Catholicism seemed to be in real danger. Yet the moment passed, and its passing seemed only to underline the robust strength of the old religion. The Scottish establishment would not countenance the linked religious reform and diplomatic revolution which the Earl of Arran had briefly tried to implement.

The Protestants' hopes of 1543 were unambiguously defeated, and the next decade did not bring them much comfort. The underground Protestant movement survived, and grew, but not dramatically. Its mood and its theology both became radicalised, but this was not enough to allow it to make a bid for power. The bloody and ham-fisted English invasions, which initially seemed to bring the Protestants some hope, served only to discredit them further. However, the war also inflicted serious damage on the old Church, and (indirectly) killed its stoutest defender, Cardinal Beaton. His successor as Archbishop of St Andrews set about an ambitious programme of Catholic reform, but this coincided with a regime, under the regent Mary of Guise, which for political reasons was no longer willing to treat heresy as a threat. As a result the Protestants were emboldened to press for a religious compromise – initially, a compromise which would have gone little further than the Catholic reformers themselves were going. For a few months in the late 1550s, Catholic reformism, Protestant hopes and Guise's moderation looked as if they might combine to make such a compromise possible.

Again these hopes unravelled. The old Church was willing to set its own house in order, but not to have terms dictated to it by heretics. The radical wing of the Protestant movement undermined any talk of compromise by a succession of acts of sabotage and terrorism. The regime's political calculus shifted with the foreign-policy situation. Early 1559 seemed like 1543 all over again: a brief period of half-toleration for Protestantism was going to be ended by a sudden crackdown from a regime which had rediscovered its alliance with the old Church. Yet this time the outcome was different. A few of the newly radicalised Protestants decided to attempt armed resistance. When they did, they found that remarkably few of their countrymen were willing to oppose them. Scottish Catholicism's ability to mobilise support had been gravely undermined by its decade-long bout of public self-questioning. It was no longer clear that there was a banner to rally to. Moreover, the events of the 1550s had left some Scots uncertain of France's trustworthiness, and the behaviour of Mary of Guise and her troops as the rebellion progressed seemed to confirm the Protestants' accusation of tyranny. And, critically, the Protestants' English allies now managed to avoid the suspicion of imperial ambitions, even as Guise's French support was sapped by growing religious discord in France. The Protestants had acquired that most vital of political assets, momentum. Reformist Catholics of undoubted sincerity now converted – some enthusiastically, some reluctantly – to the Protestant cause. Before the final military victory in the summer of 1560, a new political-religious consensus had emerged in Scotland: a consensus that was pro-English and Protestant.

This was a contingent set of events. The complex three-way negotiations between reformist Catholicism, radicalising Protestantism and a non-confrontational regime in the late 1550s could have had several outcomes, depending on the mood of each party and on external events. In particular, if Guise had not dangled the possibility of a compromise so enticingly before the Protestants, and had instead moved against their leaders in 1558, there is every reason to think she would have succeeded. Her reluctance, or inability, to recognise the real danger which Protestantism posed, must stand as one of the efficient causes of the Scottish Reformation.

The unexpectedness and unpredictability of these events does not, however, mean that they were superficial or reversible. The Scottish Reformation may have come about suddenly, but it marked a change profound enough that it may sensibly be called a revolution. It was not a mass movement like the great revolutions of the eighteenth, nineteenth and twentieth centuries, but the depth of the change it engendered; the radicalism of its ideologies; and the completeness of its break with the past were all sufficient that the comparison makes sense. Several historians of the European 'revolutionary tradition' have seen radical Protestantism as the begetter of that tradition, looking to the British civil wars of the 1640s or to the Dutch revolt of the 1560s and thereafter.[1] The Scottish Reformation has a good claim to a place in the same tradition.

The change in the structures of power is obvious. It is not merely that Scotland's religious and diplomatic orientations were reversed. The Congregation suspended the Queen Regent from office without having any right to do so (as neutrals pointed out to them), and concluded a treaty with a foreign power in order to secure military support against their rightful rulers. Moreover, the parliament of August 1560, which gave the Reformation its first legal basis, was a very irregular assembly. The Anglo-French treaty of Edinburgh which concluded the war in July 1560 was accompanied by a schedule of 'concessions' in Francis and Mary's names, in effect a formula for the future government of Scotland.[2] This document conceded the reality of the Congregation's victory but tried to ensure that French rule would remain more than a legal fiction. Government was to be committed to a council of twenty-four which would be ultimately under parliamentary control, and a parliament was to convene in August 1560 to begin the process of selecting this council. However, the French negotiators were aware that this parliament would likely be dominated by the Congregation, and therefore they took steps to hobble it. They insisted that it was to be summoned 'according to custom', fearing that bishops or lords opposed to the new order would be excluded or intimidated. It was to be required to pass a general amnesty for wartime offences. It was also required to restore any property stolen from the clergy, and to act on any complaints of ill-treatment which the clergy might submit. Most importantly, they insisted that the parliament should not address the religious question. That right was reserved to Francis and Mary themselves. The parliament was to do no more than choose a delegation to come to France and negotiate on this point. However, when the assembly actually met, these requirements were first evaded and then defied.

There was, indeed, no attempt to exclude Catholics from the parliament as such – at least not at its beginning. Rather than purging it, the Protestants packed it. In the 1420s, James I had provided for lesser lairds to have a place in parliament, but this practice had fallen away: since James IV's reign, the number of lairds in parliament had never reached double figures, and often there had been none. In 1560, however, 106 attended. These lairds petitioned for, and were granted, 'free voice' and full voting rights in parliament, on the basis of fifteenth-century practice. Yet the adherence to the forms of legality (which the new regime carefully emphasised to their sovereigns) could not conceal the clear breach of the spirit of the 'concessions'.[3] This imported Protestant majority quickly asserted its dominance. Control of the parliament's business fell, as usual, to a steering committee known as the Lords of the Articles. However, in 1560, the leading Catholic bishops were expelled from this committee, and elected lairds and provosts of key towns joined it. It was an exceptionally large committee – thirty-six men – but relentlessly partisan in its composition.[4] The parliament, led by the Lords of the Articles, not only chose the governing council, but then proceeded to consider the religious question. Three acts gave Scotland a new, Protestant confession of faith, and outlawed the Mass and papal authority. It was a thorough and unambiguous Reformation.[5] The forms of parliamentary procedure, and the lip-service paid to the absent King and Queen cannot conceal the fact that this was a revolutionary assembly.

In addition, Scottish Protestantism can make a claim to being armed with a revolutionary ideology. The question is not as straightforward as it might seem. Scottish Protestantism unquestionably produced radical political theories which claimed distinctive powers for the Church on which the state could not encroach, and which legitimised defiance of secular authority, rebellion and (*in extremis*) tyrannicide. These were the theories which were later cited to justify Mary Stewart's deposition; which made James VI's relations with the Church so difficult; and which informed the rebellions against Charles I. Before 1560, however, all we have are the ideas of John Knox and his English collaborator Christopher Goodman: ideas which were formed more with a view to England's situation than to Scotland's.[6] It is difficult to claim Knox's ideas as the political ideology of the Scottish Reformation. For a start, many of the other rebels seem to have been uneasy with his radical approach. The rebel lords' own principal justification for rebellion was an appeal to that most traditional of Scottish political concepts, liberty – albeit given a radical twist through the new demand for liberty of conscience. Moreover, there was no such ideology as 'Knoxianism' to which they might appeal. Knox was no more a consistent political theorist than he was a systematic theologian.[7] He was a polemicist and a prophet, with no organised programme and no firm political theory underpinning his views. The inconsistency of Knox's thought – chaotic or creative, according to taste – is part of the man's enduring fascination.

Yet Knox's ideas cannot simply be dismissed as incoherent and unrepresentative. As we have seen, the rebels placed him, together with like-minded reformers such as Goodman and John Willock, at the heart of their counsels; allowed sermons from these men to feed into their decision-making; and used Knox, in particular, as their mouthpiece.[8] There was, at least, a tacit acceptance of Knox's approach from the leading Protestant lords. Nor did the inconsistency of that approach render it less powerful, because Knox's politics had a ruthless pragmatism to them which was more dangerous than any theory. He was instinctively in favour of monarchical government, but, if faced with a godless monarch, he was willing to call on any forces he could find to resist her (it was usually her). He followed Calvin in suggesting that the nobility, as 'lesser magistrates', had a right – indeed, a duty – to resist a godless ruler. And he went beyond Calvin in declaring that the common people had a comparable duty to act against an idolatrous ruler, and to do so alone if necessary. One consistent principle which does emerge from Knox's political writings is that of inescapable collective responsibility. If idolatry continued in Scotland, Knox feared that God would punish the whole kingdom, because all were guilty of tolerating it. We are not only our brothers' keepers but our rulers' keepers. Knox was not a monarchist, an aristocrat or a democrat. Nor was he even a theocrat in the conventional sense. His anti-Catholicism gave him a permanent distaste for any direct political involvement by the clergy – hence his own self-defined role as prophet. Knox was, if we must coin a word for him, a *deocrat*. He believed that all forms of human authority were contingent on obedience to God. If they disobeyed God, they ceased to be legitimate, and any and all other people were duty-bound to use whatever means they had to enforce God's will – God's will, that is, as interpreted by Knox. This was a pragmatic political system, in which Knox was willing to invent whatever political structures he could to get his own way. It also reinforced Knox's unsettling self-image as God's mouthpiece. But it was also extraordinarily corrosive of authority structures, perhaps more so than any other political theory of the age; for it was a view in which sovereignty was held to reside outside of the human arena altogether.

Revolutions, however, ultimately depend not on whether a list of critical ingredients is present, but on how those ingredients combine. They are a matter of flavour and of mood, characterised by a sense of reckless change in which accepted orthodoxies are shifting too quickly to be kept up with. And it is this that is clearest in Scotland in the wake of the victory in 1560, in particular, again, in the 'Reformation' parliament.

Military victory, and the successful establishment of Reformed Protestantism in significant areas of Scotland, ensured that the Protestant lords went into that irregular assembly with the facts on the ground in their favour. They were looking for a ratification of what had already been achieved. Most participants, on both sides, apparently expected some kind of local religious liberty to emerge: Catholicism and Protantism side by side in their respective nobles' spheres of influence. This was the kind of system which came to prevail in much of Europe in the second half of the sixteenth century. Yet as the parliament assembled, it caught a more self-confident and uncompromising mood. The Reformed ministers themselves did not have a formal role in the proceedings (with the important exception of John Winram, who sat in parliament as prior of Portmoak) but they were intimately involved from the start. There were Reformed sermons preached daily, with Knox at the forefront. Attendance at these does not seem to have been entirely voluntary. The English emissary Thomas Randolph commented approvingly that there was 'great audience' at the sermons, and that 'though divers of the nobles present are not resolved in religion, yet do they repair daily to the preachings'.[9] Even those who had not, yet, been swept up by the new ways found that it was best to play along.

The treaty had barred discussion of religious matters, but had permitted the parliament to send a delegation to Francis and Mary to 'remonstrate' with them on the question. The Lords of the Articles exploited this loophole so as to turn France's intentions inside out. They decided to send the delegation armed with a confession of faith, endorsed by parliament. This decision was itself taken at the last minute. The Confession was drawn up in only four days. The Lords of the Articles had apparently decided that, for symbolic reasons, they wished to pass the Confession as their first order of business, so their proceedings were stalled while Knox and his colleagues threw a text together. The result was a doctrinal hotchpotch which continues to provide hunting-ground for textual detectives. Knox was the driving force behind it, but not the sole author. We know that a section on obedience to magistrates was cut from the original draft, at the insistence of John Winram and William Maitland of Lethington. Winram and Maitland also 'did . . . mitigate the austerity of many words and sentences which sounded to proceed rather of some evil conceived opinion than of any sound judgement'. Yet perhaps because it was written in such haste, the finished document does not read like the work of a committee. It has a rousing, polemical feel, which sets it apart from Europe's other Reformed confessions of faith. The ministers presented it to the Lords of the Articles, and thereafter to the whole parliament. That they, who were not members of the parliament, should have participated as something like expert witnesses is another sign of how this assembly was inventing procedure on the hoof.[10]

The session on 17 August, when the Confession was presented to the parliament, was by all accounts a remarkable meeting. If there was a single moment when the Scottish Reformation took place, this was it. The ministers and the Lords of the Articles expected controversy. What actually happened seems to have been more like a revivalist meeting. The text was passed almost unopposed. Of nearly 200 members, at most nine registered some kind of dissent. Most of these abstained rather than actually voting against the text. A handful of others deliberately absented themselves. As for the rest of the parliament, Randolph tells us that when the ministers had read the Confession, 'The rest of the lords, with common consent and as glad a wit as ever I heard men speak, allowed the same. Divers with protestation of their conscience and faith desired rather presently to end their lives than ever to think contrary unto that, that they allowed there. Many also offered to shed their blood in defence of the same'. Walter, Lord Lindsay, 'grave and godly' and the oldest man present, said that now he had seen this day, he would happily say his *nunc dimittis*. The Laird of Lundy, whose commitment to the Protestant cause had already been proved in battle, now theatrically bewailed how long he had lived in blindness. Lord James Stewart added a veiled threat. 'God's truth', he warned, 'would never be without its adversaries'. He may have feared that this rush of new converts would include some fair-weather friends.[11]

The most extraordinary feature of the 17 August debate, however, is how quiescent the 'adversaries' were. The most telling speech was that of the Earl Marischal. He had long been sympathetic to Protestantism, he said, but now he had no doubts, because 'he saw there present the pillars of the Pope's Church, and not one of them that would speak against it'. It was true, although the explanation may have been murkier than Marischal implied. A few of the bishops – notably Archbishop Hamilton and Robert Crichton of Dunkeld – had made their opposition to the new policy clear. They had even debated with the Protestant ministers before the Lords of the Articles, although Crichton was loath to accept that he should confer with Knox, 'an old condemned heretic'. Yet when the Confession came before the whole assembly, the bishops' opposition was pusillanimous. Hamilton claimed that he had not had sufficient time to examine the document, and that he would therefore neither oppose nor endorse it: a feeble response, given that its Protestantism is manifest, and that he had had nearly as long to read it as it took Knox and his colleagues to write it. Along with Crichton and William Chisholm of Dunblane – the only bishops to register any disquiet at all – Hamilton proclaimed his willingness to 'agree to all things [that] might stand with God's word and consent to abolish all abuses crept in in the Church not agreeable with the Scriptures'. This was the language of Catholic reform, and it was laughably out of date.[12]

This pitifully weak response was partly the result of intimidation. The new regime was bullying clergy who refused to conform. Archbishop Beaton of Glasgow had already withdrawn to France. The regime was evading the royal order for the clergy to be restored to their possessions and untroubled in their persons. During the parliament, several bishops and other clergy submitted complaints of ill-treatment, demanding that property which had been seized from them during the war should be returned. Such petitions were received, but their consideration was postponed to the end of the parliament; at which point, Maitland noted with satisfaction, 'there was none of the clergy found that would prosecute the complaint or insist on it, so that if they be not fully satisfied let them impute it to no other but themselves'. This was at best a half-truth. A week after the passage of the Confession, further acts were passed against the Mass and the papacy, acts which no longer maintained the pretence that they were intended for submission to Francis and Mary. Those bishops who refused to subscribe to these new acts were promptly excluded from the parliament. Only then was the assembly asked for its view on the seizure of clerical property. The Duke of Châtelherault, not unsympathetic to the situation of his brother the archbishop, nevertheless made the new regime's position clear: 'there would no churchmen be answered, neither of their places nor rents, without that they subscribed the Articles of the new religion.' Meanwhile, preachers were demanding death for any who defied the new dispensation.[13] We know, in retrospect, that there were no Catholic martyrs, but it was less obvious to the leading clergy at the time.

However, the clergy's weakness in the face of the new regime was as much a matter of disorientation as of fear. They seem in part simply to have lost their nerve. They did not quite realise how much the world had changed – a common source of confusion in revolutionary situations. Hamilton's letters from the summer of 1560 reveal his anger at the reformers' actions and his fear that they intended violence. But he also clearly found it hard to believe that the new dispensation could last. Surely Francis and Mary would not ratify the parliament's acts. 'I neither will nor can think that our Sovereigns will let all this country be oppressed wrongfully by subjects.' If he and his fellow bishops were reluctant to go down fighting, it may be because they were clinging to a fantasy of rescue from France.[14]

Something of the same reluctance to accept profound change can afflict historians. 'Continuity and change' is one of the hoariest clichés of academic history. The two always go together, but historical fondness for finding continuities beneath apparently dramatic change can sometimes be misleading. Underlying continuities and long-term causes are of course important, intellectually appealing, and relatively susceptible of historical analysis. Yet profound changes can be sudden, and discontinuities sharp. Strikingly new political, religious or cultural moods can emerge with bewildering speed, for reasons that may be contingent or unclear. If we are to understand the origins of the Scottish Reformation, it is essential to understand that we are searching, not for the slow emergence of a revolutionary movement, but for the sudden precipitation of a revolutionary moment.

The speed and decisiveness with which that moment arrived was the result of violence. Force and the threat of force had shaped the Scottish Reformation from its beginning: the old Church's heavy-handed treatment of dissidence had helped to generate heresy, and England's much more heavy-handed interventions in the 1540s damaged the new religion at least as much as the old. In the 1550s, however, the mismatch between the Protestant activists' violent theatre and the regime's reluctance to defend the old Church had set the wind blowing in the reformers' direction. When, late in the day, Mary of Guise realised that she would have to defend Catholicism in arms, she made the opposite error. The threat of tyranny which her forces' conduct implied eventually cost her the propaganda battle. At the same time, the more finely judged approach of the Congregation and their English allies gave them the moral stature needed to win the battle for hearts, minds and souls, while retaining the military strength they needed to subdue those whose souls would not be won. This judicious mixture of persuasion and coercion effected a national transformation.

In 1559–60 that transformation was not, of course, complete. Some of what had been achieved in 1560 was rolled back when Queen Mary unexpectedly returned the following year. Like all revolutions, that of 1559–60 failed. Like all revolutions, it profoundly and permanently changed the political climate, such that its unfulfilled hopes inspired and frightened Scots for generations. They were swept into this revolution with bewildering speed. Many Scots were caught up by the process. Those who were not could not ignore it, for it had changed the rules by which politics, religion and society worked. A religious culture which was alarmingly corrosive of traditional structures of authority had grafted itself into the Scottish body politic. Unexpectedly, almost accidentally, Scotland had stumbled into a new world.

NOTES

1 Charles Tilly, *European Revolutions, 1492–1992* (Oxford, 1993); Michael Walzer, *The Revolution of the Saints: a study in the origins of radical politics* (London, 1966).

2 Reproduced in Keith, *History of the Affairs of Church and State*, I, 296–306.

3 NA SP 52/5 fos 18r–19v, 20r, 35r–36r, 40v (*CSP Scotland*, 878, 881, 884, 886); ASP, 525–6; Keith, *History of the Affairs of Church and State*, I, 316–17.

4 NA SP 52/5 fos 12r–14v (*CSP Scotland*, 879).

5 *CSP Scotland*, 831, 880; APS, 526–35.

6 Jane Dawson, 'Trumpeting resistance: Christopher Goodman and John Knox' in Roger Mason (ed.), *John Knox and the British Reformations* (Aldershot, 1998), 131–53.

7 John R. Gray, 'The political theory of John Knox', *Church History* 8 (1939), 132–47.

8 See above, 164–5.

9 NA SP 52/5 fo. 18v (*CSP Scotland*, 881).

10 Keith, *History of the Affairs of Church and State*, III, 306; NA SP 52/5 fo. 71r (*CSP Scotland*, 902); *CSP Scotland*, 880; Knox, II, 92, 121. On the Confession, see W. Ian P. Hazlitt, 'The Scots Confession 1560: context, complexion and critique', *Archiv für Reformationsgeschichte*, 78 (1987), 287–320.

11 NA SP 52/5 fos 40v–41r (*CSP Scotland*, 886); *CSP Scotland*, 892; Hazlitt, 'Scots Confession', 289–90; Knox, II, 121; VI, 106.

12 NA SP 52/5 fos 18v, 38r, 41r (*CSP Scotland*, 881, 885, 886); Knox, II, 122; Keith, *History of the Affairs of Church and State*, III, 4.

13 *CSP Scotland*, 893; NA SP 52/5 fo. 69r (*CSP Scotland*, 901); Keith, *History of the Affairs of Church and State*, III, 7.

14 Keith, *History of the Affairs of Church and State*, III, 2–7.

Select bibliography

———◆———

MANUSCRIPT SOURCES

BRITISH LIBRARY, LONDON
Additional MS 23108, 32649, 32650, 32654
Cotton MS Caligula B.vii
Egerton MS 2880
Harleian MS 289
Royal MS 7.C.xvi
Royal MS 18.A.xxxviii

CORPUS CHRISTI COLLEGE, CAMBRIDGE
MS 105 – Papers relating to Scottish affairs, c. 1559–60

EDINBURGH UNIVERSITY LIBRARY
Laing MS III.308 – Portions of a history by the Earl of Leven

LAMBETH PALACE LIBRARY, LONDON
MS 3192, 3195 – Talbot Papers

NATIONAL ARCHIVES (PUBLIC RECORD OFFICE), KEW
SP1 – State Papers, Henry VIII
SP10 – State Papers, Edward VI
SP49 – Scottish Papers, Henry VIII
SP50 – Scottish Papers, Edward VI
SP51 – Scottish Papers, Mary I
SP52 – Scottish Papers, Elizabeth I
SP59 – Border Papers, Elizabeth I
SP68 – Foreign Papers, Edward VI
SP70 – Foreign Papers, Elizabeth I

NATIONAL ARCHIVES OF SCOTLAND, EDINBURGH
B59/1/1 – Protocol Book of Henry Elder
CS7 – Registers of the Acts and Decreets of the Court of Session
JC1 – Justiciary Court Books
JC27 – Justiciary Court Processes, Supplementary

NATIONAL LIBRARY OF SCOTLAND, EDINBURGH
MS Adv. 10.1.9 – Documents relating to the trial of George Buchanan before the Lisbon Inquisition
MS 1746 – Chronicle of Adam Abell

PERTH MUSEUM AND ART GALLERY
Original Papers of the Convener Court of Perth, 1365–1717

PRINTED PRIMARY SOURCES

[Aberdeen:] *Extracts from the Council Register of the Burgh of Aberdeen 1398–1570* (Aberdeen, 1844)

[Aberdeen:] *Registrum Episcopatus Aberdonensis*, vol. I (Edinburgh, 1845)

The Acts of the Parliaments of Scotland, vol. II: 1424–1567 (1814)

Aylmer, John, *An Harborowe for Faithfull and Trewe Subiectes, Agaynst the Late Blowne Blaste* (RSTC 1005: London, 1559)

Bain, Joseph (ed.), *The Hamilton Papers: Letters and Papers Illustrating the Political Relations of England and Scotland in the XVIth Century*, 2 vols (Edinburgh, 1890–92)

Bain, Joseph, *et al.* (eds), *Calendar of State Papers relating to Scotland and Mary, Queen of Scots*, vol. I: 1547–1563 (Edinburgh, 1898)

Bodrugan, Nicholas, *An Epitome of the Title that the Kynges Maiestie of Englande, Hath to the Souereigntie of Scotlande* (RSTC 3196: London, 1548)

Buchanan, George, *The History of Scotland*, tr. and continued James Aikman, 4 vols (Glasgow, 1827)

Calderwood, David, *The History of the Kirk of Scotland*, ed. Thomas Thomson, 8 vols (Edinburgh, 1842)

Cameron, Annie I. (ed.), *The Scottish Correspondence of Mary of Lorraine* (Scottish History Society 3rd series 10: Edinburgh, 1927)

Cameron, Annie I. (ed.), *The Warrender Papers* (Scottish History Society 3rd series 18–19: Edinburgh, 1931)

Chambers, W., *Charters and Documents Relating to the Burgh of Peebles, with Extracts from the Records of the Burgh* (Edinburgh, 1872)

Clifford, Arthur (ed.), *The State Papers and Letters of Sir Ralph Sadler*, 2 vols (Edinburgh, 1809)

Craigie, W. A. (ed.), *The Maitland Folio Manuscript*, vol. I (Scottish Text Society 2nd series, 7: Edinburgh, 1919)

Dickinson, Gladys (ed.), *Two Missions of Jacques de la Brosse: An Account of the Affairs of Scotland in the Year 1543 and the Journal of the Siege of Leith, 1560* (Scottish History Society 3rd series 36: Edinburgh, 1942)

Dickson, T., *et al.* (eds), *Accounts of the Lord High Treasurer of Scotland*, 13 vols (Edinburgh, 1877–1978)

A Diurnal of Remarkable Occurents that have Passed within the Country of Scotland since the Death of King James the Fourth till the Year MD.LXXV (Edinburgh, 1833)

Donaldson, Gordon (ed.), *St Andrews Formulare 1514–1546*, vol. II (Edinburgh, 1944)

Foxe, John, *Actes and Monuments of Matters Most Speciall in the Church* (RSTC 11225: London, 1583)

Gairdner, James, and R. H. Brodie (eds), *Letters & Papers, Foreign & Domestic, of the Reign of Henry VIII*, 21 vols (London, 1862–1932)

Hamilton, John (?), *The Catechisme, That is to Say, Ane Instructioun Set Furth be Johne Aschbischop of Sanct Androus* (RSTC 12731: St Andrews, 1552)

Select bibliography

Hamilton, John (?), *Ane Godlie Exhortatioun Sett Furth be Johane Archbischope of Sanctandrous* (RSTC 12731.2: St Andrews, 1559)

Hannay, Robert Kerr (ed.), *Rentale Sancti Andree: Being the Chamberlain and Granitar Accounts of the Archbishopric in the Time of Cardinal Beaton, 1538–46* (Scottish History Society 2nd series 4: Edinburgh, 1913)

Hannay, Robert Kerr (ed.), *Acts of the Lords of the Council in Public Affairs 1501–1554* (Edinburgh, 1932)

Hannay, Robert Kerr and J. H. Pollen (eds), 'Letters of the papal legate in Scotland, 1543', *SHR*, 11 (1914), 1–26

Harryson, James, *An Exhortacion to the Scottes, to Conforme to the Vnion, betwene Englande and Scotlande* (RSTC 12857: London, 1547)

Hay Fleming, David (ed.), *Register of the Minister, Elder and Deacons of the Christian Congregation of St Andrews . . . 1559–1582* (Scottish History Society 4: Edinburgh, 1889)

Hay Fleming, David, *et al.* (eds), *Registrum Secreti Sigilli Regum Scotorum: The Register of the Privy Seal of Scotland*, 5 vols (Edinburgh, 1908–57)

Herries, John, Lord, *Historical Memoirs of the Reign of Mary Queen of Scots and a Portion of the Reign of King James the Sixth* (Edinburgh, 1836)

Hill Burton, John (ed.), *The Register of the Privy Council of Scotland*, vol. I: 1545–69 (Edinburgh, 1877)

Hume Brown, P. (ed.), *Early Travellers in Scotland* (Edinburgh, 1891)

Innes, Cosmo (ed.), *The Black Book of Taymouth, With Other Papers from the Breadalbane Charter Room* (Edinburgh, 1855)

James V, *The Letters of James V*, eds Robert Kerr Hannay and Denys Hay (Edinburgh, 1954)

Johnsone, John, *An Confortable Exhortation: of Oure Moost Holy Christen Faith, and Her Frutes* (RSTC 14667: Malmö or Antwerp, 1535)

Kennedy, Quintin, *Quintin Kennedy (1520–1564): Two Eucharistic Tracts*, ed. Cornelis Henricus Kuipers (Nijmegen, 1964)

Knox, John, *The Works of John Knox*, ed. David Laing, 6 vols (Edinburgh, 1846–64)

Laing, David (ed.), *The Miscellany of the Wodrow Society* (Edinburgh, 1844)

Lamb, William, *Ane Resonyng of ane Scottis and Inglis Merchand betuix Rowand and Lionis*, ed. Roderick J. Lyall (Aberdeen, 1985)

Lauder, William, *Ane Compendious and Breue Tractate, Concernyng ye Office and Dewtie of Kyngis* (RSTC 15314: Edinburgh, 1556)

Leslie, John, *De origine moribus, et rebus gestis Scotorum* (Rome, 1578)

Leslie, John, *The Historie of Scotland*, tr. James Dalrymple, eds E. G. Cody and William Murison, vol. II (Scottish Text Society 19, 34: Edinburgh, 1895)

Lindsay of Pitscottie, Robert, *The Historie and Cronicles of Scotland*, ed. Æ. J. G. Mackay, 3 vols (Scottish Text Society 42–3, 60: Edinburgh, 1899–1911)

Lindsay of the Mount, David, *The Works of Sir David Lindsay*, ed. J. H. Murray (Early English Text Society old series 11 *et seq.*: London, 1865–71)

Maitland, James, *Maitland's Narrative of the Principal Acts of the Regency During the Minority*, ed. W. S. Fitch (Ipswich, 1842)

Marwick, J. D., *Extracts from the Records of the Burgh of Edinburgh AD 1403–1589*, 4 vols (Edinburgh, 1869–82)

Melville of Halhill, James, *Memoirs of his own life . . . MDXLIX–MDXCIII*, ed. T. Thomson (Edinburgh, 1827)

Mitchell, Alexander F. (ed.), *A Compendious Book of Godly and Spiritual Songs, Commonly Known as 'The Gude and Godlie Ballatis'* (Scottish Text Society 39: Edinburgh, 1897)

Patrick, David (ed.), *Statutes of the Scottish Church 1225–1559* (Scottish History Society 54: Edinburgh, 1907)

Patten, William, *The Expedicion into Scotlande of Edward, Duke of Soomerset* (RSTC 19476.5: London, 1548)

Pedersen, Christiern, *The Richt Vay to the Kingdome of Heuine is Techit Heir*, trans. John Gau (RSTC 19525: Malmö, 1533)

Pitcairn, Robert, *Ancient Criminal Trials in Scotland*, 3 vols (Edinburgh, 1833)

Pollen, J. H. (ed.), *Papal Negotiations with Mary Queen of Scots During her Reign in Scotland* (Scottish History Society 37: Edinburgh, 1901)

Pryde, George S. (ed.), *Ayr Burgh Accounts 1534–1624* (Scottish History Society 3rd series, 28: Edinburgh, 1937)

Robinson, Hastings (ed.), *The Zurich Letters, Comprising the Correspondence of Several English Bishops and Others with Some of the Helvetian Reformers during the Early Part of the Reign of Queen Elizabeth*, 2 vols (Cambridge, 1842, 1845)

Robinson, Hastings (ed.), *Original Letters Relative to the English Reformation* (Cambridge, 1846)

Rogers, Charles (ed.), *Three Scottish Reformers* (London, 1874)

Row, John, *The History of the Kirk of Scotland* (Edinburgh, 1842)

Seymour, Edward, *An Epistle or Exhortaction, to Unitie & Peace* (RSTC 22268: London, 1548)

[Spalding Club:] *Miscellany of the Spalding Club*, vol. IV (Aberdeen, 1849)

Stephenson, Joseph (ed.), *Calendar of State Papers, Foreign Series, of the Reign of Elizabeth*, vols. I–III (London, 1863–65)

Stuart, John (ed.), *Miscellany of the Spalding Club*, vol. V (Aberdeen, 1852)

Turnbull, William B. (ed.), *Calendar of State Papers, Foreign Series . . . 1547–1553* (London, 1861)

Tyler, Royall (ed.), *Calendar of Letters, Despatches and State Papers relating to the negotiations between England and Spain*, vol. X (London, 1914)

Wedderburn, Robert, *The Complaynt of Scotland*, ed. A. M. Stewart (Scottish Text Society 4th series, 11: Edinburgh, 1979)

Winzet, Ninian, *Certane Tractatis for Reformatioun of Doctryne and Maneris, Set Furth at the Desyre, and in ye Name of ye Afflictit Catholikis* (RSTC 25860: Edinburgh, 1562)

SECONDARY SOURCES

Aitken, James M., *The Trial of George Buchanan before the Lisbon Inquisition* (Edinburgh, 1939)

Alford, Stephen, *The Early Elizabethan Polity: William Cecil and the British Succession Crisis, 1558–1569* (Cambridge, 1998)

Bonner, Elizabeth, 'The recovery of St Andrews Castle in 1547: French naval policy and diplomacy in the British Isles', *English Historical Review*, III (1996), 578–98

Bryce, William Moir, *The Scottish Grey Friars* (Edinburgh and London, 1909), vol. I.

Burn, Michael, *The Debatable Land: A Study of the Motives of Spies in Two Ages* (London, 1970)

Burns, Charles, 'Papal gifts to Scottish monarchs: the Golden Rose and the Blessed Sword', *IR*, 20 (1969), 150–94

Burns, J. H., *The True Law of Kingship: Concepts of Monarchy in Early-Modern Scotland* (Oxford, 1996)

Cameron, James K., '"Catholic Reform" in Germany and the pre-1560 Church in Scotland', *RSCHS*, 20 (1979), 105–117

Cameron, James K., 'The Cologne Reformation and the Church of Scotland', *Journal of Ecclesiastical History*, 30 (1979), 39–64

Select bibliography

Cameron, James K., 'St Mary's College 1547–1574 – the second foundation: the principal-ship of John Douglas' in D. W. D. Shaw (ed.), *In Divers Manners: A St Mary's Miscellany* (St Andrews, 1990), 43–48

Cameron, Jamie, *James V: The Personal Rule 1528–42* (East Linton, 1998)

Carpenter, Sarah, 'David Lindsay and James V: court literature as current event' in Jennifer Britnell and Richard Britnell (eds), *Vernacular Literature and Current Affairs in the Early Sixteenth Century: France, England and Scotland* (Aldershot, 2000)

Cowan, Ian B., *Regional Aspects of the Scottish Reformation* (London, 1978)

Cowan, Ian B., *The Scottish Reformation: Church and Society in Sixteenth-Century Scotland* (London, 1982)

Dawson, Jane, 'The two John Knoxes: England, Scotland and the 1558 tracts', *Journal of Ecclesiastical History*, 42 (1991), 123–40

Dawson, Jane, 'The Scottish Reformation and the theatre of martyrdom' in Diana Wood (ed.), *Martyrs and Martyrologies* (Studies in Church History 30: Oxford, 1993)

Dawson, Jane, *The Politics of Religion in the Age of Mary, Queen of Scots* (Cambridge, 2002)

Dilworth, Mark, *Scottish Monasteries in the Late Middle Ages* (Edinburgh, 1995)

Dolff, Scott, 'The two John Knoxes and the justification of non-revolution: a response to Dawson's argument from covenant', *Journal of Ecclesiastical History* 55 (2004), 58–74

Donaldson, Gordon, '"Flitting Friday": the Beggars' Summons and Knox's sermon at Perth', *SHR*, 39 (1960), 175–6

Donaldson, Gordon, *The Scottish Reformation* (Cambridge, 1960)

Donaldson, Gordon, *All the Queen's Men: Power and Politics in Mary Stewart's Scotland* (London, 1983)

Dunbar, Linda J., *Reforming the Scottish Church: John Winram (c. 1492–1582) and the example of Fife* (Aldershot, 2002)

Durkan, John, 'The beginnings of humanism in Scotland', *IR*, 4 (1953), 5–24

Durkan, John, 'Scottish "Evangelicals" in the patronage of Thomas Cromwell', *RSCHS*, 21 (1982), 127–56

Durkan, John, 'James, Third Earl of Arran: the hidden years', *SHR*, 65 (1986), 154–66

Durkan, John, 'Heresy in Scotland: the second phase, 1546–58', *RSCHS*, 24 (1992), 320–65

Edington, Carol, *Court and Culture in Renaissance Scotland: Sir David Lindsay of the Mount* (Amherst, MA, 1994)

Foggie, Janet P., *Renaissance Religion in Urban Scotland: the Dominican order, 1450–1560* (Leiden and Boston, 2003)

Freeman, Thomas, '"The reik of Maister Patrik Hammyltoun": John Foxe, John Winram and the martyrs of the Scottish Reformation', *Sixteenth Century Journal*, 27 (1996), 43–60

Gunn, Dr, *The Book of Peebles Church: St Andrews Collegiate Parish Church, AD 1195–1560* (Galashiels, 1908)

Hannay, Robert Kerr, 'Some papal bulls among the Hamilton Papers', *SHR*, 22 (1925), 25–41

Hay Fleming, David, *The Reformation in Scotland: Causes, Characteristics, Consequences* (London, 1910)

Hazlitt, W. Ian P., 'The Scots Confession 1560: context, complexion and critique', *Archiv für Reformationsgeschichte*, 78 (1987), 287–320

Herkless, John, and Robert Kerr Hannay (eds), *The College of St Leonard* (Edinburgh and London, 1905)

Hoyle, R. W. and J. B. Ramsdale, 'The Royal progress of 1541, the North of England, and Anglo–Scottish relations, 1534–1542' in *Northern History* 41 (2004), 239–65

Keith, Robert, *History of the Affairs of Church and State in Scotland from the Beginning of the Reformation to the year 1568*, 3 vols (Edinburgh, 1844)

Kellar, Clare, *Scotland, England and the Reformation 1534–1561* (Oxford, 2003)

Kenneth, Brother, 'The popular literature of the Scottish Reformation' in David McRoberts (ed.), *Essays on the Scottish Reformation* (Glasgow, 1962), 169–84

Kirk, James, *Patterns of Reform: Continuity and Change in the Reformation Kirk* (Edinburgh, 1989)

Kirk, James, 'Iconoclasm and reform', *RSCHS*, 24 (1992), 366–83

Lee, Maurice, *James Stewart, Earl of Moray* (New York, 1953)

Lee, Maurice, 'John Knox and his History', *SHR*, 45 (1966), 79–88

Lorimer, Peter, *John Knox and the Church of England* (London, 1875)

Lynch, Michael, *Edinburgh and the Reformation* (Edinburgh, 1981)

Lynch, Michael (ed.), *The Early Modern Town in Scotland* (London, 1987)

McLennan, Bruce, 'The Reformation in the burgh of Aberdeen', *Northern Scotland* 2:2 (1976–77), 119–144

McRoberts, David, 'Material destruction caused by the Scottish Reformation' in David McRoberts (ed.), *Essays on the Scottish Reformation* (Glasgow, 1962), 415–62

McRoberts, David (ed.), *Essays on the Scottish Reformation* (Glasgow, 1962)

Mason, Roger, 'Scotching the Brut: politics, history and national myth in sixteenth-century Britain' in Roger Mason (ed.), *Scotland and England 1285–1815* (Edinburgh, 1987), 60–84

Mason, Roger, 'Usable pasts: history and identity in Reformation Scotland', *SHR*, 76 (1997), 54–68

Mason, Roger, *Kingship and the Commonweal: Political Thought in Renaissance and Reformation Scotland* (East Linton, 1998)

Mason, Roger (ed.), *John Knox and the British Reformations* (Aldershot, 1998)

Merriman, Marcus, 'James Henrisoun and "Great Britain": British union and the Scottish commonweal' in Roger Mason (ed.), *Scotland and England 1285–1815* (Edinburgh, 1987), 85–112

Merriman, Marcus, *The Rough Wooings: Mary Queen of Scots, 1542–1551* (East Linton, 2000)

Mullett, Michael, *Catholics in Britain and Ireland, 1558–1829* (Basingstoke, 1998)

Murray, Peter J., 'The excommunication of Edinburgh town council in 1558', *IR*, 27 (1976), 24–34

Ridley, Jasper, *John Knox* (Oxford, 1968)

Ritchie, Pamela E., *Mary of Guise in Scotland, 1548–1560: A Political Career* (East Linton, 2002)

Ryrie, Alec, 'Reform without frontiers in the last years of Catholic Scotland', *English Historical Review*, 119 (2004), 27–56

Ryrie, Alec, 'Clubs, congregations and the nature of early Protestantism in Scotland', *Past and Present* (2006)

Sanderson, Margaret H. B., *Cardinal of Scotland: David Beaton, c. 1494–1546* (Edinburgh, 1986)

Sanderson, Margaret H. B., *Ayrshire and the Reformation: People and Culture 1490–1600* (East Linton, 1997)

Sanderson, Margaret H. B., *A Kindly Place? Living in Sixteenth-Century Scotland* (East Linton, 2002)

Todd, Margo, *The Culture of Protestantism in Early Modern Scotland* (New Haven and London, 2002)

White, Allan, 'The impact of the Reformation on a burgh community: the case of Aberdeen' in Michael Lynch (ed.), *The Early Modern Town in Scotland* (London, 1987)

Winning, Thomas, 'Church councils in sixteenth-century Scotland' in David McRoberts (ed.), *Essays on the Scottish Reformation* (Glasgow, 1962), 332–58

Wormald, Jenny, *Court, Kirk and Community: Scotland 1470–1625* (Edinburgh, 1981)

UNPUBLISHED THESES AND DISSERTATIONS

Dotterweich, Martin, 'The Emergence of Evangelical Theology in Scotland to 1550' (PhD thesis, University of Edinburgh, 2002)

Flett, Iain E. F., 'The Conflict of the Reformation and Democracy in the Geneva of Scotland, 1443–1610' (MPhil dissertation, University of St Andrews, 1981)

Verschuur, Mary Black, 'Perth and the Reformation: Society and Reform 1540–1560' (PhD thesis, University of Glasgow, 1985)

Yellowlees, Michael, 'Dunkeld and the Reformation' (PhD thesis, University of Edinburgh, 1990)

Index

Index

Lightning Source UK Ltd.
Milton Keynes UK
UKOW05f1940041014

239561UK00001B/32/P